FREDERICK THE GREAT

FREDERICK THE GREAT.

AFTER THE PAINTING BY CARLO VANLOO.

FREDERICK THE GREAT

AND THE RISE OF PRUSSIA

BY

W. F. REDDAWAY, M.A.

GREENWOOD PRESS, PUBLISHERS
NEW YORK

Originally published in 1904
by G. P. Putnam's Sons

First Greenwood Reprinting 1969

Library of Congress Catalogue Card Number 69-14046

SBN 8371-1974-X

PRINTED IN UNITED STATES OF AMERICA

TO THE

NON-COLLEGIATE STUDENTS

OF THE

UNIVERSITY OF CAMBRIDGE

PREFACE

IN attempting to sketch the career of Frederick the Great and to define its relation to the rise of Prussia, I have made free use of many printed works, especially of Frederick's own *Œuvres* and of the elaborate *Politische Correspondenz* of his reign. With these great "primary" authorities may perhaps be ranked the face and voice of modern Germany, rich in evidence of Frederick's work, which have doubtless influenced my opinions more than I am aware of. Among "secondary" authorities I owe most to the opulent treasure-house of Carlyle's *Frederick the Great* and to the more systematic narrative of Professor Koser. His *Friedrich der Grosse als Kronprinz*, which largely inspired the work of Lavisse translated under the title *The Youth of Frederick the Great*, forms my chief source for much of Frederick's early life, as does the last volume of the *König Friedrich der Grosse* (1903), for the domestic labours after 1763. Mr. Herbert Tuttle's judicious *History of Prussia* gave me much assistance down to the outbreak of the Seven Years' War, and I have often referred to Mr. Lodge's *Modern Europe* and Mr. Henderson's *Short History of Germany.*

At critical points in the record of the years 1712

to 1786 I was influenced successively by the *Mémoires de la Margravine de Baireuth*, the trenchant *Frédéric II et Marie-Thérèse* of the Duc de Broglie, the *Politische Staatsschriften*, Schäfer's *Der Siebenjährige Krieg*, von Arneth's *Oesterreichische Geschichte*, and Sorel's *The Eastern Question in the Eighteenth Century*. Many of the battles in Saxony, Brandenburg, Bohemia, and Silesia form the subject of monographs which it was interesting to study on the field, sometimes with the aid of collections of maps and plans preserved in the neighbourhood.

It would be impossible without a false pretence of erudition to name more than a small portion of the books to which some reference must be made in writing of the rise of Prussia. Students will recognise the debt that I owe to such well-known works as those of Ranke, Droysen, Philippson, Förster, Seeley, Isaacsohn, Oncken, Vitzthum, Archenholtz, and many more, as well as to the *Essays* of Macaulay and Lord Mahon. My account of the early history of Brandenburg is in part based on my paper of April, 1901, in the *Transactions* of the Royal Historical Society.

I offer my grateful thanks to Mr. G. H. Putnam and to Mr. H. W. C. Davis for their counsel, to Mr. G. H. M. Gray for minute scrutiny of the proof-sheets, and to Messrs. Ernest and Harold Temperley, my indulgent comrades in Silesia. To the latter this book owes much at every stage.

W. F. R.

King's College, Cambridge,
Jan. 9th, 1904.

CONTENTS

ILLUSTRATIONS

ix

FREDERICK THE GREAT

INTRODUCTION

IN the Austrian and Prussian capitals to-day the
traveller may mark the contrast between two
great statues, in each of which the meaning of a
reign is set forth with happy instinct. In the heart
of imperial Vienna is seated the colossal figure of
Maria Theresa, the Victoria of an age when a Pompadour could sway the fate of nations. Her effigy
presents her as the mother of her people, displaying
rather than obscuring the scholars, statesmen, and
warriors who cluster round her feet, sharing harmoni-
ously the glory which neither Queen nor people
could have won without the other's aid.

In Berlin the superb monument of the Great
Frederick is instinct with a different spirit. Raised
high above the throng, the King seems to gaze with
his inscrutable mask-face at the astounding works of
his successors. At the base of his lofty pedestal are
stationed generals and civilians of renown, numerous
enough almost to confute the Cassius who should infer of Frederick's Prussia that there was in it but one

only man. The statue none the less suggests the truth. Between monarch and people there was ever a great gulf fixed. Through all his life—in his counsels, in his despair, in his triumph, and in his death—Frederick, almost beyond parallel in the record of human history, was alone.

CHAPTER I

THE RISE OF PRUSSIA

THE first task of the student of Frederick's life-story is to rid himself of the idea that the solitary King was either wholly original or wholly free. To seize Silesia, to quarter Poland, to rival Austria, to humble France, each was no doubt a feat which no Prussian ruler before him had dared to attempt. Yet in each of these, as will presently be shown, the hand of the living was at once nerved and guided by the dead. From his House Frederick inherited his might, to his House he turned for inspiration in the use of it, and to it he dedicated his conquests. He who would appreciate Frederick must first survey the road trodden for three centuries before him by the Hohenzollerns from whom he sprang.

"Why should I serve the Hohenzollerns?" Bismarck is said to have exclaimed. "My family is as good as theirs." It was the complaint of the yeoman against his fellow who has saved money and bought the lordship of the manor.

The early history of the state now called Prussia is chiefly the record of a thrifty family—the Hohenzollerns. Since the year 1415, when the overlordship

3

of the sandy tract lying between the middle Elbe and lower Oder and stretching across their banks was conferred upon him by the Emperor for cash down, Frederick of Hohenzollern and his descendants had remained lords of Brandenburg. From Nuremberg, where Frederick had been Burggrave, they had brought with them the vital energy and business ability of successful townsmen. So poor was their new estate that for many generations relaxation would have meant ruin. There was therefore no temptation to depart from that policy of adding field to field which is the natural law of the industrious countryman. Whether from native superiority or from greater need, the Hohenzollerns were usually a little wiser than their neighbours. With the aid of a family statute of 1473, which made primogeniture the rule of succession for Brandenburg, they avoided the consequences of that custom of equal inheritance which has been the bane of Germany. By careful watching of opportunities, by windfalls, by purchase, and by covenants for mutual succession on failure of heirs made with neighbours whose lines died out, the domain of the rulers of Brandenburg was in two centuries increased fourfold. When the Thirty Years' War broke out and the modern history of Prussia began, the head of the Hohenzollern family, who had long since become one of the seven Electors of the Empire, held sway over an area almost as great as that of Ireland.

Of the territories by which the original Mark of Brandenburg had been augmented, two were of special importance. In 1525 East Prussia had been acquired. This province, which throughout this book will be called by its German name of Ost-Preussen, was richer by far than the Mark, the kernel of the Hohenzollern possessions. It had an important city, Königsberg, for its capital and a coast-line on the Baltic. It constituted the domain of the old Order of Teutonic Knights, permanent crusaders whose task had been to spread the faith and civilisation of their fatherland among the heathen Slavs. But the Baltic lands had all submitted to the Cross, and the Knights became in their turn the objects of a religious mission. Early in the sixteenth century, the doctrines of the Reformation penetrated the minds of their High Master, Albert of Hohenzollern. He turned for counsel to Luther himself. In a celibate Order which had no more heathen to convert, the husband of the nun Catherine Bora could see only a standing defiance of the laws of nature and of God. By his advice Ost-Preussen was " secularised," that is, taken from the service of religion to form a Hohenzollern estate, and in time (1618), though still submissive to the suzerainty of Poland, it was added to the main body of the Electoral dominions. The Hohenzollerns thus became distinguished from the mass of German princes by ruling territories to which the Empire had never possessed any claim. Ost-Preussen was to them on a small scale what England became in 1688 to the House of Orange, or in 1714 to the House of Hanover. Their policy acquired a new breadth and a new weight. Hitherto provincial, it became more and more cosmopolitan, and commerce with the Baltic lands and England began to hint to the lord of Pillau and Memel that his future lay upon the water.

A makeweight to Ost-Preussen, which would prevent the centre of gravity of the Hohenzollern lands from shifting eastwards, was found in 1609, when the family inherited Cleves, Mark, and Ravensberg in Western Germany. This acquisition, made on the very eve of the Thirty Years' War, was accompanied in 1613 by the conversion of the Elector, John Sigismund, from the Lutheranism which his grandfather, Joachim II., had established in 1539 to the sterner and more militant creed of Calvin. This meant that at the very moment when all Germany was taking up arms for the greatest religious war of modern times, the court and people of Brandenburg were hopelessly at variance with one another. A Calvinist prince ruled a Lutheran people, and the new Elector, George William (1619–1640), "of Christmild memory" but the weakest of his line, proved to be a puppet in the hands of Schwarzenburg, his Romanist prime-minister. Under such guidance did Brandenburg, ill-knit and ill-armed, become the battle-ground between Swede and Hapsburg in their struggle for faith and empire.

What Brandenburg suffered in the terrible decade 1630–1640, between the landing of Gustavus Adolphus in Germany and the accession of the Great Elector, can never be fully calculated. The State was rudderless, defenceless, and poor; the combatants on both sides brigands, whom years of license had habituated to every kind of cruelty. What passed could be described by no more patently truthful eye-

witness than Andreas Rittner, the cheery burgo-
master of Tangermünde, a little town on the Elbe
with a royal history of its own. In his pages may
be traced the swift descent of the afflicted people
through every depth of misery down to despair or
even annihilation. The invaders — it mattered little
whether Swedes or Imperialists — exacted in endless sequence contributions, lodging, forage, and loot,
drove off the cattle, broke up the coffins of the
dead, laid waste the land, and hunted down the
inhabitants. The mischief was only increased by
the feeble efforts of the home government to call
out and support a militia. The maddened peasants
turned guerilla. Food failed, for who could sow or
reap? Men fed on carrion, even, it was whispered,
on human flesh, and soon pestilence seized on persecutors and persecuted alike.

Anarchy and degradation brought forth torture.
The name of the Swedish Drink attests the cruelty
of the degenerate deliverers of Germany. "They
laid men awhile upon the fire," writes Rittner,

" baked them in ovens, flung them into wells, hung them
up by the feet, fastened thumb-screws upon them, drove
sharp spikes under their nails, bound round their heads so
tight that their eyes started out, gagged them and sealed
their mouths. Matrons and virgins were oft-times put to
shame. Husbands must often leave their wives and wives
their husbands, parents their children and children their
parents, even on the bed of sickness, for they were powerless to save them from abuse, and sometimes when they
came back they found nought of them save some few
bones, for all else had the dogs mangled and eaten up."

Not less graphic is the story told in stone in some of the tormented cities. Round the giant church, spared by the Swedes to uphold the Lutheran faith of which it was then the temple and by the Imperialists for the sake of the Roman faith which they hoped to establish anew within its walls, there may be seen the tombs of many generations of citizens. Those of the sixteenth century are covered with quaint adornment and graven with artistic skill. Then, as war sweeps over the land, the series is broken, to be resumed after many decades with a rude clumsiness which shows that wealth and art had fled from Brandenburg together.

Though it would be rash to assume that any single part of the Mark may be regarded as typical of the whole, there seems to be no reason to call in question the dictum of Frederick the Great, that his ancestors needed a century to repair the damage of the Thirty Years' War. This great task was confided to a youth of twenty years, an only son, yet no favourite of his father, the Elector George William, whom he succeeded in 1640. Frederick William, known to history as the Great Elector, was the great-grandfather of Frederick the Great. By common consent he is reputed the founder of the glory of the House of Hohenzollern in modern times. He found Brandenburg prostrate and threatened with dissolution. It is from the low-water mark of these earliest years, when he with reason bewailed difficulties greater than those of David or Solomon, that the progress of his State is to be measured and his own achievement thereby understood.

He found his exchequer empty, his palace half-ruined, the court seeking safety and even sustenance at far-off Königsberg, the Austrian papist, Schwarzenburg, supreme in the state, the Mark trampled underfoot by alien hosts. How should an open country like his, the highroad between Sweden and Austria, be delivered from the endless war? Even if, by miracle, a peace could be devised, which Calvinists and Lutherans could both accept, what prospect, nay what possibility existed that territories so ill-compacted as his could be welded into a single, solid state? All the needful bonds of union seemed to be lacking. What common tie of blood, of faith, of speech was there strong enough to bind together Cleves and Brandenburg and Ost-Preussen, units gathered by the chance of recent history into one hand but dissevered by hundreds of miles of alien soil and by chasms of sentiment still harder to bridge over? The constituent parts of Frederick William's domain were in 1640 dissimilar in race, in history, and in interest. They had no desire for closer relations; they had not even a uniform calendar ; their only common political aim seemed to be to flout the Elector, who was the bugbear of them all.

Even were he to make himself master of the centre, dangers clustered thick on either wing, while behind the Polish problems of the East and the Netherlandish problems of the West a seer might have discerned the double peril that encompasses modern Germany. Peter the Great and his Russia lay yet in the womb of time, but Richelieu and his France were in the

full flood of successful ambition. Thus the organ-
iser of a North German power must work while
his horizon was already darkening. In grasping the
lands which formed his birthright the Great Elector
was defying, though as yet he knew it not, two of
the greatest forces of modern times. Hohenzollern
rule on the Niemen was to become a challenge to
Russia and to the Slavic advance, while the Hohenzollern lord of Cleves must ultimately reckon with
the belief of Frenchmen that the Rhine is the
boundary designed by nature for their state.

During the first critical years of his rule, however,
the plans of the Great Elector were of the humblest.
Striving for existence rather than for empire, he
was not too proud to beg for help in every likely
quarter. Among our own State-papers are to be
seen his letters suing for petty favours which Charles
I., so long as diplomacy would serve, was very willing to grant. The King of England marked the
small esteem in which he held the untried and obscure Elector by pressing upon him the hand of his
niece, a princess of the fugitive and bankrupt House
of the Palatinate. Frederick William's relations
with Poland, the suzerain of whom he held Ost-
Preussen, show yet more clearly how slight was his
power at his accession. When the Lutherans of
Königsberg threatened riot because a Calvinist was
chosen to preach the funeral sermon of George
William, the Elector did not blush to solicit the
Papist King, Wladislaus IV., to admonish these
unruly Protestants. To this end he bade his minister at Warsaw " make humble request to His Maj-

FREDERICK THE GREAT.
AFTER THE PAINTING BY CHRISTIAN WOLFFGANG.

esty that His Majesty would in friendly—cousinly fashion let it please him to send a letter to our chief Councillors (but as if His Majesty had been informed of this from other quarters and not from us) and thereby to order them to reprové and repress this folly of the unquiet theologians. . . . It will perhaps be best if you solicit this work only after the departure of the Diet." The request was made and granted, and the minister instructs the Elector how he may palm off the document as a mandate approved by the Diet behind whose backs it had been obtained.

Where charity was to be looked for, Frederick William was not too proud to beg. But of all powers the least likely to be charitable was Sweden, whose armies had for nearly ten years been fighting solely for material compensation. To Sweden therefore the Elector offered money and was allowed to purchase that deliverance from the war which was essential to all his plans (1641). He could now begin the task of his life—to reduce all his provinces into dependence upon himself and to render Brandenburg, augmented and centralised, a formidable military power.

During forty-eight years (1640–1688) he pursued the old Hohenzollern policy of family aggrandisement. His success has earned him the title of the Great Elector, and the place of the first hero of the Prussian state. Yet he is remarkable chiefly for his commercial instinct, imbibed perhaps during his education among the Dutch, the neighbours to whom he always looked for example and alliance. On

occasion he could display the soldierly instinct of
his race, but in time of peace he was hardly a heroic
figure. With domestic virtues specially to be praised
in a monarch of that time he combined a weakness
for strong drink which damaged his health and temper. He took pride in being abreast of the times,
reverenced London and Amsterdam, and was ready
to haggle with foreigners for preferential rates. He
wrote a good commercial hand, planted cabbages in
his garden, and hammered out verses which with a
little doctoring might have graced the poet's corner
of a provincial newspaper. He was a thrifty house-
holder, save when he deemed it necessary to
keep up his position by building a massive palace or
giving a pompous feast. A convinced Protestant,
he welcomed serviceable Huguenots to his capital
with more good-will than serviceable papists. It is
not impossible to believe that as a German patriot
he took favours from the Emperor with more inward
pleasure than from Louis XIV. In what Dr. Proth-
ero terms " the ocean of recognised mendacity which
we call diplomacy " he floundered without either
repugnance or great success. He spent his life in
unifying his dominions and made a will which if
carried into effect would have dismembered them
at his death. That a man of this stamp is desig-
nated Great suggests that he was not only diligent
but that he was also fortunate in the conditions
under which he lived and worked.

In his early years he owed much to the weakness
and insignificance which have already been described.
What rival state was thrown into the shade if Bran-

denburg was allowed to grow? Thus, at the close of the Thirty Years' War, the Hohenzollern line received indulgent treatment. Their claim to Pomerania was admitted for the eastern half of the duchy. The western half was indispensable to Sweden, but the rights of the Elector were bought up at the price of more valuable ecclesiastical lands scattered between the Mark and his possessions in the West. The bishoprics of Halberstadt and Minden and the reversion of the rich archbishopric of Magdeburg were given to Brandenburg, whose part in the war had been contemptible, by the great Peace of Westphalia, the fundamental pact of modern Europe. Yet its sacredness was so little appreciated by the Elector that a few years later he would have renewed the war, had not outraged Germany held him in.

The Peace of Westphalia had bestowed upon Brandenburg and other German states a gift of more value than many bishoprics—the gift of independence. In outward show Frederick William was still a vassal of the Emperor. He continued to be one of the seven Electors who chose the head of the Holy Roman Empire and honoured him with lowly homage. In virtue of his hereditary office of Grand Chamberlain it was the duty of the Elector of Brandenburg, prescribed by the Golden Bull of 1356, to appear at solemn courts "on horseback, having in his hands a silver basin with water, and a beautiful towel, and descending from his horse, to present the water to the Emperor or King of the Romans to wash his hands." As a German prince, moreover, he had still to look to the Emperor for investiture, leadership, and advice. But his right to determine the creed of his subjects, which the Peace of Westphalia confirmed, and the right to choose allies outside the Empire, which it expressly granted, were inconsistent with real vassalage. The gift of these admitted Brandenburg to a place in the commonwealth of nations. The Elector had become undisputed master in his own house. Soon his horizon expanded far beyond the bounds of Germany. Europe, nay more, as his colonial ventures were to prove, the wide world lay open to the Hohenzollern. Both at home and abroad he could strike with a freer hand. But his power, though irresistible in Brandenburg, was made respectable in Europe only by years of toil. Hence the home policy of the Great Elector was as straightforward as his foreign policy was tortuous. To beat down all competing authority, to establish an armed autocracy, to develop to the utmost all the resources of the State — such was the plan which the Great Elector designed, which his son and grandson perfected, and the fruits of which Frederick the Great enjoyed.

By steady pressure, by force, and at times by fraud, the Great Elector guarded the future of the Hohenzollern power against the danger of obstructive provincial parliaments. To make the men of Cleves, Brandenburg, and Ost-Preussen feel themselves brethren was indeed beyond his power. But he ruthlessly suppressed the institutions which symbolised their mutual independence of each other and of himself. Carlyle, the great panegyrist of *coups d'état*, thus describes one example of

" his measures, soft but strong, and ever stronger to the needful pitch, with mutinous spirits. One Bürgermeister of Königsberg, after much stroking on the back, was at length seized in open Hall, by Electoral writ,—soldiers having first gently barricaded the principal streets, and brought cannon to bear upon them. This Bürgermeister, seized in such brief way, lay prisoner for life ; refusing to ask his liberty, though it was thought he might have had it on asking."

The Great Elector's chief legacy was, however, the Prussian army. The ruler of mere patches of the great northern plain, " a country by nature the least defensible of all countries," he girdled it laboriously with a wall of men. In an age when France alone possessed a large standing army, this obscure German prince raised his force from a few garrisons to a host some twenty-seven thousand strong, well drilled and well appointed.

The lord of Brandenburg now became a *condottiere* of ever-increasing reputation. His regiments brought security to his dominions and gold to his exchequer. In every European struggle their aid was welcome. On the frozen lagoons by the Baltic and on the shores of Torbay, on the torrid plain of Warsaw, and in the vine-clad valley of the Rhine— everywhere the men of the Mark approved themselves good soldiers and punctual allies. In 1660 the Great Elector netted his profit from the Northern war by receiving Ost-Preussen free from Polish suzerainty. The heroic moment of the whole reign

came, however, in 1675, when all the threads of the
Elector's policy—ambition, vengeance against the
Swedes, military creation, domestic organisation—
guided him to the stricken field of Fehrbellin.
While playing his part in the West as a member of
the coalition against France, he learned that the
Swedes, his hated neighbours in Pomerania, had
been hurled upon his domains by their patron
Louis XIV. He straightway turned his back upon
the Rhine and stalked silently across Germany to
rescue his helpless people. His troops had been
beaten by Turenne and exhausted by the long struggle with rain and mud. Yet he dared to overrule
his generals and to strike straight at superior forces
trained in the school of Gustavus and posted with a
river in their rear.

The bold move succeeded. In a hand-to-hand
struggle, amid bogs and dunes, Brandenburg was
saved by its chief. At the crisis of the fight he put
himself at the head of a wavering squadron, and
with one wild charge shattered the Swedes and their
prestige together. The result of Fehrbellin was that
Brandenburg took rank as the first military power
of Northern Europe and that the land had rest for
many years.

Fehrbellin forms a conspicuous landmark on the
road to Hohenzollern greatness, but it is separated
by no great interval of time from a double demon-
stration of the insignificance of Brandenburg when
confronted with states of the first order. The Emperor flatly refused to admit the claim of the Elector
to portions of Silesia. The King of France dashed

from his lips the cup of triumph over the Swedes. In an age when rivers were of even greater value than at present, the great waterway of Brandenburg was the Oder. Ere she could draw full profit from the Oder, Stettin, with its splendid harbourage and strong strategic position, must be wrested from alien hands. At Fehrbellin hope sprang up that the time was come. With all the tenacity of his nature the Great Elector clung to the task. In 1677 Stettin fell, after enduring one of the most desolating bombardments in history. Before the close of 1678 the Swedes were driven from all Western Pomerania. They descended upon Ost-Preussen, but Frederick William set at naught the winter cold and his own infirmity, hurried from Cleves to the Vistula, put his troops on sledges, and dashed at the enemy across the frozen sea (January, 1679). The triumph of the Elector was complete, but at the Peace of S. Germain (1679) he was compelled to surrender all his conquests at the behest of Louis XIV.

In spite of some failures, however, Frederick William by dogged perseverance accomplished enough to justify his reputation as the founder of the Prussian State. He is still a force in Germany. Frederick the Great and all the later Hohenzollerns of renown have paid homage to his memory. William II. embittered the downfall of Bismarck by applauding a drama which represented the Great Elector deposing Schwarzenburg, the hated counsellor of his father. Throughout Prussia the imperious features of the little hero of Fehrbellin are as familiar to the people as his deeds.

With the death of the Great Elector in 1688 the
age of iron gave way to the age of tinsel. Frederick, who ruled in his father's place for a quarter
of a century (1688–1713), was a prince who prized
culture above character and strove to imitate in
his provincial court the splendours of Versailles.
From time to time, though less often than in
other royal lines, the business instinct of the Hohenzollerns fails, and of such a lapse Frederick is an
example. Despising the domestic labours of the
Great Elector, he was captivated by those ceremonious shadows which the German nation is always wont
to pursue. Frail, even maimed, since childhood, he
developed a passion for pageants, robes, and titles.
He could not endure the promotion of his equals to
rank higher than his own. If the Dutch Statthalter
rose to be William III. of England and the Duke
of Brunswick-Lüneburg to be Elector George of
Hanover, might not he himself, as master of the best
troops in Germany, also claim to rise? When in
1696 he was about to visit William of Orange at the
Hague he declared that he could not consent to sit
upon an ordinary seat while an armchair was placed
for the King. The interview therefore was accomplished standing, and when William returned the
visit he found armchairs of equal dignity set for the
Elector and for himself.

Seldom has a ruler's weakness done better service
to his State. Brandenburg was shielded by its
poverty from the ordinary fate of German states
whose rulers tried to copy the profusion of the kings
of France. Frederick, moreover, had not the force

of will to break with all the traditions of the Great
Elector. He continued to take part in every struggle
as an auxiliary, but in none as a principal. His
country thus enjoyed the glories of war without its
penalties. It was under the command of Prince
Eugene, Austria's greatest general, that Branden-
burgers helped to overthrow the French before
Turin (1706). And since a large army is the most
splendid trapping of monarchy, Frederick made his
army very large. He inherited 27,000 men, he bequeathed nearly 50,000 to his son.

The climax of his reign was reached in 1701, when
he prevailed upon the Emperor to make him King
of Prussia. In a double sense it may be said with
truth that he owed his crown to his weakness. It is
generally believed that the chief motive which
prompted him to sue for it was vanity. For months
he could think and speak of nothing else. When
at last the imperial license came, the enraptured
Elector quitted Berlin in midwinter and spent twelve
days in moving with a pompous train to Königsberg.
There, with every detail of ceremony that his imagination could suggest, he placed the crown upon
his head. It is doubtful whether a more sober ruler
would have prized a throne as he did, and doubtful
too whether the Emperor would have consented to
the elevation of a prince less obviously feeble. But
Frederick had carried on without reserve the old
Hohenzollern tradition of standing well with the
head of the German world. He had even given back
to Austria the territory of Schwiebus, which the Emperor had assigned to the Great Elector in settlement

of whatever claim the Hohenzollerns possessed to portions of Silesia. Now he was prepared to uphold the Hapsburg cause in the War of the Spanish Succession. What harm could there be, the Emperor may well have asked himself, in promoting a vassal so devoted as this?

Forty years later, Austria had bitter cause to rue the error of her chief. From the very first the crown aggrandised the Hohenzollern dynasty. It consecrated their ambition, enlarged their horizon, and gave them, as the Lord's anointed, a new claim upon the devotion of their subjects. The Order of the Black Eagle, which for two centuries has been the coveted prize of service to their state, signalised the coronation of Frederick I.

The Great Elector and the first king of Prussia have this in common — that whatever may be thought of their achievements it is difficult to mistake the men themselves. Of the second king, Frederick William I. (1713–1740), the father of Frederick the Great, the exact opposite is true. His life-work, the establishment of the royal power "like a rock of bronze," is patent to all. He himself, on the other hand, was a mystery to his own children. His most gifted admirer, Carlyle, sets out to paint a prophet and ends by portraying something very like a madman. His theory of his own sovereign office was as mystical as his practice of ruling was simple. He regarded himself, it has been said, as the servant of an imaginary master — the King of Prussia — under whose eye he lived and worked. Baser princes looked on their royalty as a privilege to be enjoyed. To

Frederick William it was a duty calling for endless toil. He struggled to check every detail of government with his own hand, as though Prussia were a single manor and he the squire. A French critic (Lavisse) thus portrays him wrestling with his ever-multiplying tasks :

"Have we not too many officials," the King enquires. "Could not several places be merged into one? We must see if some of the officials cannot be put down. Why is not the beer so good everywhere as at Potsdam? In order to have wool we must have sheep. Now in Prussia there are nearly as many wolves as sheep. Quick, let me have a minute upon the destruction of wolves. How comes it that the salt tax has brought in less money this year than last from the district of Halberstadt? The number of officials has not diminished, has it? They must have eaten as much salt as last year. There must therefore be fraud or waste somewhere. The Superintendent of the Salt Department must be warned to manage matters better than he has done of late. Can it be that my subjects buy salt in Hanover or Poland? Every importer of salt must be hanged."

His violence was and still is notorious. He flung plates at his children, caned his son in public, cudgelled the inhabitants of his capital, and flung the judges down-stairs. He forced his queen, the sister of the English King, to drink to the downfall of England. He vilified everything French, and insulted the British Ambassador so seriously that he conceived himself bound to leave Berlin. Yet he kept Prussia at peace steadily enough to earn for himself the reputation of a mere bully whom the Emperor could lead by the nose.

In spite of the contradictions of his character, however, the broad principles of his reign are clear. Having stripped the state of the veneer of luxury with which Frederick I. had disguised its poverty, he took up and developed further the ideals of the Great Elector. He made the royal power absolute in the state, and increased the army till a population of about two and a half million souls supported the unheard-of number of 83,000 men under arms. These were drilled to such a pitch of perfection that Macaulay could say that, placed beside them, the household regiments of Versailles and St. James's would have appeared an awkward squad. Yet this mighty force was used for little save to secure the frontiers of Prussia and the rights of all German Protestants. In territory the "Sergeant King" gained only from the wreck of Sweden part of the prize which the Great Elector had grudgingly relinquished at the behest of Louis XIV.—the mouth of the Oder and with it the islands of Usedom and Wollin, and Western Pomerania as far as the river Peene (1720).

In the home department, on the other hand, Frederick William I. made a conspicuous advance from the point reached by his grandfather. He showed the same military zeal, the same practical insight, the same determination to set to rights with his own hand whatever in his dominion was governed amiss, the same contempt for higher education, the same benevolence towards the persecuted of other lands who might be made useful to Prussia. But he showed also a power of grasping and of simplifying the whole system of administration such as few rulers

have ever possessed. His great Edict of 1723 removed friction from the working of the Prussian state. Thanks to this, his son Frederick found the organisation described in the sixth chapter of this book—a machine of government answering to every touch of the royal hand. He found at the same time a firm tradition in favour of thrift, diligence, and activity in the steersman of the state. We have traced the growth of Prussia to 1740; let us now turn to the story of the prince who in that year linked her fortunes with his own.

CHAPTER II

WHAT manner of man was the first-born son of Frederick William, known to history as Frederick the Great, and what were the causes that made him such as he was? To answer either question is a task of uncommon difficulty. Even to those who were regarded as his intimates Frederick remained an enigma all his life. In his early trials he acquired, as Carlyle happily expresses it, "the art of wearing among his fellow-creatures a polite cloak-of-darkness," and became what he in great measure still remains, "a man politely impregnable to the intrusion of human curiosity." And if it passes our wit adequately to describe his personality, how shall we determine and distinguish the factors which created it? No adding together of influences will suffice. Such enquiries lead us far beyond the bounds of mere arithmetic. Of Frederick's nature, as of every man's, a greater share was built up in ages which have left no record than in the generations whose history we can trace. If therefore we next endeavour to indicate the influences of his parentage and his surroundings, let us avoid the delusion

24

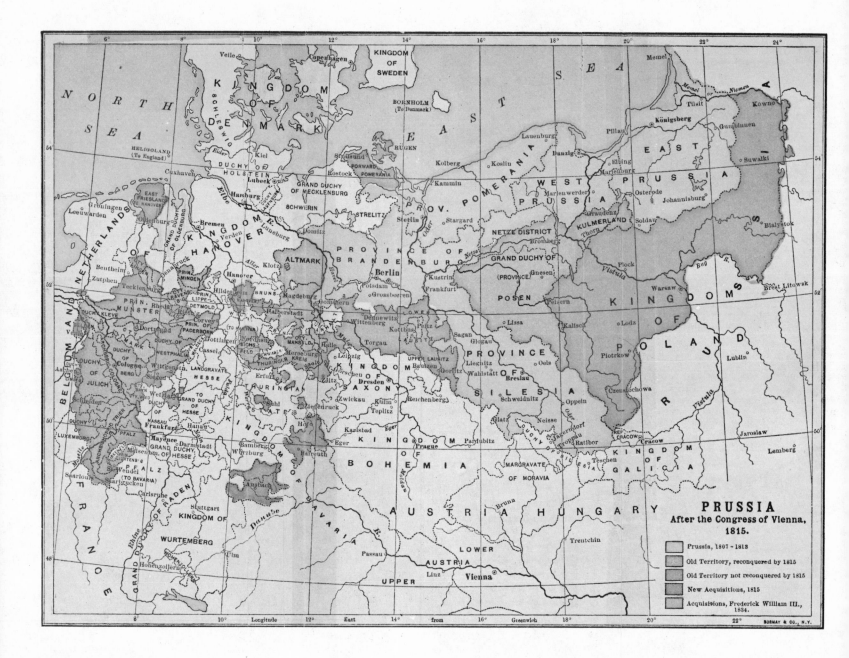

PRUSSIA
After the Congress of Vienna,
1815.

Prussia, 1807–1813
Old Territory, reconquered by 1815
Old Territory not reconquered by 1815
New Acquisitions, 1815
Acquisitions, Frederick William III.,
1834.

BORMAY & CO., N.Y.

that these alone made him what he was. In Frederick's case, too, it is perhaps equally needful to beware of the converse error. His personality, like his policy, was not untouched by ordinary influences. Parents, tutors, friends, nation, home, even religion— each bestowed something upon one who might on a too hasty scrutiny be pronounced a freak of nature —the ugly duckling of the Hohenzollern brood.

Frederick's birth, on January 24, 1712, remedied the anxieties of a line which had gained too much from the extinction of allied lines not to be keenly sensitive to its own lack of heirs. His father, Frederick William, gave vent to rude transports of joy at the arrival of a male heir. Frederick I., the royal grandfather, who had himself a third time plunged into wedlock in the hope of safeguarding the succession to the new Prussian crown, seized the opportunity to astonish Berlin by the pomp of the infant's christening. The Prussian nation, living in tranquillity under the Hohenzollerns, shared in their rejoicing.

The infant prince represented many noble lines, and, it might almost be said, two separate civilisations. Frederick William was a kind of Prussian Squire Western. His wife, Sophia Dorothea, was a princess of the rising House of Hanover, a lady soon to be nicknamed Olympia from her majestic bearing as queen. Through her and through his grandmother, a clever daughter of Sophia of Hanover, a thin strain of Stuart blood flowed in Frederick's veins. His great-grandmother, the wife of the Great Elector, was a daughter of the House of Orange, born at the moment of its triumph over Spain. A generation farther back the Hohenzollerns had married into the House of the Palatinate, which in 1618 threw for the Bohemian crown and lost. But the virtues of every Protestant House in Europe could not compensate for the infirm health which had assailed both the father and the son of the Great Elector, and which there seemed reason to fear had descended to the offspring of his grandson Frederick William. Two older sons had died in infancy, a daughter, Wilhelmina, though she grew up and married, was never robust, and Frederick himself seems in his childhood to have been often ailing.

The home circle of this delicate prince was surely the strangest in the world. The royal family of Prussia in the reign of Frederick William I. was hardly a family and hardly royal. The monarch seemed to regard his sceptre chiefly as a superior kind of cudgel. As Prussian King, and therefore *ex officio* the father of his people, he could treat them as children, could order them to be anything or to build anything or to pay anything, with even less risk of resistance than an Elector of Brandenburg might have had to fear. He was, it is true, on a footing of equality with foreign kings in negotiating for a treaty or a province or a bride. But apart from his acceptance of the perquisites of royalty, his life was one long protest against all that the world associated with the name of king. Intolerant of state and ceremony, he agonised his chamberlains by his behaviour. His recreations were such as befitted a bargeman on the Havel or an overgrown loafer kidnapped to serve in the King of Prussia's giant grenadiers. In that snuff-taking age, a king whose hobby was to smoke pipes in a kind of glorified tavern-circle known as the Tobacco Parliament earned the reputation that would fall in our own day to a king who should chew and spit.

Frederick William drank himself to death before he was fifty-two. Though an artist, if not a scholar, he drove Wolf, the philosopher, from his dominions and made Gundling President of the Academy of Letters because he amused the Tobacco Parliament when in his cups. As a sportsman he slew wild swine by the thousand and forced his subjects to buy their carcasses at a fixed price. He ordered his officials to spend only six thousand thalers on the entertainment of Peter the Great, but to give out that it cost him thirty or forty thousand. His mixture of fervent piety and immorality suggests that he was hardly sane, and his foreign policy does not discountenance the suggestion. In some of his officials he placed complete confidence, even when proofs that they were bribing his envoys abroad to send home false news were in his hands. He rushed upon others with his cudgel, first breaking their heads and then cashiering them. What he was to his children may be inferred from the fact that his daughter became his bitter satirist and his son his bitter foe.

Such was the father who directed Frederick's education. His talent for detail was always at the service of the state. It could be devoted to no worthier object than the training of the future king. At the age of nine years, therefore, Frederick found every hour of the day assigned to some part of the

scheme of education by which the crowned Podsnap
designed to make him such another as himself.

For all its minuteness, the scheme failed in its
main object. It failed because Frederick William
was not the sole factor in moulding and inspiring
his son. In the royal household were two trembling
conspirators against the tyrant—his wife and his
daughter. Sophia Dorothea and Wilhelmina formed
with Frederick a trio who sighed after the genteel.
Loathing the pipe-clayed Teutonism in which their
lord delighted, they longed for newer fashions and
society more polite, for the wit and gallantry of the
French court, and for the splendour of their own
opulent kinsfolk at Saint James's. Their lines
had fallen in far less pleasant places. In Berlin,
a quiet country town with dull surroundings and a
trying climate, they had at least palaces, parties, and
scandal. In Wusterhausen, to this day a lonely village, they were in exile; and Wusterhausen was the
favourite residence of the King. The Europe in
which they lived, it must be remembered, was a
Europe which believed with all its heart that whatever Louis XIV. might have been in politics, he was
beyond doubt the Apollo of culture. German princes
prided themselves on speaking French, on dressing
à la française, on building palaces that might be
named in the same breath with Versailles. Frederick's mother spoke French so well that a Huguenot
refugee paid her the supreme compliment of enquir-
ing whether she understood German. His sister's
memoirs, like his own, are French in language and
in inspiration. What sympathy, we may wonder,

could there be between these ladies and a boor who
hated everything French, whether language, literature, art, cookery, or dress, and whose ideal of life was
to sleep on straw in a barn, wash at daybreak in a tub,
don a plain uniform, inspect farms, account-books,
and soldiers, gorge himself with rude German dishes
in the middle of the day, snore under a tree in the
afternoon, and devote the evening to tobacco, buf-
foonery, and strong drink?

It is not surprising that, when the King's scheme
of discipline outraged his son instead of moulding him, mother and sister were at hand with ready
sympathy. The wayward boy never forgot their
kindness, nor the indulgence of the tutors who
connived at a more humane education than Frederick William had commanded them to inflict.
Cordially as the King detested French culture, he
did not venture to exclude it from a leading
part in the education of his son. A French lady,
Madame de Roucoulle, was entrusted with the
oversight of his earliest years. Madame de Camas,
whom he called Mamma, was the wife of a Frenchman. His tutor, Duhan, was a Huguenot. French
was at that time the universal language of the polite
and learned world. Frederick, who never learned
English and was forbidden to learn Latin, therefore
drew all his mental supplies from French originals
or French translations.

German he never spoke or wrote with ease. To
him it stood for whatever was dull in his education,
—for windy sermons every Sunday, lessons of nearly
two hours a day in the Christian religion, books

full of dismal pedantry, the speech of boors and
of his father. Thus he early acquired from France
ideas which he proclaimed throughout his life.
That literary creation is the highest achievement
of man, and that next to creation stand patronage
and culture; that religion is superstition; that the
enlightened man is he who views with calm not
only the rubs of fortune but also the frailties of
mankind—such were the abiding traces of Frederick's education. The King, as may readily be believed, did not fail to remark something of this and
to loathe it. He leaped to the conclusion that a
boy who preferred French to German, and flute-
playing to parades, was a monster who would ruin
Prussia. It never occurred to him that his own
scheme could be imperfect, and life became one long
collision between father and son.

Yet Frederick's most irritating delinquencies —
his delight in soft living and secret dissipation, his
distaste for the uniform and duty of a soldier,
his contempt for Germans and their tongue — may
fairly be ascribed in great part to mere youthful
squeamishness and to the tyranny of the King. Had
Frederick William been wise enough to trust to the
future and to the past, to reflect that in the long
line of Hohenzollerns none had been traitor to his
House, that a lad who could think for himself would
be more easily influenced than coerced, that at the
worst he himself was not twenty-four years older
than his son and might train the state to survive
Frederick II. as after the Great Elector it had survived Frederick I.—had he in short been either a

sympathetic father or a man of real penetration, then history might have heard nothing of either the new Junius Brutus or the Ogre of Potsdam, and the million victims of Frederick's wars might have been spared.

Unhappily for his son and for the world, Frederick William was neither sensible nor sympathetic. His aversion to an heir who refused to resemble himself was doubled when the heir became the advocate of a matrimonial policy which he came to regard with loathing. From the hour of Frederick's birth the dearest wish of the Hanoverian House, and of Sophia Dorothea most of all, had been to unite more closely the royal lines of England and Prussia. At length a double marriage was proposed. The Prince of Wales was to marry Wilhelmina, and Frederick his cousin Amelia, daughter of George II. In 1730, however, England and Prussia were estranged, yet Frederick William knew that his household had not given up their darling project. Flouted as a father and as a statesman, he treated his son so ill as to lend colour to the suspicion that he wished him dead. Not content with impounding his books, forbidding him the flute, compelling him to see his mother only by stealth, the tyrant actually rained blows upon him in public, even in the camp of the Saxon King. " Had I been so treated by my father," he is said to have exclaimed, " I would have blown my brains out, but this fellow has no honour."

Unfortunately for Frederick William, the youth whom he thus outraged was Crown Prince of Prussia, and as such by no means lacked friends. To

England, to Austria, and to his father's ministers he was an important pawn in the game of politics. Some of the younger officers lent him countenance in the hope of favours to come. But the dearest friend of his life, Lieutenant von Katte, loved him for himself rather than for what he might be able to bestow. To Katte the prince confided his fixed purpose to flee from a tyranny that was past endurance. Together they planned to make use of the opportunity of escape which might arise when Frederick should approach the French frontier in the course of a forthcoming tour with his father among the German courts.

On August 4, 1730, the attempt was made. The confederates tried to steal from the royal camp at dawn and to ride into France. Such a flight was not without precedent in Hohenzollern history. Frederick's grandfather, sharing the general belief that his stepmother had poisoned his brother and meant to poison himself, had first sought shelter at Cassel with his aunt and at a later date had quitted the Great Elector's court altogether. But for the heir to a crown to flee beyond the bounds of Germany was a still graver step. The youth of eighteen had hardly calculated the probable consequences of success. Where was Frederick William's heir to find a safe asylum? Louis XV. was not likely to be to him what Louis XIV. had been to the Old Pretender. George of England would hardly expose Hanover to the vengeance of the King of Prussia. His envoy had in fact refused to countenance the scheme. Nor would the Emperor care to sacrifice

PRINCESS SOPHIA DOROTHEA, DAUGHTER OF KING GEORGE THE FIRST.
AFTER THE PAINTING BY HIRSEMAN.

the Prussian alliance to mere sentiment. Even if
Frederick should succeed in finding a refuge for
himself, he would none the less have left two dear
hostages at the mercy of the King. "Your mother
would have got into the greatest misery," declared
Frederick William a year later. "Your sister I
would have cast for life into a place where she
would never have seen sun and moon again."

Thanks, however, to the vigilance of Colonel von
Rochow, his keeper, and to the panic of his page,
Frederick did not even mount the horse that was to
have borne him out of Germany. His abortive attempt inaugurated one of the strangest tragedies in
history. From the very fact that he was the guest
of other princes Frederick William could not act in
haste. The scheme was betrayed to him at Mann-
heim on August 6th, and he ordered von Rochow to
deliver his son to him at his own town of Wesel,
alive or dead. In this mood they continued the
tour of pleasure, sailing down the Rhine and visiting
the potentates upon its shores. At last, on the evening of the 12th, they reached Wesel. Frederick
William at once interrogated his son, who lied and
protested his submission. The King replied by
despatching him to Spandau under the care of a
general, who was enjoined to frustrate any attempt
at rescue by killing his prisoner.

Spandau is the fortress near Berlin where to-day the
Prussian sentries guard some millions of the treasure
wrung from France. It was not deemed safe enough
to keep the Prince of Prussia. "He is very cunning,"
wrote the King, "and will have a hundred inventions

for making his escape." A stronger gaol was sought for. In a sombre plain east of the capital lies Cüstrin, whose grim fortress marks the spot where the sluggish Wartha gliding down from Poland silently joins the Oder. There, on September 4th, Frederick was imprisoned. On the way he had faced a tribunal of soldiers and lawyers with a jaunty confidence which showed that though he might cower before the King he had not forgotten that he was still Crown Prince of Prussia. It was rumoured that he had poked fun at Grumbkow, his father's most trusted counsellor. For himself he asked no favours, but avowed his responsibility for all that Katte had done amiss.

A fortnight later, on September 16th, the commission examined him again. In the meantime he had begun to understand the nature of a gaol. His father, who lived in such a state of frenzy that he ordered that the tongue which spoke of this affair should be cut out, had not scrupled to condemn him to solitary confinement, a penalty often destructive of health and not seldom of reason. He was clad in brown prison dress, fed on the humblest fare, and deprived of light at seven o'clock in the evening. Thus prepared, he was subjected to a merciless inquisition. After more than one hundred and eighty questions of fact, came two which the King had commanded the interrogators to add. "Do you wish that your life should be granted to you or not?" "I submit to the King's mercy," answered Frederick, adding in pencil, when the report was laid before him, "and to his will."

"Since by violating your honour," ran the last question of all, "you have made yourself incapable of succeeding to the throne, will you renounce the succession by an abdication that shall be confirmed by the whole Roman Empire—to save your life?" "My life is not over-dear to me," replied the Prince, "but Your Majesty would surely not be so ungracious to me"—and he added a prayer for pardon. The King tore up the petition and applied his genius for detail to a code of rules for the torment of his heir. No one was to speak to the prisoner. Three times a day the door of his room might be opened, but within four minutes it must be made fast again. Mute attendants were to set before Frederick food which they had cut in pieces, since the royal command deprived him of knife and fork. For Katte Frederick William had ordered the rack, but on the representations of Grumbkow the order was cancelled. For his son he discovered a torture which Grumbkow himself was to apply. "He must be told," decreed the King, "that no one thinks of him any more; that my wife will not hear his name; that his sister Wilhelmina has fallen under my displeasure, that she is shut up in Berlin, and will very soon be sent into the country."

The problem before Frederick William, whose wrath increased as he experienced the difficulty of laying to his son's account any definite crime, was to crush his heir without imperilling Prussia. On October 11th Frederick declared to the commission that he was ready to renounce the succession. On October 16th the King avowed in writing his desire to make his second son his heir. But to do this while Frederick lived was dangerous, and on what charge could he be put to death? Assassination, though it might rectify the succession to Philip of Spain or Peter of Russia, was to a Hohenzollern simply impossible. And Frederick William was not entirely sovereign over his son. It was true that a Prussian subject had no longer any right of appeal from the decrees of the Prussian King. But the Prussian King was also Elector of Brandenburg, and therefore a vassal of the Emperor. The heir to the Electorate of Brandenburg was equally a prince of the Empire and as such could appeal unto Cæsar. Moreover, no proof could be found that Frederick was a traitor. He had neither acted nor tried to act in collusion with any foreign Power. His father suspected that England was at the bottom of the plot, but no evidence of this could be found. By no severity could his son be brought to confess more than a design to run away. Foreign sovereigns protested against violence which degraded the royal caste.

It is difficult to see with what hope the baffled King insisted on a quibble which might make out his son to be technically a criminal. Frederick, by no choice of his own, was a colonel in the Prussian army. On October 25th a military court met at the King's bidding to try him and his accomplices for desertion.

The court consisted of fifteen officers, three from each of five grades. The members of each grade, after deliberating apart, handed their votes to a president, the aged Lieutenant-Colonel von Schulen-

burg, who summed up their verdicts and added a
sixth vote of his own. With regard to the Crown
Prince, all were unanimous. Declaring themselves
incompetent to pronounce upon affairs of state and
of the royal family, they commended the exalted
penitent to His Majesty's supreme and paternal
mercy. Katte was condemned by three grades to
death, by two to lifelong imprisonment. Von Schulenburg voted for the latter, which by military law
carried the day, since it was less severe. The King
denounced their criminal leniency and clamoured
for "justice," but von Schulenburg stood firm, ap-
pealing to a Higher Power. Thereupon Frederick
William decreed "that Katte, although in conformity with the laws he has deserved to be torn with
red-hot pincers and hanged for the crime of high-
treason which he has committed, be removed from
life to eternity by the sword, out of consideration
for his family. In informing Katte of this sentence,
the Council will tell him that it grieves His Majesty,
but that it is better that he should die than that
justice should entirely leave the world."

Under a sentence which no consensus of civilised
opinion, no high-placed appeal, no murmur of disaffection could reduce, the doomed man journeyed
slowly to Cüstrin. Frederick, who believed that all
would go well with himself and his friend, was
cheerful still. At five o'clock on the morning of
November 6th he was awakened by two officers who
told him that Katte was that morning to be put to
death and that he must witness it. "What are
these ill tidings that you bring me?" he is said to

have exclaimed. " Lord Jesus! rather take my
life." Before his judges he had steadfastly declared
that Katte's guilt lay at his door. Now for two
terrible hours he wailed, wrung his hands, burst into
tears, sent to his friend to beg forgiveness, prayed
for a respite while a courier should lay at the King's
feet whatever he might desire from his son—renun-
ciation of the succession, consent to lifelong imprisonment, nay, his own life if Katte's might be
spared. His honourable clamour moves the heart
of posterity, but it could vary no line upon the
parchment on which the King had set down even
the numbers of the soldiers who were to attend the
execution. Seven o'clock struck, and the dismal
procession filed into the courtyard which stretched
from the fortress-wall to the Oder. As the King
had commanded, Frederick was led to the window
of his cell. He saw his friend, who had received
the communion, standing calm and brave amid the
soldiers and awaiting with bared head the recital
of the sentence of death. The prince kissed his
hand to him and cried aloud for his forgiveness.
Katte laid his finger upon his lips, bowed respect-
fully, and answered that there was nothing to for-
give. He then bade his comrades farewell, knelt to
receive the chaplain's blessing, and with prayer upon
his lips submitted to the fatal stroke.

Frederick had fainted. It was the duty of the
chaplain to pass straight from the dead offender to
the living, and to exhort him to repent. But nature
made this royal order of none effect. The prince,
when he came to, could only stare dumbly at the

FREDERICK THE SECOND.
AFTER THE PAINTING BY CUNNINGHAM.

gloomy pall which draped the body of his friend. At two o'clock some citizens brought a coffin and bore away the corpse, but Frederick could not withdraw his gaze from the place of execution. All that day he took no food. At night he passed from delirium into a second swoon—then fell to raving anew. When morning broke he declared that Katte was standing before him. But the very violence of his emotion made the reaction swift. On the same day he told the doctor that he was well and asked him for a certain powder. Next day, after much talk with the chaplain on matters of religion, he learned from him that Katte's fate was not to be his own. Nine days later he made peace with Grumbkow, who came at the head of yet another Commission to exact an oath of strict obedience to the King, and to open the prison doors a little wider. Before Christmas he was reported to be " as merry as a lark."

The conduct of father and son during this crisis is peculiarly worthy of attention because each was his own counsellor, and because Frederick never again lay under a scrutiny so searching. In the summer of 1730 the King reaped all that he had sown during his son's boyhood. He found in his heir a youth whom he distrusted and despised but could not get rid of. He therefore began the task anew and inaugurated a second education sterner than the first. He had slain his son's friend, not, as he professed, " that justice should not entirely leave the world," but that he might, in spite of past failures, fashion an heir after his own heart. The loyal father of the dead man found consolation in viewing his loss as a sacrifice to this design. That this, which he believed to be indispensable to the welfare of Prussia, was the leading motive of the King's policy, grew clearer as his outbursts of wrath against his son became less frequent and less fierce. It inspired Frederick also with a leading motive—to beguile his father into believing that he had his way.

His first education made him a rebel; his second, a hypocrite. Katte's death had taught him once and for all that life would be tolerable only if he gained his father's confidence. To this end he applied every art which a fertile brain could devise and an unscrupulous actor could practise. He exhausted the language of contrition for the past. He promised full amendment for the future. He sent letters, as many as his father would consent to receive, and the burden of all was that he was indeed a new man, a second Frederick William, adoring the things that he had burned and burning those that he had adored. The new Frederick is interested in tall soldiers, his father's hobby, and longs to put on the uniform which he had been wont to call his winding-sheet. He relishes theology and after argument abandons what his father calls " the damned heresy " of predestination. He professes to find pleasure in the work of the estates committee and informs his father with ecstasy that the rent of some royal domains can be raised. He tries to propitiate the King of Prussia as Philip of Spain tried to propitiate the English people, by pretending to a taste for beer. Even his opinion of his own family has swiftly changed. He now pretends to realise that his mother is a mischievous

intriguer ; to be content that his sister shall abjure
the throne of England and marry an obscure Hohenzollern of Baireuth ; to desire that his father may
live to see his children's children grow up around
him. Finally he receives at the hands of Frederick
William a regiment and a wife and withdraws into
the marshy solitudes of Brandenburg to make the
best of both.

It is the duty of Frederick's biographer to mark
from Frederick's point of view the stages of this
second education. The first period lasted rather
more than two and a half years, from November,
1730, to June, 1733, and therefore roughly corre-
sponds with the period of residence at an English
university which is usually enjoyed at the age at
which the Crown Prince had then arrived. This
course began and ended with a crime. Katte was
done to death for a military offence which a tribunal
representing the most sternly disciplined army in
the world had declared not to be death-worthy—
though their commander-in-chief and king demanded another verdict. A fortnight later, that is,
on November 20, 1730, Frederick was admitted as a
humble participant in the proceedings of the local
Chamber of War and Domains—to assist in duties
which he privately styled the work of brigands.
He was to study agriculture under the Director,
Hille, and in general to survey the foundations of
the Prussian State.

He was still a close prisoner living at Cüstrin
under the heavy cloud of the King's displeasure.
At Christmas he fell ill and his father wrote on the

margin of a report which told him of it: "If there were any good in him he would die, but I am certain that he will not die, for weeds never disappear." He was forbidden all books save bible, hymn-book, and Arndt's *True Christianity*, a work of devotion dear to humble believers in many lands. Geometry and fortifications were classed as "amusement" and forbidden, along with cards, music, dancing, summer-clothing, and meals outside the house. Again, as in the early days of August, Frederick William entrusted him to the care of three nobles. These were to refuse to converse with him on any subject save "the Word of God, the constitution of the land, manufactures, police, agriculture, accounts, leases, and lawsuits." Such a scheme of education, aimed at compounding a king out of a recluse and an attorney, it is hardly necessary to discuss. We hardly know whether to think the King a simpleton for imagining that he would be obeyed, or a fool for continuing to issue minute directions if he knew that he would not. What is certain is that Frederick's household revelled in forbidden gifts, diverted itself as best it could, and pressed unceasingly for further freedom. One pleasure, as Frederick William knew in his heart, sweetened his son's captivity,—in exile he was at least safe from the sight of his father.

The first dawn of forgiveness took place on August 15, 1731, the King's forty-third birthday. Then Frederick received his father in his shabby lodging, kissed his feet, listened to his reproaches, confessed once more that it was he who had led Katte astray, and finally received the royal embrace before all the people. Soon came permission to engage in the practical study of agriculture, attended by an increase of liberty and even of amusement. The King still imposed restrictions upon Frederick's reading and ordered him to sing hymns. He was never to be alone or to speak privately to anybody, especially to any girl or woman. Within a fortnight of his father's visit he had begun his courtship of the young wife of Colonel von Wreech.

The remaining months of the year 1731 brought Frederick great pleasure and a heavy blow. He grew in favour with his father, who in November summoned him to appear for a short time at Berlin and at last promised to restore to him his rank in the army. But at the same time he lost his sister. Wilhelmina was forced by her father into an unhappy marriage with the Margrave of Baireuth, a humble cousin whose title to the favour of his bride was that by accepting him she propitiated her father and freed herself from a still less bearable suitor. Elated by the progress of his own fortunes, Frederick seems for the moment to have been insensible to her trouble and to his own loss. By the King's order he paid his sister a visit. But he treated her coldly when they met, broke off the conversation abruptly, and walked into the room to which her husband had courteously withdrawn. "He scanned him for some time from head to foot," writes Wilhelmina, "and after addressing to him a few words of cold politeness he withdrew. . . . I could not recognise that dear brother who had cost

me so many tears and for whom I had sacrificed myself." Frederick's standard of behaviour towards his
social inferiors was however revealed by other incidents at this time. His tutor, Hille, was a man of
the middle classes. In his official position he received reports from a Landrat, or Sheriff, who was
of noble birth. A reference by Hille to these reports drew from the Crown Prince the remark that
it was singular that a nobleman should render account to a man of the middle class. Next year he
wrote to Grumbkow that his daughter was "without
charms and without ancestors."

In 1732 Frederick experienced another·pleasure
and a far severer blow. He was allowed to leave
Cüstrin, but he left it under sentence of marriage.
This had been decreed in consequence of a curious
chain of events. Frederick's preceptors had remarked that he scorned administrative detail but
displayed a taste for high politics. This was evident
in his suggestions for the disposal of his hand. Now
he would marry, if he must marry at all, Anne of
Russia; now the Archduchess Maria Theresa, re-
nouncing his succession in Prussia. This suggestion
was reported by Grumbkow to the Emperor's great
minister, Eugene. The old diplomat scented danger
in such large ideas and urged that the Crown Prince
of Prussia should be bound to the car of Austria.
He might be encouraged to borrow money from the
Emperor, and married to Elizabeth of Brunswick-
Bevern, a niece of the Empress. Frederick William,
still hot against England, with whose Court his queen
continued to intrigue, cheerfully assented to the match.

ELIZABETH CHRISTINA OF BRUNSWICK.
FROM AN OLD PRINT.

In a honeyed letter of February 4, 1732, the King broke the news to his son. " She is a creature who fears God," he wrote, "and that is everything." The bridegroom elect thought othérwise. He wrote to Grumbkow that he hated severe virtue, and rather than marry a fanatic, always grimacing and looking shocked, he would prefer the worst character in Berlin. " When all is said and done he cried, there will be one more unhappy princess in the world." " I shall put her away as soon as I am master," he twice declared. " Am I of the wood out of which they carve good husbands? " " I love the fair sex, my love is very inconstant; I am for enjoyment, afterwards I despise it. I will keep my word, I will marry, but that is enough ; *Bonjour, Madame, et bon chemin.*"

Frederick's marriage, by which he brought to an end the sternest period of his second education, was a crime, but the bridegroom was not guiltless. All his outcry was made in secret. To the King, in whose hands his fate lay, he showed himself all submission. Frederick William had in his own young days received the names of three princesses from whom his father desired him to choose a bride. He protested with success against such compulsion and his marriage with Sophia Dorothea was something of a love-match. Here was an argument to which he could hardly shut his ears. His son preferred to purchase greater liberty for himself by condemning to a life of misery an innocent creature who had never harmed him. At the same time, by making a happy home-life impossible, he shut out what was perhaps the last chance that he might become in any sense of the words a good man.

For the moment, however, his submission brought him freedom. On March 10, 1732, he went through the formal ceremony of betrothal. Some of the guests remarked that his eyes were filled with tears and that he turned abruptly from his betrothed to a lady who was supposed to be the mistress of his heart. But a year's respite was granted him. While Austrian statesmen schemed to turn the timid, ignorant Elizabeth of Brunswick-Bevern into a woman of the world, who might make her husband a Hapsburg partisan, Frederick was learning his work as colonel not far from the field of Fehrbellin. It was drudgery, but it was not Cüstrin. After a year of it he wrote: "I have just drilled, I drill, I shall drill. That is all the news. But it is delightful to indulge in a few moments' breathing-space, and I would rather drill here from dawn to dusk than live as a rich man at Berlin."

June 12, 1733, was Frederick's wedding-day. The Austrian diplomats, who had made the match, went far towards flinging away their advantage. At the last moment they dared to suggest that Frederick William should accommodate the Emperor by entering into a new combination which assigned an English bride to his son. The King was furious at the slight, and the marriage was only another step towards the alienation of the Hapsburgs and the Hohenzollerns.

After his marriage Frederick's father still dictated his movements and kept him short of money. But

the period of dragooning was over, and it becomes
important to enquire what Frederick William had
achieved by this stage of the second education begun with crime and carried on with cruelty. One
answer to this question must be mentioned because
it is supported by the authority of Carlyle. He
holds that the execution of Katte was just, that the
imprisonment of Frederick was salutary, that the
King was a father yearning to reconcile his son with
God and with himself, and that he was not only just
and affectionate but also successful. An opinion
more widely held is that the execution and imprisonment were unjust but politic, that reasons of
state excused them, that their righteousness was
proved by their success, and that by them Prussia
gained a hero who made her great among the nations of the earth as none but he was able.

On reflection we may think it strange that results
so great should have been achieved by a scheme of
education so stupid. The King owed the best features
of his plan to suggestions from outside. He had condemned his son to tedious, nay, dangerous idleness:
it was Wolden who obtained for him a grudging
permission to work. He had set him to learn agriculture by attending board meetings: it was Hille
who urged that he should be allowed to see how
farming was carried on. The united efforts of Hille
and Wolden could not convince him that the heir to
the throne needed any books save books of devotion. These faults, though significant, were errors
of detail. But the King's whole plan is open to
graver objections. It is in fact based on three of

the commonest yet most fatal errors with regard to education. That boys are dough or putty to be placed in a mould and beaten till they take the exact shape of it, that a youth who is destined for a given career will succeed best by trying to make himself a facsimile of some one else who has been successful in it, and that it is good to limit training to the acquisition of professional aptitude — these are errors which Frederick William held in common with pedants and doctrinaires of every era.

From Frederick's birth onwards he had laboured to give him his own characteristics, even his own vices, in the hope that as his son's conduct grew like his own, so also would his policy. This was still the aim of all his measures. But the second education is distinguished from the first by the ghastly object-lesson with which it opens and by its appearance of success. The death of Katte affords the measure of Frederick William's powers as a teacher. It imperilled the health, even the reason of his pupil, but assuredly it was not forgotten. Are we then to infer that the King's system atoned for its faults by its triumph? That Frederick was bullied into love for his father seems incredible. It is true that in public he spoke little ill of him, either before his death, when it would have been dangerous to himself, or after it, when it would have been detrimental to the office which he had inherited. But neither his motto nor his conduct after 1730 betokened love. "Far from love, far from the thunderbolt," are not words of affection, nor is it filial piety to cozen, to flatter, and to shun. He addressed the King as "most all-gracious Father," while he secretly petitioned the foes of Prussia for funds wherewith to play upon his weakness for tall recruits. It was like a foretaste of death, he said, when a hussar appeared to command his presence at Berlin.

It may at once be granted that in conduct Frederick was transformed. Before his disgrace he had been a trifler, after it he worked hard till the day of his death. What is doubtful is that this result could not have been obtained at a less cost. There is no evidence that the King had ever tried the normal method of giving his son a fitting task and a reasonable independence in performing it. Frederick, moreover, was nearing the age at which many triflers develop a new spirit. During his year of exile his health improved. He became stouter in body and firmer in gait, so that at first even Wilhelmina did not recognise him. This change at least was not designed by the father who wished him dead, yet to this may be ascribed much of his novel energy.

It is still less certain that his character had gained from the second education. Many of the striking traits of old reappear. Frederick is still before all else brilliant—a gay and versatile young man with elastic spirits and a passion for music, society, and intellectual conversation. Despite his father's hatred of all things French, Frederick still looked on Paris as the Mecca of civilisation. His literary ambitions were more pronounced than ever. At Cüstrin he had gone back to verses—verses always

Gallic, copious, and bad. A Prussian patriot lamented that while he knew not whether his ancestors had won Magdeburg at cards or in some other way, he had Aristotle's rules of composition by heart. Yet, for all his perseverance, Lord Mahon speaks with justice of "his two kinds of prose, the rhymed and unrhymed." In the darkest hours of his struggle against all Europe, he sat down to rhyme in French. "He does not really know the Germans at all," complained his tutors. Though sometimes brutal, he prided himself on his ceremonious politeness—a German version of Louis XIV. All through his career he was wont at times to put on the great monarch. "Hush, gentlemen," once exclaimed Voltaire when his royal host thus suddenly stiffened, "the King of Prussia has just come in." His morals were no better after confronting death than before. "The flesh is weak," he writes to his mother, "but I do not believe that Cato was Cato when he was young." It was said that the motive of his amours was vainglory rather than the satisfaction of vicious desires. No one, wrote harsh critics, could rely upon his word, and few if any could tell of a disinterested act that he had done.

Yet in some respects Frederick had gained. His talent for diplomacy grew with the need for it. His father's schooling had this effect—that he learned to outwit his father. The closing years of Frederick William's life were cheered by the mirage of a good son and a good husband, which of all Frederick's fabrications was perhaps the cleverest. Progress in diplomacy was attended by increase of self-control. Frederick learned in a hard school to disguise his true emotions and to feign what he did not feel. Hence arises a difficulty which Carlyle constantly encounters as he strives to approach his hero with paternal sympathy and to penetrate into his inner man. He is forced to speak of Frederick's " polished panoply," and to describe him as " outwardly a radiant but metallic object to mankind."

The King's handiwork may be discerned in the increasing poverty of affection that his son displayed. Frederick William had killed his friend, proscribed his associates, banished his sister, placed his mother under a cloud, and forced upon him a wife whom he despised. It is not surprising that Frederick's heart, never of the tenderest, grew harder year by year. He turned to the friendship of men, always difficult for kings to win, and doubly difficult for an autocrat who was not prone to self-sacrifice. It was remarked of him in later life that he softened only in illness, and that the sure sign of his recovery was renewed harshness towards those about him. His intimates were chiefly devotees of art and letters, among whom Voltaire was chief. But the very name of Voltaire, whom Frederick first adored and then expelled, hints at the transient nature of these ties. As his sister, his mother, and Madame de Camas were one by one removed by death, he became bankrupt of affection, and his old age was consoled only by the fidelity of his servants and of his dogs.

Such was Frederick at his marriage, but his very defects contributed for a time to his social success.

An accomplished man, with great flashing eyes and flexible, resonant voice, "musical even in cursing," he had a genuine relish for the circle of which he was the centre. His schooling had given him skill in seeming what he pleased, and whatever affection he possessed was given to his friends. At Rheinsberg, where he built himself a house and lived from 1736 till 1740, he was gay, hospitable, and refined, living in apparent amity with his wife and fitting himself by study and by administration to fill the throne in his turn.

The year after Frederick's marriage, the year 1734, was of high importance in his career. The war of the Polish Succession had broken out between France and the Empire, and Prussia fulfilled her obligations by sending an auxiliary force of ten thousand men to serve on the Rhine under Eugene. In this campaign, which proved inglorious, Frederick played the part of an eager novice, dogging the footsteps of the aged hero and copying even his curt manner. There he laid to heart several fruitful facts—that the great commander never accepted praise to his face, that the enemy feared him more than they feared his army, and that other German troops cut a sorry figure beside the men of Prussia. And—though his father had ordered him to keep out of harm's way—he proved by his calm while cannon-balls were splintering trees around him that the traditional courage of the Hohenzollerns had descended to him.

Next year (1735) he begged to go to the war again, but the King, who had been near death from dropsy,

put him off with a journey to Ost-Preussen. This
was the first of those official tours of inspection
which later became one of the chief occupations of
Frederick's years of peace. In 1736 he began a far
more agreeable pursuit. It was then that he established himself at Rheinsberg, and, that, to quote his
own testimony, he began to live.

To live, in Frederick's vocabulary, meant to read.
He plunged into books, comparing, annotating, an-
alysing, and learned by four days' trial the lesson of
the zealous freshman — that man needs more than
two hours' sleep a day. To the remonstrances of
the doctors he replied that he would rather suffer in
body than in mind. Books were supplemented by
conversation, the society of ladies, music, theatricals,
literary effort of every kind. His *Anti-Machiavel*,
a treatise on the duty of princes, attracted the attention of Europe, and men of liberal mind awaited
with impatience the moment at which he would be
able to put his virtuous maxims into practice. Meanwhile he revelled in intercourse with philosophers
and learned men. Frederick styled his house "the
temple of friendship," and his guests rejoiced to find
that the palace of a Crown Prince could be Liberty
Hall.

Yet the hand of Frederick William was not entirely invisible. Thrice every Sunday must the master of the house tear himself from philosophy to
go to church, and he was also compelled to read the
sermons which his father's favourite chaplains had
composed. His own select preacher was Voltaire,
with whom and with his intimates he "reasoned high

Of providence, fore-knowledge, will and fate, Passion and apathy and glory and shame." From history he learned much for every department of life; from philosophy chiefly contempt for religion and a deep-rooted fatalism which sustained him at many moments of disaster. He speaks of

" this Necessity, which orders all things, directs our intercourse and determines our fate." " I know too well that we cannot escape from the inexorable laws of fate . . . and that it would be folly to desire to oppose what is Necessity and was so arranged from all eternity. I admit that consolation drawn from the impossibility of avoiding an evil is not very well fitted to make the evil lighter, but still there is something calming in the thought that the bitter which we must taste is not the result of our fault, but pertains to the design and arrangement of Providence."

In such discussions passed many hours of the halcyon period, 1736–1740. Of perhaps higher value was the insight into the possibilities of human providence which Frederick gained during his visits to Ost-Preussen. There he saw how the hand of his father had turned a wilderness into the most blooming of his provinces, so that a land which the King had found swept bare of men by the plague now contained half a million prosperous inhabitants. When at last (May 31, 1740) he took the place of the father whose last hours his presence had consoled, it was with a conviction that if his foreign policy had been contemptible, he had shown himself heroic at home.

VOLTAIRE.
FROM THE STATUE BY HOUDON AT THE COMÉDIE FRANÇAIS.

The time had come when the domestic organisation of Prussia was to acquire a new significance in Europe. At Rheinsberg, while protesting that he desired nothing more in life than to be left in peace with his books and his friends, Frederick had been steadily pursuing the study of politics. In 1738 he had set down on paper "Considerations" which pointed to the need of a new champion to defend the liberties of Europe against the stealthy and menacing expansion of France. It remained to be seen whether Prussian foreign policy would in future be influenced by her singular constitution. To appreciate the meaning and the value of Frederick's innovations in both systems we must portray the situation that he found on his accession. This demands in the first place a brief scrutiny of Europe as it was at Frederick William's death.

CHAPTER III

THE PROBLEM OF 1740

IN his instructions for the education of his successor, Frederick prescribed a thorough course of European history from the time of the Emperor Charles V. (1519–1556) to his own reign. This had been the favourite study of his own youth, so that at his accession he realised to the full that modern Europe owed little of its political contour to chance, but much to the aspirations and struggles of the several states during the last two centuries. For modern Europe was no older than Charles V. Right through the Middle Ages the Christian world maintained that supreme authority, like truth, ought to be one, and that every Christian should look up to the Emperor in matters temporal as he looked up to the Pope in matters spiritual. On the secular side, however, this theory had crumbled beneath its own weight. Even a Charlemagne could not really rule the world. As the various races of mankind who lived in England, France, Spain, and Scandinavia gradually came under the sway of a few national rulers, the Emperor dwindled into a dignified president of German princes. His lordship of the world survived only in distracting. claims to rule more widely and more exclusively than his attenuated power could warrant. Two sharp shocks heralded modern times. First Columbus bestowed upon his masters, the Kings of Spain, a new world which had never heard of Pope and Emperor and which the Emperor at least did not pretend to sway. Then Luther, wrestling blindly with the papacy, shattered the central pillar of the mediæval world, and modern history, the biography of a group of independent states, began.

These states, however, did not enjoy unchallenged independence. Each had to work out its own religious settlement, and—if it embraced the Reformation—had to repel, with whatever help it could find, the rescue-work of the Pope and his allies. To the end of the sixteenth century, through the careers of Charles V., Elizabeth, William of Orange, Henry of Navarre, Romanist and Protestant States always tended to fall apart into two hostile camps. Even in Frederick's time religious affinity always counted for something. He had laid history to heart and, as we shall see, profited in his dealings with England by the old cry of "Church in danger." On his lips the cry was a mere ruse. The day of crusades was over. In the sixteenth century Spain, Austria, and Italy rejected the Reformation ; England established its own Church; France came to terms with the Huguenots. At the great Peace of Westphalia Germany established parity between the warring creeds, a boon tardily won by thirty years of desolation. Thenceforward affairs of state came first in every

land.   Louis XIV.'s revocation of the Edict of
Nantes in 1685 proved that religious aggression was
to be feared only as the sequel of undue political preponderance.   From the birth of modern
states down to our own time, the bugbear of the
nations has been world-rule and their watchword
equilibrium.

The first prince who threatened to restore in fact
if not in form the world-rule which had broken down
in the Middle Ages was Charles V., the scion and
pattern of the House of Hapsburg, whose career is
the narrative of European politics from 1519 to 1556.
France, which he threatened most, took the lead
against him, began the long duel between Bourbon
and Hapsburg, and thus guarded the liberties of
Europe till the close of the Thirty Years' War
(1648).   Then Louis XIV. threatened to make
France in her turn mistress of the world.   The equilibrium which he, as absolute ruler of the foremost
State of Europe, seemed to have overthrown, was
painfully re-established at Utrecht (1713).   A new
and greater Thirty Years' War was thus brought to
an end.   It left the States weary and timid, dread-
ing France as a century earlier they had dreaded
Spain, clinging to peace lest the whole fabric of Europe should collapse and with it the gains which
they had made or hoped to make should vanish.
France, conscious of weakness in spite of the glories
of Louis XIV., turned to diplomacy and won Lorraine.   England, ridden on a loose rein by Walpole,
followed her natural bent towards the sea.   For
Austria and the Hapsburg Charles VI., the great

problem was to keep what had already been heaped
together. Only Spain was not afraid to break the
peace, and in the long run she gained parts of Italy
by her boldness.

Most of the territorial profits made by European Powers during the years 1713–1740 were made
at the expense of Charles VI., either as head of
the Hapsburgs or as Emperor. As it became certain that he would have no son, he grew more
and more reckless in sacrificing the welfare of the
Empire to that of his House. The future of his
heir was indeed precarious. For there was not
and never had been an Austria in the same sense
in which there was an England, a France, or a Spain ;
that is, a well-knit nation, preferring ruin to dismem-
berment. "Austria" meant the dominions of the
elder branch of the House of Hapsburg just as
"Prussia" under Frederick I. meant the dominions
of the elder branch of the House of Hohenzollern.
In the case of the Hapsburg agglomeration, however, the subjects were too many, too miscellaneous,
and too rich for the work of a Frederick William to
be possible. Germans, Hungarians, and Italians
were only the chief among a motley crowd of races
which had come under the sceptre of Charles VI.'s
ancestors and which he strained every nerve to hand
down to his daughter undispersed.

The method which Charles selected was to proclaim that his dominions were one and indivisible,
and descended to a female heir if no male were forthcoming. This he did by the famous Pragmatic
Sanction, a document which for fifteen years, from

1725 to 1740, was the pivot of European politics.
From State after State Charles purchased a guarantee of the Pragmatic Sanction, which amounted to
an undertaking to recognise his daughter, Maria
Theresa, as heir to the Hapsburg dominions. For
this he yielded to Spain broad lands in Italy, for
this he sacrificed commercial prospects to the sea-
powers England and Holland, for this he consented that Lorraine should pass from Germany to
France, for this he followed Russia into a Turkish
war which cost him great tracts on either side the
Danube. For this, too, he committed what was perhaps the most dangerous of all his blunders. He
played fast and loose with a time-honoured ally, and
estranged the King of Prussia.

Ever since the Peace of Westphalia had given
them freedom to make alliances where they would,
the policy of the Hohenzollerns had been to maintain a good understanding with Austria. It might,
indeed, happen, as after 1679, when Louis XIV.
hired them, that some other course became so advantageous that for the moment they adopted it. In
general however, the Emperor had most to give.
To him the German princes still looked for investiture, for arbitration, and for promotion, and if a State
desired to exercise its troops, who was so likely as
the lord of the long Hapsburg frontiers to be at war?
King Frederick William might reasonably hope that
the Power which had given his father the crown,
which had led Prussians to victory before Turin, and
which had permitted him to keep conquests in
Swedish Pomerania (1720), would reward his devoted

service by favouring his pretensions to inheritance on the Rhine.

Though a forceful squire, as a statesman the King lacked imagination. He was master of the finest soldiers in Europe, yet he dared not vindicate his claims to Jülich-Berg without the help of the Emperor, and he could not understand that the Emperor might be reluctant to help the master of the finest soldiers in Europe. Such was, however, the truth. The rise of the Hohenzollerns had long been watched at Vienna with not unnatural jealousy. Even against the Turk Prussians were but sparingly enlisted. The gift of the crown had been hotly opposed and bitterly regretted. When Frederick William cried, "The Emperor will have to spurn me from him with his feet: I am his unto death, faithful to the last drop of my blood," it was already a Hapsburg maxim that a new Vandal kingdom must not arise on the shores of the Baltic.

The statesmen at Vienna valued the Prussian alliance enough to employ Grumbkow and the Austrian ministers at Berlin to hoodwink Frederick William. As we have seen, they lavished pocket-money and sacrificed a bride in the hope of securing ascendancy over his son. But they blundered greatly when to please England and thereby to further the Pragmatic Sanction, they bade the King break off a marriage which all the world knew was fixed for the very next day, and they blundered still more when to please France and Holland with the same end in view they withdrew the promise of supporting him in Jülich-Berg. In 1732 Frederick William, for the only time

in his life, met Charles VI. face to face and the truth
with regard to the relations between Hapsburg and
Hohenzollern began to dawn upon him. All his life
he had been the vassal of an Emperor whom he had
imagined as a German overlord, heir to the dignity
of the Cæsars, who when the time was ripe would
look with paternal complacency upon the Prussian
claims. The vision faded and revealed a rival monarch, pompous, contemptuous, and shifty. The shock
of disillusionment was terrible, but before his death
he saw clearly. Once, it is said, he pointed to Frederick with the words, "There stands one who will
avenge me." It is certain that with failing breath he
warned his son against the policy of Vienna.

Thus, even supposing that Frederick's view of
politics had been no wider than his father's, that he
had come to the throne resolved merely to keep up
a great army and to win Jülich-Berg, he would none
the less have possessed remarkable freedom of action.
In foreign politics he was fettered by only one great
treaty, that of Berlin (December, 1728), by which
Prussia undertook to maintain the Pragmatic Sanction. But it was possible to contend that this agreement, which was made in secret to secure the
Emperor's assistance in Jülich-Berg, became void in
1739, when Austria entered into conflicting engagements with France.

Circumstances, too, were favourable to Frederick's liberty. The very existence of the Pragmatic Sanction, a violent remedy against dissolution,
was a guarantee that Austria would be harmless
for years to come. If Charles VI. and his heir were

loath to uphold Prussia on the Rhine, they would
be very unlikely to risk their own existence by
taking up arms against her. In other quarters
Prussia had little to fear. Hanover, the parvenu
electorate which lay like a broad barrier across the
direct road from Berlin to the West, had become
a dependency of England in 1714, and therefore
was not dangerous. Whatever might be the wishes
of George II., it was certain that Walpole would
not spend blood and treasure to maintain the House
of Pfalz-Sulzbach, Prussia's rival in Jülich-Berg, at
Düsseldorf. The Dutch, it is true, felt themselves
menaced by a Prussian garrison in Cleves, but
their course had by this time become that of a
mere cock-boat in the wake of Great Britain. France
alone remained to be considered, and France, with a
frontier fifty leagues from Berg, was guided by a
Walpole of her own, Cardinal Fleury, now nearing
the close of his eighty-seventh year. If then Frederick elected to make Prussia more considerable
among the Powers of the West by pressing his claims
to Berg he could fling his sword into the scales of
justice without great fear that a stronger hand would
turn the balance against him.

Adventure in the Rhine countries had much to
commend it to the young King. His House undoubtedly possessed some title to Berg, and it had been
the secular policy of the Hohenzollerns to forego no
claim without arguing to the death. The busy and
fertile Rhineland was a gold-mine in comparison
with the sterile Mark. Frederick, as an enthusiast
for the higher civilisation of the West, might well

feel drawn towards a duchy which lay more than half-way along the direct line from his capital to Paris. And, greatest merit of all in the eyes of a dynasty of merchants, Berg was eminently salable. The Rhenish duchies were like good accommodation-lands in the midst of thriving farms. Many rulers would always be glad of them and their price would therefore be high.

But the arguments against staking all on Berg were also strong. A statesman trained between the Elbe and the Oder could hardly be unaware that Prussia's heritage in the West was a mere windfall and that by interest as by situation she belonged to the system of the North. Her natural outlook was towards the Baltic, which formed the only free road between her centre and her eastern wing. It was by foregoing lands on the Baltic that she had gained rich bishoprics to the westward in 1648. Baltic Powers, Poland, Russia, and above all Sweden, had steadily influenced her politics since the advent of the Great Elector. History and geography alike seemed to beckon young Frederick to the sea. Let us therefore cast a glance at those among his neighbours whom he had to take account of, whatever plan he might devise.

Just as the traditional enemy of the Bourbon was the Hapsburg, so the traditional enemy of the Hohenzollern was the Vasa. This gifted House had ruled in Sweden since 1520 and had chosen for their country a path which it was not strong enough to follow to the end. They had striven to turn the Baltic into a Swedish lake by conquering all its

FREDERICK WILLIAM THE FIRST.
AFTER THE PAINTING BY F. W. WEIDEMAN.

coasts. Success seemed nearest when in 1630 Gustavus landed in Germany, and at the point of the sword compelled his kinsman of Brandenburg to favour his adventure. The result of these bold steps was for Sweden a swift blaze of glory; for Brandenburg a decade of misery inflicted in great part by Swedish hands. In 1648 the great treaty compensated the Swedes for their work by driving the Great Elector from the mouth of the Oder. Their ambition to be masters of the Baltic shores, however, remained, and the Great Elector suffered much at their hands before the Peace of Oliva (1660) confirmed his sovereignty over Ost-Preussen. What happened at Fehrbellin and after it has been already told. The meteoric career of Charles XII. (1697–1718), who began by humbling Prussia, but ended by losing Stettin to her, is no part of our story, except in so far as it interested and influenced young Frederick. It suffices that in 1740 Sweden was factious and impotent, and that her aged King still held that part of Pomerania which Prussia did not possess. To acquire Western Pomerania was therefore a possible object for Frederick's ambition.

The central mass of the Hohenzollern dominions touched along almost the whole of its eastern frontier a Power whose decline was even more visible than that of Sweden. The Polish Republic, which almost encircled Ost-Preussen, formed perhaps the strangest spectacle that Europe has ever seen. A vaster country than any of the Western Powers, Poland remained in the Middle Ages. Her constitution, indeed, seemed to have no other end than to make progress impossible. There were only two classes, nobles and serfs, the free and the unfree. But where every freeman was noble, many nobles were poor. These served for hire, and were distinguished, it is said, from men of lower birth by the privilege of being flogged upon a Turkey carpet. The direction of this vast country rested with a few thousand feudal chiefs who elected a nominal King from within their own body or outside it. They made the laws themselves, but a single dissentient voice could wreck the work of a whole Diet, as the annual session of Parliament was termed, and of late years this right had commonly been exercised. What trade there was, was left to the despised class of German burghers. The fighting force grew every year more feeble. While Austria could boast a Eugene and Russia a Peter, while the parade-ground at Potsdam was trodden by ever-growing masses of men who handled modern weapons with the precision given by daily practice, the Poles were blindly trusting in feudal levies generalled by a puppet King.

At Frederick's accession, however, Poland still possessed two elements of strength besides her vast bulk and the knightly courage of her sons. These were the Saxon connexion and the port of Danzig. Two years earlier, at the price of war with France (1733–1738) and loss of lands in Italy, Charles VI. had secured the Polish crown for the son of the late King, Augustus III., the Elector of Saxony. The Emperor made this sacrifice to win support for the Pragmatic Sanction and to propitiate Russia, who looked upon Poland as her own if the French candidate were expelled. And, as the road from Dresden to Warsaw passed through the Hapsburg province of Silesia, Augustus had good reason to be faithful to the daughter of Charles VI.

Poland none the less promised much to a king of Prussia who could wait. Her artificial connexion with Saxony, established by foreign Powers against the will of a majority of the Poles, could only weaken the frail bonds which bound the State together. Poland, all the world had long known, would one day fall in pieces, and who should hinder Prussia from gathering some of them? For the moment, however, Augustus could defend his new dominions. A king of Prussia in a fever to act at once could not assail Poland without laying bare his flank to Saxony and to her Imperial ally.

But could Prussia in 1740 afford to wait? If Augustus's dream were to be fulfilled would not she be in jeopardy? The Elector hoped that the Emperor would cede to him a part of Lower Silesia, so that Prussia might be for ever divided and hemmed in by a Saxon-Polish State. Had we no other guide than the map, we might be tempted to guess that it was to avert this peril that Frederick seized Silesia. If it were true it were a grievous fault. Augustus, who was no statesman, might dream of a hereditary crown, but a firm Saxony-Poland was in fact impossible. Dresden and Warsaw were centuries apart. Out of two such halves no strong whole could be compounded. The one was German, the other Slav; the one industrial, the other primitive; the one Lutheran, the other partly Romanist and partly

Orthodox. Compounds so discordant could have found no abiding unity in a monarchy based on the treason of their common head against the constitution of each. Nor could such a State have barred for a decade the path of the Muscovite Colossus which Peter had already roused and which Catherine and Alexander were soon to reinspire.

In weighing Frederick's wisdom we must not forget that the share of Poland which he might expect that Prussia was destined to acquire, and which did, in fact, fall to her during his own lifetime, would change Ost-Preussen from an isolated province into a strong limb of a well-knit State. It gave her the lower waters of a third great arterial river—the Vistula. But it came to her in 1774 shorn of its chief glory, the old portal of the Vistula and strong tower of Poland, the matchless town of Danzig. Frederick had seen that fair city, a hearth of German culture among the Slavs, with its giant Marien-kirche towering over a mass of battlements and gates and churches of stately civic halls and mansions hardly less stately, the whole forming a Venice of the North beside which his capital was but a market town. He must have taken note of the foundation of all this grandeur, great warehouses on busy wharves, canals crowded with masts and hulls from many lands. And he cannot have been blind to the fact that within a few miles of this prize lay Ost-Preussen, and that, since Augustus had surrendered Curland, within a few miles of Ost-Preussen lay Russia. Seldom has a king had clearer warning to look before he leaped.

Thus, without departing from the policy of the men who had made Prussia what she was, the young King had his choice between adventure on the Rhine or across the Peene and a policy of expectant watchfulness on the Vistula. But if he were capable of building upon the foundations of his forefathers the loftiest structure that they would bear, then a still more glorious conquest might be his. Lord of Stettin and of the ports of Ost-Preussen, he might claim a share in what all the nations coveted, the empire of the sea.

It is one of the most grotesque facts in history that the Emperor William II., when he cried, " Our future lies upon the water," should have been uttering as prophecy what ought to have been commonplace for a century and a half. Even in 1740 the truth that the New World offered a fairer career than the Old was not hidden from statesmen less astute than Frederick. Since the Armada foundered in 1588, the nations of Europe had been realising it one by one. Spain and Portugal, the first in the field, still held a vast heritage across the ocean, but their monopoly was not as unchallenged as of old. First the Dutch, who as subjects of Spain had monopolised that carrying-trade which seemed to be beneath the dignity of an Iberian gentleman, enriched themselves so rapidly that they were able to throw off the yoke of Philip II. and to establish a colonial and commercial empire of their own. Then England, tardily comprehending the changing conditions of life, grappled with their little republic in a long and doubtful struggle. Finally weight told, and after the Revolution of 1688 England under her Dutch King led the way and Holland followed in a campaign against a rival dangerous to both. For France had been guided by Colbert into the path of greatness beyond the seas, and it was by grasping at Spain and the Indies that Louis XIV. aroused the keenest apprehensions that he might become dictator of the world. Only at the cost of two mighty wars had the danger from France been averted for a generation. By the Peace of Utrecht (1713) the Sea Powers gained security for themselves and for their commerce, but the prize of North America still remained to be fought for between France and England.

In the early years of the eighteenth century other competitors put to sea. Under Peter the Great, the new land Power, Russia, struggled to become maritime, though her horizon, as yet, hardly extended beyond European waters. But in 1722 the Emperor Charles VI. made his port of Ostend the headquarters of a new Imperial East India Company, and England, France, and Holland joined in an outcry against German competition. Nine years later they were appeased. The Hapsburg sacrificed the future of his House to its past. To purchase guarantees of the Pragmatic Sanction he withdrew his support from the Company, which none the less was able to maintain itself for more than sixty years.

If then the tide had set so strongly towards distant continents that even conservative ill-knit Austria was swept along with it, we may well ask, what of Prussia? The history of our own time makes the question more pertinent. North Germany has shown beyond dispute not only that she can now build ships, a fact which proves little or nothing as to her powers in the past, but also that she can fill them with brave and skilful seamen, whose character only many generations of worthy forefathers could create. These forefathers were the Prussians of Frederick's day, poor, fearless, and docile, living on the borders of the Baltic, speeding and welcoming its fleets at Memel, at Pillau, at Colberg, and above all at Stettin. Why, it may be wondered, was Frederick blind to the signs of the times? Why did not he at the very outset of his reign hasten to employ the power of the Crown, which Frederick William had raised so high, to equip a Prussian Baltic Company, a Prussian West Africa Company, even a Prussian East India Company?

Never was the political situation more favourable to such an enterprise than when Frederick grasped the reins. No neighbour could enforce a veto upon Prussian maritime enterprise. Poland was in the last stage of impotence and decay. Russia, who might form a good customer, was not yet equipped for conquest. Austria could not afford to offend a German ally. Sweden had lost her sting and her province of Pomerania was a hostage at Frederick's mercy. The Sea Powers would view the enterprise askance, but they too had given hostages to Prussia. If England played foul, the master of eighty thousand men could overrun Hanover in a fortnight and the Dutch would think twice ere they provoked the lord of Cleves. Of all Powers Denmark, the surly janitor of the Baltic, was perhaps the best able to injure Prussian commerce with impunity, but the heir of the Great Elector might be trusted to find a way with Denmark.   Thus Europe seemed to invite Prussia to follow the destiny which nature prescribed, and which led to wealth.   Firmly governed, armed to the teeth, learned, Protestant, and rich, she might have pursued her old opportunist policy on the mainland with full confidence that the future would bring her wider boundaries and yet greater strength.

In an earlier generation and with smaller means the Great Elector had perceived that the true path for Prussia lay across the seas.   Balked of Stettin, he strove to make Pillau and Memel his London and Amsterdam.   His little Armada of ten frigates attacked the Spaniards with success.   In a humble way there began to be Brandenburgish West Indies, and in 1683 Fort Great-Fredericksburgh was built upon the Brandenburgish Gold Coast.   But the Great Elector's son and grandson lacked either his firm hand or his imagination.   While Frederick I. was squabbling with the Dutch about armchairs, the Dutch were driving his subjects from West Africa. Frederick William, the apostle of domestic economy, was impatient of flunkeys, universities, and colonies, the several extravagances of his father and of his grandfather.   Would Frederick II. prove himself more enlightened?

We see with amazement that he did not.   A prince who was accounted clever, who had spent the first decade of manhood in pondering on high politics, who revered the memory of the Great

Elector, and followed the fortunes of England with keen interest — how could such an one ignore what the movement of the times and the course of after events seem to point out so clearly? Among his first acts was the establishment of a new department of manufactures. He commanded the head of it to take measures for improving the condition of existing industries, for introducing new ones, and for bringing in foreign capital and foreign hands. Why did he not at the same time establish a department of marine? Why did he wait till East Frisia fell to Prussia before making even a half-hearted effort to win profit from the sea?

A partial explanation may lie in the fact that Frederick lacked the inspiration drawn from travel. The stupid fears of Frederick William that his son would become too Frenchified in his life or too Austrian in his politics had closed to Frederick the doors of the best school of his time. Who knows how much profit the Great Elector brought to his State from his education in Holland, or Peter the Great from his journeys in the West? Save at Danzig, Frederick had hardly seen with his own eyes the dignity which commerce might create. Save for two stolen days in Strasburg in the first months of his reign, a secret visit to Holland in 1755, and a meeting with the Emperor in Moravia in 1770, he was fated never to gain fresh knowledge of what would now be foreign lands except at the head of his army.

Again, Frederick's political economy was unfavourable to Prussian commerce. At Cüstrin he learned from Hille that the only trade by which a

country can profit is that which adds to its stock
of gold and silver.   His father had carried this idea
to its logical conclusion.   He had seized the precious metals and locked them up.   Like a timid
farmer who thinks that the bank will break, he had
hidden in his cellars the hoard which represented
the economies of a lifetime. Frederick therefore
found a treasure of more than twenty-six million
marks, at a time when the weekly wage of a common soldier hardly exceeded one.

It seems clear that a policy of hoarding could be
wise only when war was in sight.   In time of war
that Government would be happiest which had most
coined money with which to pay its troops.   But in
time of peace not even Frederick William could
take a breed from barren metal by keeping it locked
up.   Profit could be drawn from it in either of two
ways.   The coined metal might be spent to advantage, so that the State bought something, such
as a school, or a farm, or a flock of sheep, which
would in the future be worth more than the sum
laid out.   Or it might be lent to citizens who would
pay for the use of it and establish with its aid some
business which might be taxed.   By locking up the
surplus funds of the country, however, the King
stifled commerce at the birth.   Frederick did not
detect the fallacy, and Germany waited till the
nineteenth century for her commercial rise.

Though nimble-witted and fond of philosophy,
the King was hardly profound.   His lector, the
Swiss de Catt, tells a significant story of his first
discussion   with   a   singular   stranger   on   a   Dutch

vessel, whom he did not suspect to be the lord of Prussia. Frederick, he says,

"tried to prove that creation was impossible. At this last point I stood out in opposition. 'But how can one create something out of nothing?' said he. 'That is not the question,' answered I, 'the question is, whether such a Being as God can or cannot give existence to what has yet none?' He seemed embarrassed and added, 'But the Universe is eternal.' 'You are in a circle,' said I, 'how will you get out of it?' 'I skip over it,' said he, laughing; and then began to speak of other things."

He wrote incessantly on history and politics, always with the clearness and sprightliness that seem inseparable from the French tongue which he employed, and always with the confidence of a journalist and of a king. Of his ancestor Joachim I. he says: "He received the surname of Nestor in the same way as Louis XIII. that of 'the Just'; that is, for no reason that any one can discover" — and this is a very fair example of his style. Sense, lucidity, concise statement, even wit, distinguish his writings. He made so many confident generalisations on political affairs that some have almost of necessity proved correct. But of deep insight, still less of great constructive power, there is little trace.

In freedom from illusions, however, Frederick surpassed some rival statesmen. This was abundantly illustrated at the very outset of his reign. He saw, as Charles VI. could not, that the claim of the Emperor to be lord of the world rested on no firm basis. Early in 1737 he had written: "If the Emperor dies to-day or to-morrow, what revolutions will come to pass! Every one will wish to share his estate, and we shall see as many factions as there are sovereigns." The discovery, indeed, was by no means new. More than a century earlier Gustavus Adolphus had told the Germans that their constitution was rotten. But Frederick informs the Emperor pointedly that he is only first among his peers. He was equally clear-sighted in the choice of means to spread his views. William the Silent had perceived a fact dark to many statesmen since his time — that the public opinion of Europe is worth much and that it may be courted through the Press. Frederick had already composed the earliest of his many pamphlets, which he intended to publish anonymously as the work of an Englishman, to rouse the Sea Powers against France.

More significant than all else was the fact that he viewed his own strength with clearer eyes than his father's. Frederick William had never been able to convince himself that Prussia was a strong State: Frederick wears no blinkers and with his accession the day of half measures is over. Two years before this he had written to Grumbkow words which express his real opinion of the old policy of his House. The affair of Berg, which he as Crown Prince earnestly hoped would enable him to win fame on the battle-field, had then entered upon a phase adverse to Prussian expectations. Austria had been prevailed on to join with France and the Sea Powers in claiming that it should be referred to the arbitration of a congress, and Frederick William, though disgusted, had decided to give way. Of this decision Grumbkow approved, writing, " I am persuaded that a King of Prussia, like a King of Sardinia, will always have more need of the fox's hide than of the lion's." Frederick replies (March, 1738) :

" I confess that I perceive in the answer a conflict between greatness and humiliation to which I can never agree. The answer is like the declaration of a man who has no stomach for fighting and yet wishes to seem as if he had. There were only two solutions, either to reply with noble pride, with no evasions in the shape of petty negotiations whose real value will soon be recognised, or to bow ourselves under the degrading yoke that they wish to lay upon us. I am no subtle politician to couple together a set of contradictory threats and submissions, I am young, I would perhaps follow the impetuosity of my nature; under no circumstances would I do anything by halves."

Close observers held that a change of king would be followed by a change of policy and that Frederick was likely to attempt great things. What these would be no one, with the possible exception of the young King himself, had the least idea. What in the opinion of the present writer they should have been is sufficiently indicated above. What they were, will be shown in the following chapter.

At first, for all his determination to lose no time, the results of his accession seemed but small. No

human being could maintain that he was swayed
by his affections. Though Duhan, Keith, and
Katte's father received some measure of compensation for their sufferings, Frederick's behaviour
towards those concerned in his early struggles em-
boldened the wits to say that his memory was
excellent as far back as 1730. His Rheinsberg
friends expected to share the spoils of office. They
were disappointed in a way that has reminded
Macaulay of the treatment of Falstaff by Henry V.
Frederick was as masterful as his father. The aged
Prince of Anhalt-Dessau, who had created the
Prussian army, and the aged General von Schulenburg, who had risked all rather than condemn Katte
to death, were humiliated by royal reprimands.
Grumbkow, with whom he had corresponded for
more than eight years in terms of affectionate
intimacy, might have caused him a moment's em-
barrassment, but he had just died — "for me the
greatest conceivable gain," the King assured his
sister. He broke up his father's useless and costly
regiment of giant grenadiers, a measure which Frederick William had himself advised, but he increased
the effective strength of the army by nearly ten
thousand men. At the same time he sounded, more
clearly even than his ancestor George William, the
note of religious toleration for which Brandenburg
had been honourably distinguished in the time of
her greatest peril. "In this country," he instructed
his officials, "every one shall get to heaven in his
own way."

The crowned philosopher always recognised the

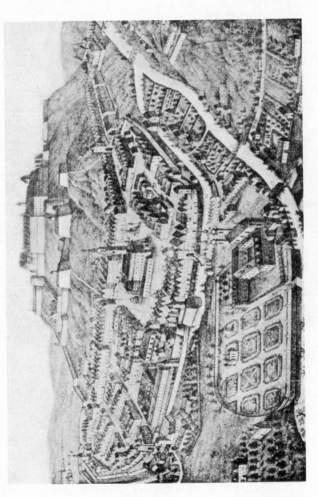

VIEW OF GLATZ IN THE EIGHTEENTH CENTURY.

FROM AN OLD PRINT.

difference between the things which were Cæsar's and the things which were God's. The scion of a Calvinist House, he began his reign by authorising the Lutherans to restore their ritual, which had been arbitrarily simplified by his father. He was soon to court the favour of Breslau by supplying her with Protestant preachers, and of Glatz by bestowing vestments upon a statue of the Virgin. When Romanist Europe expelled the Jesuits, he seized the opportunity of picking up well-trained teachers cheap. Some of his papist subjects had a fancy for buying handkerchiefs which bore the effigies of saints. Frederick, eager to encourage the linen manufacture, bade his officials find out which saints were the most popular and adjust the supply to the demand.

A story cited by Carlyle illuminates Frederick's views upon the relations between Church and State. He was questioning the monks of Cleve, to whom the old dukes had assigned an income from the royal forest-dues for masses to be said on their behalf. "'You still say those masses then?' 'Certainly, your Majesty.' 'And what good does anybody get out of them?' 'Your Majesty, those old sovereigns are to obtain heavenly mercy by them, to be delivered out of purgatory by them.' 'Purgatory? It is a sore thing for the Forests, all this while! And they are not yet out, those poor souls, after so many hundred years of praying?' Monks have a fatal apprehension, No. 'When will they be out, and the thing complete?' Monks cannot say. 'Send me a courier whenever it *is* complete!'

sneers the King," and leaves them to finish the *Te
Deum* which they had begun to greet his arrival.

Lastly, the forms with which Frederick took up
the kingship showed that the fears of his father and
the hopes of enlightened men were alike without
foundation. It became clear that the philosopher-
king, though he relieved famine and tempted learned
foreigners to Berlin, would not revert to the ill-timed
pageantry of his grandfather. Nor—though he freed
the press and restricted to a few cases the use of
torture—would he anticipate the glory of some
Hohenzollern who is still unborn by fostering a spirit
of individual liberty among his people. Impatient
of coronation, which he classed among the "useless
and frivolous ceremonies which ignorance and superstition have established," he received the homage of
his subjects by proxy everywhere save in Ost-Preussen, Brandenburg, and Cleve. At Königsberg he
paid homage to the memory of liberties which his
ancestors had crushed, and which he had no intention of animating anew. The ceremony at Berlin
was made memorable by one of his rare displays of
feeling. When he appeared on the balcony of the
Castle and looked down upon the surging crowd in
the square below, he was so affected that he remained standing many minutes, silent and buried in
thought. Then, recovering himself, he bowed to the
multitude, and rode off to attend a military review.

It is, however, on his journey to Wesel, his Rhenish
capital, that he reveals most clearly how the Crown
Prince has changed into the King. Wilhelmina had
found him of late so careless, even so uncivil, a cor-

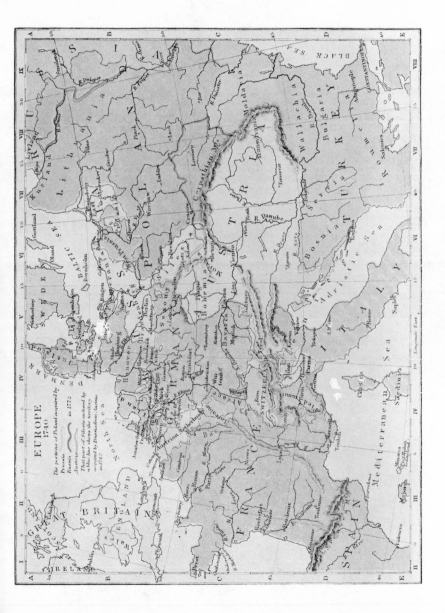

EUROPE
1740

The partition of Poland marked by
Prussia
Russia
Austria   in 1772.

That part of Silesia enclosed by
a blue line shows the territory
acquired by Prussia from Austria
in 1742.

respondent that the news of his coming to Baireuth
prostrated her with joy. He seemed to her so altered
in countenance and developed in form that, just as
after his imprisonment at Cüstrin, she hardly recognised him. But a less welcome change was only
too perceptible. Wilhelmina found her brother's
caresses forced, his conversation trivial, their sister,
the Margravine of Ansbach, more favoured than
herself. The remainder of the journey proved that
Frederick at least remained true to the French. At
Frankfort he disguised himself for a flying visit to
Strasburg. There his little party put up at an inn,
sent the landlord to invite officers to their table, and
visited the theatre. The mask was penetrated by a
runaway Prussian whose tall brother had been kidnapped for the army and who recognised the son of
his former King. The greatest pleasure of all came
last. At Wesel, besides dealing with the affair of
Herstal, which will be described in the next chapter,
Frederick for the first time paid homage in person
to Voltaire.

At the end of October Wilhelmina visited Berlin,
but her brother welcomed her coldly. She found
abundant proofs that he had become inscrutable.
She describes in her *Memoirs* how the Queen
Mother had shut herself up, equally astonished and
mortified at her complete exclusion from affairs of
State. "Some complained of the little care he had
to reward those who had been attached to him as
prince royal; others, of his avarice, which they said
surpassed that of the late King; others of his pas-
sions; others again of his suspicions, of his mistrust,

of his pride, and of his dissimulation." This criticism from an unwonted quarter may possibly be explained away. It has been suggested that the King's treatment of his sister at Baireuth was due to the same policy of repelling every possible claimant to influence his policy, which may be held to excuse the snubs inflicted upon Dessau and Schulenburg and the dignified exile of Frederick's mother and wife. His conduct at Rheinsberg, whither Wilhelmina followed him, does not admit of the same excuse.

" The little spare time that he had," she complains, " was spent in the company of wits or men of letters. Such were Voltaire, Maupertuis, Algarotti, and Jordan. I saw the King but seldom. I had no ground for being satisfied with our interviews. The greater part of them was spent either in embarrassed words of politeness or in outrageous witticisms on the bad state of the Margrave's finances; indeed he often ridiculed him and the princes of the empire, which I felt very much."

CHAPTER IV

THE SILESIAN ADVENTURE, 1740–1742

THE proceedings of Frederick in 1740, trivial as
some of them are, reveal him as a statesman,
just as the events of 1730 revealed him as
a man. They therefore possess an interest such as
hardly any other part of his reign can claim. For a
few months he is free to choose his own path in life,
guided only by instinct and education. Thus an
element of free-will is present which is to some extent lacking in two notable crises of his fortunes—
the tragedy of 1730 and the miracle of 1757. This
year sums up, as it were, the eight and twenty
which had gone to make Frederick what he was : it
shapes his course in the six and forty that were to
follow.

In the story of Prussia, 1740 inevitably suggests
comparison with 1640, when the Great Elector likewise stood at the parting of the ways. Then and
for years afterwards the choice had lain between
existence and ruin ; now it was between increase by
natural growth and perhaps speedier increase by
speculation. For a century Prussia had seldom de-
parted from a policy of thrift and autocracy at home

and opportunism abroad. Would she now abandon it? Frederick's early measures showed that he intended no sweeping changes in domestic politics. We may therefore postpone an examination of the system which he there pursued. For us he is at present only the lord of ninety thousand of the best-drilled troops in the world, entangled in no alliances and hampered by no fears. What choice would be for him the wisest?

Calm reflection on the situation of Europe in 1740 seems to show that Frederick's strength was to sit still. Signs were abundant that the peace which had prevailed almost from his birth could not endure much longer. Apart from the problem of Austria, grave questions had arisen which not even a Walpole and a Fleury could settle otherwise than by the sword. France and England, it was felt, would soon resume the duel which the Peace of Utrecht had but interrupted, and would struggle for primacy in America and in the world. Spain and England were already at war, and Europe knew that the Bourbon Kings of Spain and France, who were uncle and nephew, were joined in close alliance. To strike at King George without crossing the sea France must aim at Hanover, and the sword of Frederick, the neighbour of Hanover, would be bid for by both sides. According to the convenient theory then current, a prince could hire out an army without committing his State to war, so that Frederick stood to gain much,—money, military glory, experience for his men, perhaps even territory for his House,— while he need stake nothing save that which he had

long desired to hazard,—his own life and the lives
of his soldiers.

A Hohenzollern was the last man in the world to
undervalue what he might wish to sell. Frederick
strove to persuade Europe that in him a new and
greater Gustavus had appeared. He increased his
army ostentatiously and bade his representative at
Versailles speak of his active and impetuous way
of thinking.

"You can say," he continues, "that it is to be feared
that this increase kindles a fire which may set all
Europe in a blaze; that it is the way of youth to be
adventurous, and that the alluring visions of heroic
fame may disturb and have disturbed the peace of
countless nations in the world."

The prospect of acquisitions in the Rhineland
seemed first to engage his thoughts. In hopes of
winning Berg he not only made overtures to France,
but even invited the help of Russia. The fruit of
these negotiations was small. Their significance,
however, is great, since they showed that Frederick
intended to choose his allies without regard to the
tradition of his House in favour of Austria, and also
that he would not shrink from favouring Muscovite
development by employing Cossacks in Western
Germany.

At the same time that he bargained in this spirit
with foreign Powers, Frederick compelled his brother
Germans to mark the change of accent which he was
introducing into the old language of his House.
Brandenburg had taken up the informal protectorate

of the German Protestants when the Saxon Elector by becoming Romanist (1697) resigned it. Frederick William devised a safe but effective method of checking Romanist aggression. If any German prince persecuted Protestants, the King of Prussia used forthwith to apply similar oppression to his own papist subjects. Thus, without stirring from Berlin, he stayed the hand of persecutors in the distant valleys of the Neckar and the Salzach. His son soon proved himself ready to go to greater lengths.

Claims and counter-claims as to territory had arisen between one of the great Romanist princes, the Archbishop of Mainz, and the Landgrave of Hesse-Cassel, the heir of one of the earliest champions of the Reformation. The former relied on his own troops and on those of neighbouring bishops, while he also possessed the support of the Emperor, whose right to judge the case had been challenged by his opponent. The Landgrave appealed to the King of Prussia and to other princes of the Empire. Frederick's reply was immediate, emphatic, and successful. "In case of need," he wrote to his brother-Elector of Mainz, "we should not know how to refrain from affording to the aforementioned His Dilection the Lord Landgrave William the necessary protection and help against unlawful force and disturbance." At these words the hostile coalition—Elector, bishops, and Emperor —melted away. The young King, it was apparent, had entered the field of German politics with *éclat*.

Equally peremptory and equally successful was Frederick's verdict for his own claims in a dispute

with the Bishop of Liège with regard to Herstal, a
tiny barony lying on the Meuse to the westward of
Aix-la-Chapelle. The inhabitants had resisted the
officers of his father, who would gladly have sold
Herstal to Liège, and the Bishop, who wished to
buy but could not come to terms, had egged them
on. Frederick, scorning the advice of his ministers,
resolved to use his strength as a giant. From Wesel
he sent the following ultimatum to the Bishop:

"Cousin! Knowing all the attacks that you have made
upon my unquestionable rights over my free barony of
Herstal, and how the seditious men of Herstal have been
supported for some years in their detestable disobedience to me, I have ordered my privy-councillor Ram-
bonnet to visit you on my behalf, to demand from you
in my name a sincere and categorical explanation within
the space of two days, whether you wish to protect the
mutineers of Herstal in their abominable disorder and
disobedience. In case you refuse, or delay that just
reply which I demand of right, you will render yourself
solely responsible before all the world for the consequences which your refusal will inevitably bring after
it. I am, etc."

"This is strong, this is lively," cried the ambassadors at Berlin when they read it; "it is the language
of Louis XIV.; it is a beginning which shows what
we must expect some day from this prince." Their
prophecy was to be fulfilled sooner than they anticipated. In the meantime the new diplomacy won
another triumph. The Bishop made no reply to the
ultimatum and in a week's time the Prussians, sow-
ing apologies broadcast over Europe, seized his

county of Hoorn. The apologies concluded with
the assertion : " His Majesty will never put from him
a just and reasonable arrangement with the said
prince, as the sole end which his justice and moderation have in view in this affair, these two invariable
principles being the pole-star of all his actions." The
"just and reasonable arrangement" proved to be
the payment of two hundred thousand thalers to
the King.

Frederick could therefore congratulate himself
that within five months of his accession he had
taught both Prussia and Europe that he was stronger
than his father. It was clear that he was resolved
not to be hoodwinked by man or woman. He had rejected the advice of his cautious ministers with the
pleasantry that when they spoke of war they resembled an Iroquois talking of astronomy. The
event had gone far towards silencing the taunt of
Europe that "the Prussians never shoot," and towards establishing the truth of Frederick's well-
known simile, " The Emperor is an old phantom of
an idol and has no longer any nerves."

A king of Prussia with such a spirit as Frederick
had already shown was not likely to rest long upon
his oars. But it was chance that determined the
course that he was next to steer. The Herstal
treaty, which confirmed his second diplomatic victory, was signed on October 20th. Six days later a
swift courier brought to Rheinsberg the news that
on that same day the Emperor, Charles VI., had
died. Frederick lay ill of fever. He defied his
doctors, took quinine, and was well. He sent for

his cautious minister Podewils and for the dauntless soldier Schwerin, and wrote to Voltaire:

"The least expected event in the world forbids me this time to open my soul to yours as is my wont. . . . I believe that in June it will be powder, soldiers and trenches rather than actresses, ballets and theatres. . . . This is the moment of the entire transformation of the old system of politics: the stone is loosed which Nebuchadnezzar beheld when it rolled upon the image of four metals and destroyed it."

Two days later he expressed himself with still greater confidence: "I am not going to Berlin, a trifle like the Emperor's death does not demand great commotions. All was foreseen, all was thought out in advance. So it is only a question of carrying out designs which I have long had in my mind."

These designs were, in brief, so to use the political situation created by the death of Charles VI. as to add to Prussia the whole, or at least the north-western part, of the Hapsburg province of Silesia— the fertile basin of the upper Oder. In conception and in execution the idea was Frederick's own. It is the pediment of his fame as a hero of his nation. All the world knows that the capture of Silesia converted Frederick the Second into Frederick the Great. It is therefore imperative that at this point, with judgment unclouded by the smoke of battle and the incense of victory, we should address ourselves to the double enquiry, Was it necessary? and Was it right? postponing but not evading the further question, Was it wise?

The plea that Silesia was necessary to Prussia, that the existence of Prussia could only be prolonged or her people safeguarded or fed if Silesia were hers, may be dismissed at once. Necessity is the usual pillar of a claim to extend the area of dominion over lands lately rescued from barbarism. The Law of Nations declares that, when under such conditions two civilised states desire the same territory, one may further its claim by showing that without this addition the territory which it already has would be rendered worthless. But what might give a good title to Fashoda would be absurd if applied to Breslau. Frederick had himself investigated the subject nine years before when studying under Hille at Cüstrin. He then concluded that Silesia did Prussia commercial injury by exporting to her goods at lower rates than the merchants of Brandenburg could afford to take. This state of things, he and Hille thought, demanded a protective tariff. It could not by any stretch of imagination dictate or justify the annexation of a province. Nor from a military point of view was there imperative necessity for acquiring Silesia. It was no doubt desirable for Prussia that she should avert future danger by thrusting a wedge between Saxony and Poland, and that more than one-fifth of the road from Vienna to Berlin, by way of Breslau, should be in Prussian hands. But no Prussian could maintain in 1740 that if Glogau and Breslau remained Austrian his state would be imperilled in the same sense as the German Empire would have been imperilled if Metz and Strasburg had remained French in 1871, or as the British Empire

THE RATHHAUS IN BRESLAU.
FROM A STEEL ENGRAVING.

would be imperilled to-day if Pretoria and Johannesburg were still in hostile hands. The plea of hereditary right, not that of necessity, was put forward by Frederick as the basis of his claims. In 1740 the latter would have seemed equally absurd in law and in fact.

The second question, Was it right for Prussia to attempt to acquire Silesia for her own profit? may seem to have little claim to discussion by Frederick's biographers, because considerations of right and wrong counted for little with Frederick himself. There seems to be no evidence that Frederick either in his public or private life practised the stale hypocrisies of truth and morality. What it seemed to him profitable to do, that he did; what it seemed to him profitable to say, that he said. "If there is anything to be gained by being honest, let us be honest; if it is necessary to deceive, let us deceive," are his own words. In the case of Silesia, his avowal to Podewils, who urged that some legal claim could be furbished up, is sufficiently explicit. On November 7th the King writes: "The question of right (*droit*) is the affair of the ministers; it is your affair; it is time to work at it in secret, for the orders to the troops are given." Two days later he received the news of the death of the Empress of Russia, which was worth more to him than a thousand title-deeds. Russia had no clear rule of succession, and usually fell into anarchy at the demise of the Crown. Frederick could therefore strike southward with confidence that his flank was safe.

The question, Was it right? has, however, a deeper

historical interest than that involved in the biography of a king of Prussia. Frederick's indifference to all right renders it unnecessary to reflect in his case upon the spectacle of a good man cheerfully doing evil in the service of the State—of Sir Henry Wotton setting out with a jest "to lie abroad," or of Cavour exclaiming, "If we did for ourselves what we do for Italy, what scoundrels we should be!" But it is to be borne in mind that in 1740 it was impossible to lay down with certainty the duty of a state towards its neighbours. The standard of right and wrong for states in their dealings with one another was not yet fixed. Nearly a quarter of a century later it was possible for Frederick to write, "The jurisprudence of sovereigns is commonly the right of the stronger." But Maria Theresa was taught that sovereigns must rule their peoples as branches of one Christian family.

Hitherto the old idea that a state was the property —the estate—of the king had not lost all its influence. Even in England, which was already the leader of the world in politics, the dynasty elected by the nation had great weight in determining foreign policy. Without the knowledge of any Englishman, William III. had committed England to the partition of Spain, and in defiance of most Englishmen George II. was soon to commit her to the defence of the Pragmatic Sanction. But if England was not yet wholly free from the ancient notion, much more did Austria and Prussia, bundles of Hapsburg and Hohenzollern lands, resemble the estates of their rulers.

From this two consequences followed, vital in that day, almost incomprehensible in ours. It was, in the first place, a maxim universally accepted among the rulers of the Continent that the inhabitants of a province had little or no share in choosing their overlord. They might possess rights, even the right not to be divided between several lords, but they could be sold or exchanged or given away by one overlord to another without their own desire or even consent. This maxim was accepted to the full by both Hapsburgs and Hohenzollerns, whose fortunes had been made by the union of family estates, and who never hesitated to barter those estates to advance their own fortunes. Thus the fact that a province would be happier under an overlord who professed the same religion with itself would, according to the ideas prevalent in 1740, afford no good reason for change. Religious oppression by a ruler, it was universally admitted, entitled other rulers to interfere. But religious differences between ruler and ruled gave no such right.

In so far, then, as States still resembled estates, the relations between them varied according to the personal character of their kings and princes. The nation ruled by an honourable king observed its engagement strictly, at whatever inconvenience to itself. If a State evaded its engagements the king's honour was held to have been tarnished. Unfortunately for Europe, this theory had been shaken, if not shattered, by the reign of Louis XIV. The Apollo of France, the cynosure of the Christian world, the king who was the very fount of honour and in person the very pattern of chivalry, had in his dealings with the Dutch and the Germans shown himself a

kinsman of Machiavelli and of Bismarck. His conspicuous severance of political from personal morality
shook the faith of the world, and in the corrupt generation which followed Louis XIV. and nurtured
Frederick even the standard of personal morality
sank low.

At the death of Charles VI., therefore, men were
perplexed about the source of law as between State
and State. It seemed no longer sufficient to trust
in princes, and yet what new code could be set up?
Frederick's attack upon Silesia struck a deadly blow
at the remnant of the old system. His whole career
was to influence the new profoundly.

In answer to our two first questions it would therefore appear that the attack upon Silesia was not dictated to Frederick by hard necessity, and that, tried
by the old standard of honour between princes, it
was clearly wrong. The third question—Was it
wise?—is of a different order, for it is far from certain
that the wisdom or folly of Frederick's act has been
sufficiently tested by time. A safe step towards the
truth, indeed, is to examine the international situation and calculate Frederick's chances of success, as a
statesman would compute them from the facts which
lay before him in 1740. First of all, however, we
must account for the fact that Frederick, who was
only the third Hohenzollern to wear a crown, found
himself in a position to assail the dynasty which had
held for centuries the foremost place in Germany.

The House of Hapsburg, perhaps to a greater extent than any other of the ruling families in Europe,
lay under the spell of its own past. This was due in

part to its native pride and sluggish blood, in part
to its long association with the oldest and most dignified institution of the Christian world — the Holy
Roman Empire.   From 1438 onwards the descendants of Rudolf of Hapsburg had been chosen in
unbroken sequence to fill the office which entitled
its possessor to style himself Lord of the World.
The radiance of old Rome had gilded Vienna for so
long a time that it seemed to have transfigured the
race that reigned there.   Thus the Hapsburgs grew
proud with a pride which no other House could
rival, and no Hapsburg was prouder than Charles
VI., the Anglo-Austrian candidate in the War of
the Spanish Succession.   His pride was fatal, for it
banished him from the world of fact.   He could
never comprehend how Europe could leave off fighting to make him King of Spain, nor how the King
of Prussia, who served him with towel and basin as
Grand Chamberlain of the Empire, could cherish
aims and aspirations which conflicted with his own.
Pompous ceremonies and parchments made up so
large a part of his own life that he came to believe
that they expressed realities.   Hence he made the
cardinal error of his life.   He committed the future
of his House to the Pragmatic Sanction.   Domestic
economy was beneath his notice.   While Frederick
William was crying out because his son's tutors
permitted an item " for the housemaids at Wusterhausen," to appear in the accounts, dishonest stew-
ards were debiting the Emperor with twelve buckets
of the best wine for the Emperor's bath and two
casks of old Tokay for Her Majesty's parrots.   When

Charles VI. died the treasury was almost empty; the army seemed to have passed away with Prince Eugene; the ministers were blunderers of seventy and the sovereign a woman of twenty-three.

Maria Theresa had, however, much in her favour. Though untried in affairs of State, it was certain that her birth, her beauty, her piety, her courage, her wifely devotion, and her unfailing goodness of heart would win the affection of her subjects. And the realm of the Hapsburgs needed only loyalty to be strong. Its broad and smiling provinces could furnish inexhaustible supplies of men and food, and the rank and file had proved their courage in a hundred wars. Besides, after all the trouble and sacrifices of Charles VI., in what quarter could immediate danger arise? The rulers of Bavaria, Saxony, Spain, and Sardinia had each a claim to some part of his inheritance, but they could each and all be confuted or bought off. A miscellaneous empire like that of the Hapsburgs could never be wholly free from such disputes. What might well give confidence for the future was the fact that France, so long the moving spirit of Europe and the implacable foe of Austria, had in 1738 given to the Pragmatic Sanction the most ample guarantee that the wit of man could devise. What her king had then undertaken, her all-powerful minister had lately confirmed. In January, Fleury had written to the Emperor:

"The King will observe with the most exact and inviolable fidelity the engagements which he has made with you, and if I may speak of myself after a name so

worthy, I venture to flatter myself that my pacific intentions are well enough known for it to be supposed that
I am very far from thinking of setting Europe on fire."

Both King and Cardinal were sincere, and the best
proofs of their sincerity were the signs of coming
strife between them and England. It was clearly to
the interest of France that they should keep their
pledge.

If she had nothing to fear from France, Maria
Theresa had everything to hope from Prussia. It is
hardly necessary to say that Frederick William, the
devoted vassal of the Emperor, had been among the
first to guarantee the Pragmatic Sanction. His son,
so Austrian statesmen might argue, had to thank
the Emperor for protection when he lay in prison,
for secret supplies of money, for experience in the
field, above all for admission by way of marriage to
the outer circle of the Imperial family itself. Now
he expressed himself in terms which convinced the
consort of the Queen, Francis of Lorraine, that his
attitude towards the young couple was that of a
father. Francis even flattered himself with expectations of Prussian support in his candidature for the
office of Emperor. Although the Austrian resident
at Berlin wrote towards the end of October, 1740,
that the gossips spoke of dangerous designs upon a
portion of Silesia, and although, on November 19th,
Maria Theresa gave utterance to a fear that the price
of Prussian protection would be a slice of her hereditary dominions, still no one at Vienna had the least
suspicion of the blow that Frederick was preparing.

What was hidden from the victims was hidden also from Europe and from Berlin. Till the end of November, the only clear fact was that Prussia was arming fast. Envoys besieged Podewils and the King, and even Voltaire journeyed to Rheinsberg in the hope of piercing the veil. All their efforts were vain. The conviction that Silesia was in danger gathered strength, but no one could be sure that Frederick would move at all, or that if he moved it would not be towards the Rhine. He astutely feinted in the direction of Berg by strengthening the garrisons in Cleves and repairing the roads to the West. At the same time he toiled hard to baffle official curiosity at home and abroad and to feel the pulses of the Powers, especially that of France. Wilhelmina, who saw her brother revelling in the social pleasures of Rheinsberg, had no idea of what was in the wind.

At last, when secrecy was no longer profitable, the King's design was allowed to appear. On November 29th, the English ambassador wrote from Berlin that the project of invading Silesia was as good as avowed. Frederick had yet to meet and to brave the Marquis di Botta, who came from Vienna on a special mission to the Prussian Court and encountered the stream of troops flowing towards Silesia. At their meeting the King dropped the mask of friendship. " I am resolved," he said in effect, " to safeguard my rights over parts of Silesia by occupying it. Yield it to me and I will support the throne of Maria Theresa and procure the imperial crown for her husband." " Impossible for us," urged the

Austrian, "and for you, criminal in the eyes of all Europe." Argument was plainly futile, and both fell to threats. "The Prussian troops make a handsomer show than the Austrian," said Botta, "but ours have smelt powder." "The Prussian troops will prove themselves as brave as they are handsome," replied the King. Three days later, on December 12th, he attended a masquerade in the apartments of the Queen, questioned the French ambassador with regard to the disposition of Fleury, and afterwards supped in public. To the last moment the routine of pleasure was performed.

Next morning Frederick set out for Silesia. He had first to shake off two lads of fourteen and ten, his brothers Henry and Ferdinand, the youngest colonels in his army, who seized the skirts of his coat and begged him to take them to the war. A day's drive brought him to Frankfurt-on-Oder, and between Frankfurt and the frontier of Silesia was encamped an army of 19,000 men with seventy-four guns. The heart of the despot not yet twenty-nine years old beat high with lust of adventure and with confidence of success. On the evening of December 16th, he wrote to Podewils from Silesian soil:

"I have crossed the Rubicon with waving banners and resounding music ; my troops are full of good-will, the officers ambitious and our generals consumed with greed for fame ; all will go as we wish and I have reason to promise myself all possible good from this undertaking. . . . I will either perish or have honour from it."

Frederick's next step was to issue to the world

a document, of which one thousand copies had been printed in deepest secrecy exactly a month before. This was designed to reassure the people of Silesia as to the intentions of the King of Prussia. It was dated December 1st and gave out that a general war was threatening, in which Silesia, " our safeguard and outwork," would be involved and the security of Prussia threatened. To avert this peril the King saw himself compelled to despatch troops to Silesia.

" This is by no means intended to injure Her Majesty of Hungary, with whom and with the worshipful House of Austria we rather most eagerly desire to maintain the strictest friendship and to promote their true interest and maintenance according to the example of our glorious forefathers in our realm and electorate. That such is our sole intention in this affair, time will show clearly enough, for we are actually in course of explanation and agreement with Her Majesty."

Commentary on this profession, if not sufficiently supplied by Frederick's interviews with Botta, was afforded two days after his entry into Silesia. Then for the first time a Prussian representative, Borcke, informed the rulers of Austria of his master's proceedings. Shamefaced and without hope of success, he began the unwelcome task by offering to the Archduke Francis his master's guarantee for the Hapsburg lands in Germany, a place in the Prussian alliance with England, Holland, and Russia, his vote at the Imperial election, and a loan of two million florins. Then he named the price—the cession of all Silesia. " Rather the Turks before Vienna," cried

the Archduke, " rather the Netherlands to France,
rather any concession to Bavaria and Saxony."
And when he grew calmer and spoke of negotiation,
the door opened and Maria Theresa asked whether
her husband was there.

Next day the subject was broached anew by a
more Olympian plenipotentiary, Oberhofmarschall
Gotter, who had arrived after Borcke's message was
made known. He found Vienna stirred to its depths
and the English ambassador declaring that if such a
thing were done Frederick would be excommunicated
from the society of Governments. None the less
he took the high tone and strove to intimidate the
pliable Archduke.

" ' I bear,' he said, ' in one hand safety for the House
of Austria and in the other, for Your Highness, the
Imperial crown. The treasures of the King my master
are at the service of the Queen, and he brings her the
succour of his allies, England, Holland and Russia.
As a return for these offers and as compensation for the
peril which he incurs by them, he asks for all Silesia,
and will take no less. The King's resolve is immovable.
He has the will and the power to possess himself of
Silesia, and if it be not offered to him with a good grace
these same troops and treasures will be given to Saxony
and Bavaria, who are asking for them.' "

Gotter's words seem to strike the keynote of the
Silesian adventure. His silence as to legal claim
throws into strange relief the preposterous character
of the moral claim which he advances. Saxony and
Bavaria had made no overtures to Frederick, and

Frederick, as soon became apparent, was willing to accept much less than the whole of Silesia. The spirit of Maria Theresa breathed in the calm and dignified reply of the Archduke. Her high-minded confidence in Providence, her allies, her people, and herself blunted all the weapons of Prussia—the threats and cajolings addressed to the sovereign and the three hundred thousand thalers offered to the ministers. Austria declared that the invasion must cease or she would not even negotiate. Thereupon Gotter and Borcke joined their voices to the loud and unceasing chorus of remonstrance with which Prussia and Europe assailed the ears of Frederick in vain.

The young King's firmness may be ascribed in part to an overweening confidence in his own talents and in part to the favourable progress of his enterprise. He knew himself to be a cleverer man than his father and he had boundless faith in prompt and decided action. His success in the affairs of Mainz and Herstal could not but have augmented his self-esteem. The sight of the well-found and eager army which a word from him had assembled filled him with a sense of omnipotence. He declared that it must not be said that the King of Prussia marched with a tutor at his elbow. The minister of France, who admitted his great power of becoming what he wished, smiled maliciously at what he wished to become.

" Fully convinced of his superiority in every department, he already thinks himself a clever statesman and a great general. Alert and masterful, he always decides upon the spot and according to his own fancy. His generals will never be anything but adjutants, his councillors anything but clerks, his finance-ministers anything but tax-gatherers, his allies among the German princes anything but his slaves."

Frederick's whole career is a vindication of this estimate.

Already, both in Silesia and in Europe, good progress had been made. No Austrian armies disputed Frederick's advance, for Charles VI's grandiose projects had denuded his home provinces of troops. The natural defences of Silesia, too, were all on the wrong side. Mountains formidable though by no means impassable screened it from loyal Bohemia and loyal Moravia, and thus blocked the direct paths to Vienna. Only a few hills and streams barred an attack from the side of Saxony and no natural obstacle intervened between Breslau and Berlin. The strong portal looking towards Prussia was Glogau, which closed the Oder, the great natural highway of Silesia. Breslau, the capital, a city which Frederick could praise as the finest in Germany, was too big to be a fortress by nature and too independent to be made one by art. In the main Protestant, and therefore ill-disposed towards Austrian rule, it stood firmly upon its right to provide for its own defence and refused to receive a garrison. Glogau was therefore the only formidable fortress in Lower Silesia, the half of Silesia where Protestant feeling was strongest and which was most exposed to the Prussian invasion. The south-eastern half, Upper Silesia, contained two other strong places of

high importance -- Brieg, which commanded the upper Oder, and Neisse, which secured the backdoor of
the province towards Austria.   But Glogau, Brieg,
and Neisse were all iil-supplied and undermanned.
Without a field army to use them as bases and supports they could not oppose a serious obstacle to
the army of the King.

Frederick's worst foe, indeed, was the weather,
which tested the endurance of the Prussians and
found it great.   Torrents of rain fell from the
eighteenth of December to the twentieth.

"Waters all out," says Carlyle of the latter day,
"bridges down, the country one wild lake of eddying
mud.   Up to the knee for many miles together ; up to
the middle for long spaces; sometimes even up to the
chin or deeper, where your bridge was washed away.
The Prussians marched through it, as if they had been
slate or iron. . . .   Ten hours some of them were out,
their march being twenty or twenty-five miles; ten to
fifteen was the average distance come."

Their unshaken discipline was the trophy of Frederick William and the best omen for the adventure of
his son.   On December 22d he knocked at the door
of Silesia and was not dismayed at finding it shut.
Wallis, the Governor of the province, had thrown
himself into Glogau, had worked manfully to make it
defensible, and now stood firm.   Without siege-guns
Frederick could hardly hope to take the place, and
for a few days his own command was brought to a
standstill.   He summoned the reserve under the
younger Prince of Anhalt-Dessau to join him at

THE BOARD OF FINANCES AT NEISSE.
FROM A STEEL ENGRAVING.

Glogau and used the delay to organise a system by which Silesia should feed his troops for the future, but should feed them with the minimum of inconvenience and waste. Meanwhile the enterprise continued to be fortunate. On December 27th Schwerin and the right wing surprised Liegnitz, an industrial town within sight of the western wall of mountains, and on the same day the Young Dessauer brought the reserve to Glogau and set Frederick free. "Thou wilt shortly see Silesia ranked in the list of our provinces," wrote the King. "Religion and our brave soldiers will do the rest."

In Silesia and in Europe alike the philosopher-king counted much on religion. He cheerfully accepted the rôle of Protestant hero assigned him by the people, first of Berlin, then of Silesia, and finally of England. Never was this rôle more serviceable than in his dealings with Breslau. Leaving the Young Dessauer to blockade Glogau, he pressed on to the capital and, aided by the frost, accomplished the journey of seventy miles in three days. Much display of friendship and a little sharp practice sufficed to win the city, and Frederick, gracious and debonair, entered it in great state. Thus in three weeks from his departure from Berlin the King destroyed the Austrian civil government of Silesia. Half the province lay almost passive in his grasp, and he had secured a base for the conquest of the other half.

The remainder of the month of January, 1741, was spent in pressing home the advantage already won. The smaller towns, Ohlau, which would be useful as a base till Brieg could be acquired, Ottmachau, and Namslau, capitulated one by one. It was true that the activity of the young Austrian general, Browne, produced an ever-increasing disposition to resist, and that Glatz, hedged in by hills, defied the besiegers. But the area under Prussian control was steadily increased. Brieg was masked as Glogau had been, and Neisse, after a futile bombardment of four days, was treated in the same way. Schwerin was set free to drive Browne through the mountains into Moravia and to lead the army into winter quarters. On the 29th of January, Frederick returned to Berlin and plunged with zest into the whirlpool of diplomacy which had been stirred to its depths by his adventure.

Great as was his trust in resolute action and in accomplished facts, he could not disguise from himself the truth that on one side his calculations had broken down. Austria, inspired by a Queen whose high soul it was not in Frederick's power to measure, was not one whit nearer to compliance with his demands. Russia, as he foresaw, was likely to do little to help her, but the action of the Western Powers was less easy to calculate. Frederick felt sure of one thing above all else—that under no circumstances would France and England be on the same side. He therefore devoted himself to the task of winning the alliance of one and the neutrality of the other.

Frederick's simultaneous courtship of two Powers whose latent enmity to each other was beginning to reappear throws valuable light on his diplomatic methods and upon his regard for the truth.

"A veracious man he was, at all points," says Frederick's greatest biographer; "not even conscious of his veracity; but had it in the blood of him; and never looked upon 'mendacity' but from a very great height indeed. He does not, except where suitable, at least he never should, express his whole meaning, but you will never find him expressing what is not his meaning. Reticence, not dissimulation . . . Facts are a kind of divine thing to Frederick; much more so than to common men; this is essentially what Religion I have found in Frederick."

By his verdict that Frederick was a "veracious" man and his seizure of Silesia a righteous act, Carlyle robs the story of his life of half its value. The plain meaning of the facts which he adduces seems to be that he was an astute man, careless of truth and right. Hence we may enquire with keen interest, How far can such means lead to lasting success? In deference to a great name, however, two of Frederick's letters may be placed side by side. It will then be unnecessary to recur to this ungracious topic. From this time forward it will be assumed that the reader has formed his own opinion of Frederick's truthfulness.

So soon as he realised that his negotiation with Austria might break down, Frederick turned to France. On January 5, 1741, he wrote to Fleury from Breslau:

"My dear Cardinal, I am deeply impressed by all the assurances of friendship which you give me and I will always reply to them with the same sincerity. It depends only upon you, by favouring the justice of my title to Silesia, to make eternal the bonds which will unite us. If I did not make you a sharer in my plans at first it was through forgetfulness rather than for any other reason. It is not everyone who is as unfettered amid his work as yourself, and to Cardinal Fleury alone is it granted to think of and to provide for everything."

And in sending the letter he added:

"I ask nothing better than a close union with His Most Christian Majesty, whose interests will always be dear to me, and I flatter myself that he will have no less regard for mine."

At the same time he was making proposals for a close union with the natural enemy of France. In the same month, January, 1741, he addressed the following sentences to George II.:

"My Brother! I am delighted to see that I have not deceived myself in placing confidence in Your Majesty.

"As I have had no alliance with anyone I have not been able to open my mind to anyone; but as I see Your Majesty's good intentions I regard you as already my ally, from whom I ought in future to have nothing secret or concealed. Far from desiring to disturb Europe, I demand only that heed be paid to the justice of my uncontestable rights. I place unbounded confidence in Your Majesty's friendship and in the common interests of Protestant princes, which require that those oppressed for their religion should be succoured. The tyranny under which the Silesians have groaned is frightful, and the barbarity of the Catholics towards them inexpressible. If the Protestants lose me they have no other resort.

" If Your Majesty desires to attach to yourself a faithful ally of inviolable constancy, this is the time: our interests, our religion, our blood is the same, and it would be sad to see ourselves acting against each other: it would be still more grievous to oblige me to concur in the great plans of France, which I intend to do only if I am compelled."

The question of alliances was still unsettled on February 19th, when Frederick again left Berlin for the scene of war. Prussia might be doomed to act alone; her safety lay in her own right hand. New armies were set on foot, but a skirmish at Baumgarten, in which he narrowly escaped capture, proved to Frederick that the Austrians were moving and that his own troops were not all that could be desired. Nor was the Prussian strategy above criticism. The Old Dessauer, the father of the army, held up his hands in horror at the dispositions of Schwerin. Weak detachments were cantoned everywhere and the mountain-passes not secured, although Neisse, Brieg, and Glogau were still Austrian, and the Prussians would be at the mercy of an army entering Silesia from the Bohemian side.

But soon the King's spirits, which had been depressed by the danger of a European coalition against him, were raised and the military situation greatly improved by a brilliant feat of the Young Dessauer. Glogau, Frederick had been pleased to decree, must be taken. At midnight on March 8th–9th, therefore, a combined assault was made with that perfect organisation and cool courage which already distinguished the Prussian infantry. In an hour the work was done, at a speed which made the loss on each side the merest trifle. Frederick could congratulate his lieutenant on " the prettiest military stroke that has been done in this century," and himself on the acquisition of an open high-road to Breslau. The capital now became a safe central storehouse for the Prussians, and its value as a base of operations was greatly enhanced by the gain of control over the Oder. So far as Glogau itself was concerned, it may be convenient to remark that the work had never to be done a second time. In a wall near the northern portal may be seen a stone inscribed F. R. 1741—a token of Prussian sovereignty which from that day to this has suffered no erasure.

The next task was to secure Neisse, the Glogau of Upper Silesia. The problem was complicated by the fact that the Austrians had succeeded in fling-ing a thousand men into the fortress, and that a relieving army under Marshal Neipperg was known to be on its way from Vienna. Frederick therefore determined to turn the blockade into an active siege, while one covering army was established to the westward, and Schwerin received orders to concen-trate another to the south-east. The detachments were being called in for this purpose when the King had to acknowledge a surprise which led to the first pitched battle of the war and which might have ruined his whole enterprise. While Schwerin was carefully shutting the south-eastern gate of Silesia in Neipperg's face, the marshal passed him on his right and, by a creditable march over roads supposed to be impracticable, arrived at Neisse on April 5th. The advantage of this bold move was soon apparent. Frederick and Schwerin, who had been within an ace of capture, were also marching northwards, but they were separated from their friends by the river Neisse and by a superior force of the enemy. Neipperg was strong in cavalry and longed to follow up his advantage by crushing the Prussians in detail.

Frederick was saved, however, by Neipperg's ignorance of the strength and position of his foes. With a force of less than sixteen thousand men, the marshal's plain duty was to use his temporary superiority in numbers by meeting the enemy in the field and striving to destroy him. Failing in this, he might make for Ohlau and the magazine. But after crossing the Neisse, he lost touch with Frederick's force and believed himself to be between hostile armies on the north and south-east. Snow and rain hampered his movements and chilled his men. He therefore abandoned the initiative, and on April 9th sat down within sight of friendly Brieg to await events. He was right in supposing that a Prussian force lay to the south-east of him. It was the army of Frederick and Schwerin, which had received reinforcements from all sides. It was three times as strong as he believed it could be, and it was within five miles of his camp. He was wrong, however, in supposing that a stronger force lay to the north in Ohlau. Ohlau was weak and Frederick was hastening thither to save his heavy artillery and magazine. Neipperg lay right across his path and a battle was inevitable. It would soon be proved whether the Prussian troops were indeed as brave as they were handsome, or whether Europe was right in thinking that Prussia would pay dear for the presumption of her King.

Frederick realised the importance of the crisis. For two days, it is said, he could neither eat nor sleep. On April 8th he wrote to his brother and heir, Prince Augustus William, bidding him farewell if the next day should be his last. In that event he commended to his care four of his friends, " those whom in life I have loved the most," as well as two of his servants. The next day, however, proved tempestuous and the Prussian attack was postponed till April 10th. Then the morning sun shone out upon a plain hardened by frost and covered to a depth of two feet with snow. The Prussian baggage was packed at five o'clock, and by nine the whole force had silently taken rank. An hour later, the march northward began, the army pressing slowly through the snow towards Ohlau, and feeling for the enemy who lay across their path. At last the vanguard surprised an Austrian outpost, captured twenty men, and learned that Neipperg lay encamped in and about Mollwitz, a village less than two miles ahead.

How twenty-two thousand men could have approached so close to the enemy unperceived, it is hard to understand. Neipperg, it is true, did not expect to be attacked. There was some screen of woods between the Prussians and Mollwitz, and the country-folk were Protestants who volunteered

information only to the Prussians. But the day
was clear and the scene as flat as the parade-ground
at Potsdam ; the Austrians were particularly well
supplied with scouts and their general's avowed
plan was to shape his course according to the movements of his opponents. None the less it was in
fact not till after ten o'clock that he received the
alarm, and by that time the Prussians were methodic-
ally ranking themselves for battle. Had the same
opportunity come to Frederick later in life, he would,
as he himself declares, have flung troops upon Mollwitz and the neighbouring villages and put the
Austrians to flight before they could form. But in
this first fight every traditional precaution was
carefully observed, "the faithful apprentice-hand,"
says Carlyle, "still rigorous to the rules of the old
shop."

While Neipperg was bustling and hurrying to
collect his army from three villages and to draw it
up in front of Mollwitz, the Prussians were manœuvring into place as though they were on parade.
Two long lines were formed across the plain. These
were three hundred paces apart, so that if the front
were pierced, which was hardly supposed possible,
the rear could fire their flintlocks without massacring
their comrades. Heavy guns to the front, cavalry
on the wings, were the orders, and, as the enemy
were superior in cavalry, Frederick copied an expedient of the great Gustavus by placing two regiments of grenadiers between the squadrons of horse
on either wing. At length all was ready, and at
midday the Prussian cannonade began, galling the

Austrian cavalry and as yet unanswerable by the Austrian guns.

Neipperg had ordered the cavalry to wait till a general advance could be made. But the left wing, refusing to be shot down like dogs, suddenly defied their officers and dashed at the Prussian right. They lost all formation, but they found a foe unschooled in their tactics. First pistol-shot, then a stroke with a sabre as sharp as a razor right at the head of the enemy's horse, finally, as horsé and man went down, a thrust from the rear at the rider—such an attack was beyond the experience of the Prussian cavalry, and they could not stand against it. As often as Austrian horse met Prussian on the day of Mollwitz they gained an easy victory. They captured some of the guns, plundered the baggage, tore several gaps in the line, and drove the King himself in headlong flight from his first battle.

For some time Frederick was driven helplessly here and there amid his ruined cavalry in a fight which was unlike anything that he had ever seen and which he was impotent to control. His generals begged him to quit the field. To his inexperienced eye all seemed lost, and at last Schwerin confirmed his fears. "There is still hope," said this tried captain to his sovereign, "but in case of the worst it would be well if your Majesty in person would bring troops from Ohlau and Strehlen." Bewildered and despairing, the King turned his back on the wreck of all his hopes and fled far to the south-east. Distancing many of his attendants in a swift ride of more than thirty miles, he arrived at Oppeln on the

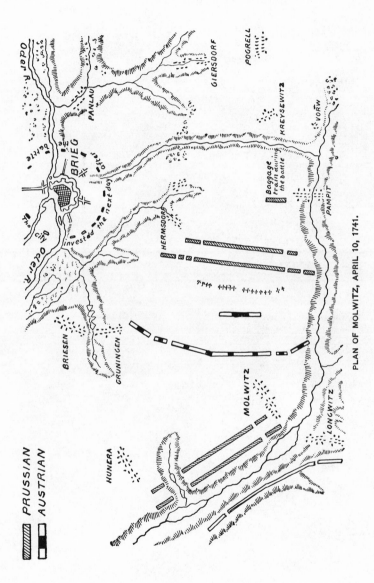

PRUSSIAN
AUSTRIAN

PLAN OF MOLWITZ, APRIL 10, 1741.

Oder, only to be repulsed by the unexpected fire of a party of Austrian hussars who had seized the town and who captured some of his worse-mounted companions. To this check, for he then doubled back towards his army, he owed the fact that at the close of a ride of nearly fifty miles he received the news of victory without delay.

When Frederick left the field it was about four o'clock. The havoc in the Prussian ranks had been wrought by unsupported charges of horse. Schwerin could still count upon his infantry, which in the midst of the whirlwind had stood firm as a rock and by sheer steadiness and speed of firing had tumbled masses of cavalry into ruin. His first act was to send to the Young Dessauer, who commanded the second line, an exhortation to do his duty and to keep his men from firing volleys into the backs of their comrades. The Young Dessauer, who hated Schwerin, replied that he needed no judge save the King and that he would do his duty without any reminders.

After this exchange of courtesies, Schwerin braced himself to the task of retrieving the day. He assured his infantry that the King was well, that no battle could be won or lost by cavalry alone, and that he placed his trust in them. He then ordered his right wing forward against the Austrian infantry. These were raw levies and gave signs of unsteadiness before the Prussians came within range. Range, in days of weak powder and clumsy muskets, was some forty-five paces, and the sight of the enemy bearing down upon them, shoulder to shoulder, was too much for undisciplined men to face. Neipperg drew supports from his right, but even his victorious cavalry soon refused to face the fire which was poured in by men perfectly trained and furnished with the iron ramrods invented by the Old Dessauer. The Austrian infantry, which was able at the best to fire less than half as fast as the enemy, hid trembling one behind another and tried to endure a torment to which they could not reply. As the sun was sinking Schwerin pressed his advantage home. With sounding music and waving banners, in irresistible advance, the Prussian left swept down upon the weakened Austrian right. Neipperg saw that the battle was lost. He retreated first behind Mollwitz then, seeing that his men would not stand, round the Prussian left and eventually to Neisse.

Except that his magazine was saved and that he was soon able to capture Brieg, Frederick derived little immediate military advantage from what he describes as "one of the rudest battles fought within the memory of man." The chief profit of Neipperg's march had evaporated before the battle, at the moment when Frederick and Schwerin became superior in numbers. In spite of Mollwitz the Austrian army remained on Silesian soil, and it was better placed near Neisse than near Brieg. In killed and wounded each side had lost about 4500 men, nearly one-fourth of the combatants engaged. And in spite of Frederick's hoarded millions and well-filled regiments, it was clear that, if the contest were to remain a duel between himself and Maria Theresa alone, the size and natural wealth of Austria must tell in the long run. After Mollwitz, Frederick would still have been glad to accept Lower Silesia as the price of his alliance with Austria and a contribution to her exchequer.

Prussia's greatest gain from Mollwitz was increase of prestige. Though her cavalry did not regain their nerve for many a day, her infantry, the backbone of the army, had proved that it was indeed as brave as it was handsome. Frederick never alluded to his own departure from the field. In later life he accustomed himself to inaugurate the Prussian military year by celebrating the anniversary of the triumph which he had not seen. Every fifth of April the Guards were twice ordered to the charge and dismissed with the words, "Thus did your forefathers at Mollwitz." The traditional Austrian contempt for Prussia had received its first signal rebuke. The story survives among the villagers of Mollwitz that when the call to arms disturbed one of Neipperg's officers at dinner he called to the landlord to keep the dishes hot. "We will come back soon," he promised, "but we have to go and dust the Prussians' jackets for them."

Victory in the field reconciled Prussian opinion to Frederick's Silesian adventure, but this was a small gain in comparison with its effect on opinion in Europe, especially in France. At the Court of Louis XV. the party opposed to Fleury and to peace had been gathering strength day by day. Hot-headed men and women, blind to the true interests of their country, could see in Austria only the hereditary enemy from whom lands and laurels were to be won.

Chief among them was Marshal Belleisle, a man who conceived great schemes and advocated them with eloquence and charm. His plan was that France should ally herself with Prussia, procure the Imperial crown for Charles Albert of Bavaria, and, in spite of all her pledges to support the Pragmatic Sanction, endow both the Bavarian and Saxon claimants with Austrian lands. Having thus humbled Austria and made the fortunes of Austria's rivals, France might gain the Netherlands and Luxemburg for herself and dictate to a divided Germany for ever.

Before Mollwitz, Belleisle had progressed with this policy so far as to be entrusted with a mission to the Diet which assembled at Frankfort to elect an Emperor. Frederick's victory encouraged all the enemies of the Hapsburgs and thus lightened the task of Belleisle. In May, 1741, Charles Albert accepted the rôle marked out for him, and early next month the King of Prussia, despairing of an alliance with England, came to terms with France. By a treaty signed at Breslau in the deepest secrecy, he agreed to renounce his claims to Jülich-Berg, and undertook to vote for Charles Albert at the Diet. France in return guaranteed him in the possession of Lower Silesia, and undertook to safeguard Prussia by sending an army to support Charles Albert within two months and by stirring up Sweden to make war on Russia. The coalition against Austria gathered strength as it proceeded, and with the exception of the English and the Dutch no nation hesitated to desert the Pragmatic Sanction.

The idea with which Frederick began the Silesian

adventure was at length realised. He had, as he anticipated, stirred up general confusion, amid which the strong man who knew his own mind could hardly fail to carry off some spoils. To France, as the moving spirit, he was all gratitude and devotion. But his real design henceforward was to leave his confederates to subdue Austria, while he himself devoted all his powers to grasping what Prussia could hope to retain. What he gained from Belleisle's work was made manifest in the summer and autumn of 1741. While the Bavarians and French were advancing in triumph down the Danube towards Vienna, the Austrians could take no thought for Silesia. Frederick, therefore, had leisure to train his cavalry and consolidate his conquest. He treacherously destroyed the municipal independence of Breslau, which he had bound himself to preserve, but did little actual fighting. Neisse, protected by Neipperg's army, seemed still too strong to be attacked.

Meanwhile the extreme peril of Maria Theresa's throne forced the Queen to make trial of desperate remedies. By throwing herself upon the generosity of the Hungarians, the traditional rebels against her House, she more than doubled the force at her disposal. Her endeavour to purchase France was futile, but a hint from Frederick was now enough to inaugurate negotiations with Prussia. Early in October these issued in the famous convention of Klein Schnellendorf. In deep secrecy, for Fleury had written that the King of Prussia was false in everything, even in his caresses, and the French ambassador kept a watchful eye upon his movements,

Frederick met Neipperg at a castle in the neighbourhood of Neisse. Each was accompanied by one companion, while the English ambassador, Lord Hyndford, who had arranged the interview, acted as clerk and witness. There Frederick, who had just written to Belleisle a letter full of encouragement, sold his allies for his own profit. It was agreed that after a sham siege of Neisse the Austrians should evacuate Silesia, and that Prussia should become neutral in fact though not in show. To Neipperg, whose army would now be free to act against the French in Bohemia, Frederick gave wise counsel for the campaign. "Unite all your troops, then strike home before they can strike you." If the Austrians should succeed, Frederick might join them; if not, he would be compelled to look to himself. To deceive the French, the English ambassador was to report him as deaf to all propositions. If any word of the convention got abroad, the King declared he would deny all and regard all as void.

This conspiracy against Frederick's allies was punctiliously carried into effect so long as it was profitable to Prussia. For fifteen days Neisse submitted to a bombardment and two hundred cannon-shot were fired off by either side. After seven days Neipperg's army made off, attended by a Prussian corps in seeming pursuit, and at the time appointed the strong fortress was surrendered. On the very same day the King accepted a treaty for the partition of Austria. The Prussians then, as arranged, went into winter quarters in Upper Silesia, which Austria was eventually to retain, and from time to

time sham skirmishes took place to hoodwink the
French.

At the beginning of November the King left
Neisse for Berlin, pausing on his way to view the
scenes of all his triumphs. At Brieg and Glogau he
inspected the fortifications, but at Breslau he drove
in state to the grand old Rathaus and received the
homage of Lower Silesia, the province secretly ceded
to him at Klein Schnellendorf. The ceremony was
immediately followed by the reorganisation of the
Government in Church and State. The province
was simply made Prussian, with absolute religious
equality, heavy but not harsh taxation, and a regular
system of conscription.

At Klein Schnellendorf Frederick had hinted that
if the Austrians were not successful in Bohemia they
could not expect him to do more than stand neutral.
The event soon showed what he meant. Before the
end of November Prague was stormed in brilliant
fashion by the Bavarians, French, and Saxons.
Frederick's allies had succeeded where he expected
them to fail. He at once proclaimed his intention
of standing by the winning side. " My fingers itch
for brilliant and useful action on behalf of my dear
Elector," he wrote to Belleisle. He broke all the
provisions of the convention of Klein Schnellendorf
and derided the suggestion that such a pact could
ever have existed. "Should I be so foolish as to
patch up a peace with enemies who hate me in their
hearts, and in whose neighbourhood I could enjoy
no safety?" the King demanded. "The true principles of the policy of my House demand a close

alliance with France." Such was the substance of the argument which Frederick addressed to Fleury.

Lord Hyndford, however, had witnessed all that passed at Klein Schnellendorf, and would not allow England to be duped by lies. Frederick therefore told him frankly that he intended to set the convention at defiance. The allies, he showed, had 150,000 men against Austria's 70,000 and could do with her what they would. If she published the convention she would only expose her own folly, and perhaps she would not be believed. Then, besides treating Upper Silesia as his own and laying hands on the adjoining county of Glatz, he ordered the conquest of Moravia. Ere the year was out Schwerin was in Olmütz, the chief town of the North, and it seemed as though the allies would filch yet another province from the Queen. "Alas!" wrote the philosopher - king on one occasion to Voltaire, "trickery, bad faith and double-dealing are the leading feature of most of the men who are at the head of the nations and who ought to set them an example."

Never was the fortitude of Maria Theresa more needed or more illustrious than in these winter months. The earlier gleams of light—Vienna spared and Frederick bought off—only made yet more black the clouds which now gathered over her throne. Her father had flattered himself that he bequeathed to her the support of united Europe. Within a year of his death the greater part of Europe was leagued to despoil her. France, Spain, Bavaria, Prussia, Saxony, the Elector Palatine, the

Elector of Cologne formed the coalition, and the accession of Sardinia was the prelude to a severe struggle on the side of Italy. The loss of Bohemia almost without a blow made the Queen well-nigh forgetful of Silesia until the perfidy of Frederick opened the former wound anew. At the same time a revolution at St. Petersburg extinguished for the time being the Austrian influence in Russia and thereby increased the King's security. Then came the attack upon Moravia, and before the end of January, 1742, the Imperial crown passed from the Hapsburg family by the election of the head of a rival House—Charles Albert of Bavaria.

Amid all these disasters, however, the courage of the young Queen, rooted as it was in her belief that right must triumph, remained unshaken. She organised new armies and inspired them with her own spirit. Before the resurgent might of Austria the new-made Emperor sank into impotence. Within a month of his election the Queen recovered her cities on the Danube and overran the hereditary lands of the Bavarian. *Et Cæsar et nihil* laughed the wags. What would his allies, France, Prussia, and Saxony, do to relieve him?

The position of affairs may be simply stated. Two Austrian armies were in the field, one conquering Bavaria, the other protecting it against an attack from the side of Bohemia, where the allies were still masters of Prague. If this second army were driven back by a superior force, the first would be recalled to support it. Thus Bavaria and Bohemia, the actual and the pretended inheritance of Charles Albert, would be freed from the Austrians together. At the same time the French in Bohemia would be relieved from the fear of being outnumbered and attacked, and the Saxons would have the simplest march possible—straight into Bohemia by the natural highroad of the Elbe. Every military consideration thus summoned Frederick to join in clearing the kingdom of Austrian troops. But this plan promised no special advantage for the King of Prussia and it opened no market in which he might barter his allies. With infinite labour he therefore secured the adoption of another, in which these defects were remedied. This was that he should lead the Saxon army into Moravia to assist the Prussians in conquering the province, and in thus creating a diversion which, he maintained, would aid the Emperor as well as any other.

The Saxons reluctantly left their country with no force, save the French, to guard its frontier against the Austrian army of Bohemia. Frederick was therefore secure against treason on his flank and could again stir the waters of politics in full confidence that his House would gain some profit. Moravia might become to Silesia what Silesia had now become to Brandenburg—a dependency and an outwork. Or if this was too much to hope for, he as conqueror of Moravia might at least dictate to Vienna the surrender of a Silesia augmented by cuttings from the Bohemian kingdom, of which Frederick regarded the Emperor or the Queen as lawful sovereign exactly according to his convenience at the moment. At the worst Moravia might pass to the Saxon House, which was a weaker and therefore a safer neighbour than the Hapsburg.

All these calculations were falsified by events. The invasion of Moravia was a far more difficult task than the invasion of Silesia. Instead of a level and fertile country inhabited in part by Protestant well-wishers, Frederick found a rugged desert whose people hated the Prussians and did them every mischief in their power. He devastated the land by way of penalty, and dragged the grumbling Saxons through clouds of guerillas to Brünn, the capital, where he induced them to join him in a siege. As leader of a composite army, however, he was no longer served with the prompt and unquestioning obedience which the unmixed Prussian forces had displayed.

Brünn made a stout resistance and Prince Charles was deputed to march to its relief. At this point the heroism of the Queen seemed to be rewarded by a sudden change of fortune. Frederick tried once more to sacrifice his allies to his own profit, but in vain. England, now guided by Carteret in place of Walpole, was actively supporting Maria Theresa. Sardinia deserted the coalition against her. At Vienna, men regained a confidence which was heightened by the news from the North. Prince Charles feinted against the French in Bohemia and Frederick dismissed the Saxons to help them. This was but the first step towards the abandonment of the whole venture. After a toilsome retreat and countless skirmishes, the exhausted Prussians crossed safely into Bohemia before the end of April and again the negotiators were set to work. Once more they failed and the Prussians found themselves between Prague and the army of Prince Charles, which was now making thither from Moravia.

A conflict was inevitable. It took place at Chotusitz, near the Elbe, within three marches of Prague, on May 17, 1742. This battle is remarkable not only because seven thousand men fell in three hours, but also because it is the first victory actually won by Frederick himself. His imperious temper had cost him the services of Schwerin, the hero of Mollwitz, while the Old Dessauer had been rebuked for disobedience and sent to the rear. But the Prussian infantry were as steady as at Mollwitz, the cavalry, who suffered terribly, much better, and the King proved that he could seize the moment for decisive action on the field as well as in the cabinet. Four thousand Prussians fell, but casualties, captures, and desertion reduced Prince Charles's force of thirty thousand by one-half.

The victory of Chotusitz assisted Frederick once more to abandon his allies. It added force to the diplomacy of England, whose policy was to help Austria a great deal against the French, but not at all against the Prussians. While the English ambassadors were urging the Queen to submit to the loss of Silesia, the Austrian troops pressed the French hard in Bohemia and thus forced Frederick to hurry on a peace. Within four weeks of Chotusitz, victor and vanquished had come to terms. Frederick withdrew from the war and received all Silesia except a fringe on the south-west, as well as

the county of Glatz in full sovereignty for ever.
On July 28th these terms were embodied in the
Treaty of Berlin, which closed the First Silesian War.
In twenty months, at a cost of two pitched battles,
Frederick had added to Prussia sixteen thousand
square miles of fertile land and a million and a
quarter of inhabitants—a greater prize than any
that his ancestors had won.   He was not yet thirty-
one years of age.

CHAPTER V

THE SECOND STRUGGLE FOR SILESIA, 1742–1745

AFTER following Frederick's career through many phases in a dozen years, we observe him with interest as he quits the whirlpool of foreign adventure for the calm of government at home. We may well enquire how far three crowded and strenuous campaigns have transformed our hero. It is impossible that the deeds done at Breslau, Mollwitz, Klein Schnellendorf, Olmütz, and Chotusitz and the strenuous toil of twenty months in departments new to him should have left no mark upon himself. The story outlined in the foregoing chapter suggests that he moved from place to place and from task to task with great speed and that his life, perhaps even his throne, were more than once in danger. But it can convey no adequate idea of the inundation of ambassadors, generals, messengers, officials, and busybodies which daily surged in upon the King. Frederick, it must be remembered, was his own commander-in-chief and his own prime minister at a time when, as he himself confessed in later years, he had not the least knowledge of war, when, owing to his father's

THE PARADE GROUND AT POTSDAM.

jealous absolutism, he had had the briefest possible experience of diplomacy, and when his powers both in war and in diplomacy were taxed by the problems of a newly-won province which must be conciliated at all costs.

The strain was indeed severe. Under it Frederick became more statesmanlike but not more humane. After a course of the waters at Aix-la-Chapelle, he diverted himself as of old with literature and the society of wits. But he made no effort to improve his domestic life. His queen had retired to Schönhausen, a modest country-house in the dreary plain which lies on the north side of Berlin — a dwelling so remote that the swift expansion of recent years has not yet brought it within the city. The King's thoughts ran already upon a bachelor establishment at Potsdam, the Sans Souci of later years, where he might escape from the society of his relations to enjoy that of his friends. For his subjects he attempted to provide few benefits beyond a codification of the law — little enough for one who had held out hope of a revolution in the art of kingship. It is true that he built the great Opera House at Berlin, that he lavished money upon actors and musicians, and that he endowed an Academy of Sciences. But he made French the only vehicle of learned and literary thought; and though Berlin might shine in Europe, the Prussian people gained little benefit thereby.

The King even enjoyed for a time the society of Voltaire, at that time the King of Letters. The transaction is characteristic of the age. The brilliant Frenchman, having quarrelled with his peers at home, obtained from Louis XV. an informal commission to pry into the secrets of Prussia. Before leaving France, he vented his spleen in a parcel of epigrams upon Louis and his subjects, which he sent in all secrecy to his affectionate admirer, Frederick. The latter, thinking to close the doors of France to his guest and so to cage him at Berlin, published them all at Paris. Both betrayals failed. As a diplomat Voltaire extracted only banter from his patron and disciple, while Frederick found that Louis XV. was indeed what Voltaire had termed him — " the most stupid of kings," for the epigrams did not sting him.

Frederick's wider experience of life, it is clear, had rather hardened his heart than softened it. As a king he had developed, faster doubtless than in time of peace, along the lines with which we are already familiar. He was still conspicuously energetic, imperious, and mercantile. His energy is the more striking by contrast with the habit of his contemporaries. Philip of Spain was sluggishly obeying his wife. Louis of France, whom Frederick termed a good man whose only fault was that he was King, was toying with mistresses, patronising sieges, and pointing out the faults in a policy which he was too indolent to cheek. Augustus of Saxony was sacrificing his armies lest he should be late for the opera. The Czarina Elizabeth has been described as " bobbing about in that unlovely whirlpool of intrigues, amours, devotions, and strong liquor, which her history is." In a word, the princes of Europe still in great part looked on their office as an inheritance to be enjoyed. Meanwhile, the King of Prussia was rising at dawn, reviewing troops, inspecting fortresses, drafting and conning despatches, superintending his players, and constituting himself a judge of appeal for all his kingdom.

Whether judge, general, or stage-manager, he was always the King of Prussia, and his naturally imperious temper mounted higher day by day. His stern treatment of the Old Dessauer and the alienation of Schwerin have already been mentioned. In time of peace his ministers met with no greater forbearance. They were treated at best as clerks, and often as dogs. The faithful Podewils, who had just rendered priceless services to his master in the negotiations with Austria, presumed to suggest that the King should remain for a time in Silesia. "Attend to your own affairs, Sir," was the reply, "and do not presume to dictate whether I ought or ought not to go. Negotiate as I order you, and do not be the weak tool of English and Austrian impudence." With the same imperious brutality Frederick wrote to the honourable nobleman who represented him at Vienna. " Do not forget, Sir, with what master you have to do, and if you take heed of nothing else, take heed for your head."

As with his dependents, so with states weaker than his own, Frederick always played the dictator. To grace his new opera he had engaged the famous dancer Barberina, who was then at Venice. Her

English lover persuaded her to break the contract and remain there and the Doge and Senate professed themselves powerless to interfere. Frederick therefore seized a Venetian ambassador in Berlin and held him as a hostage, until the Venetians in their turn violated justice by sending Barberina a prisoner to Berlin.

With an imperiousness equal to that of his father Frederick combined the traditional Hohenzollern willingness to buy and sell. He failed to buy Silesia, but he succeeded in buying Glatz. The county of Glatz belonged to Bohemia, and in 1741 Frederick recognised Charles Albert as King of Bohemia. From him he purchased territory which the Bavarian had never possessed and which he could never hope to possess without foreign aid. The Prussians conquered the country and in 1742 Maria Theresa offered to cede it. Thereupon the King accepted from Austria what he had declared to belong to Bavaria and announced that he was no longer bound to pay the purchase money agreed upon.

Frederick seems to be still in all essentials the man whose development we have traced from his birth to his accession. He is tougher, as it were, in mind and body alike. He has thrown off the feeble health of his earlier years and the lust for mere adventure which possessed him in the twenties. But experience has only added to his trust in himself, to his belief that " negotiations without arms are music without instruments," that war determines disputes, and that bravery and leadership determine war. His faith in prompt and decided action was never more conspicuous than in 1744, when on the death of its prince without lineal heirs, he seized Eastern Frisia. Hanover also had claims to the land, but nothing could withstand the speed with which the Prussians made this miniature Silesia their own and thus acquired in Emden an outlet on the North Sea.

Frederick's schemes are, indeed, so daring, and his acts so swift and decisive, that many have believed—as he himself seems to have believed at the time—that he was gifted with almost superhuman insight and rose superior to human weakness. It may, therefore, be well to cite the words in which Professor Koser of Bonn, the greatest living authority upon the subject, has set down his impression of the King as he was at the end of the First Silesian War.

"To us he seems neither superhuman nor inhuman, a man not ready made and complete, but still in process of growth. The cold 'satanic' calculator shows himself more than once a sanguine man, a man of impulse. Sometimes insolent and sometimes almost faint-hearted, he lets his bearing be easily decided by the impressions of the moment. In his haste and heat and lack of experience he makes plenty of mistakes, not only in war, but also in politics. He does not look far into the future, and sometimes, however near to his heart lies his good repute, he takes no thought for it in time to come. And as he himself later admits, he owes a great part of his successes to fortune and to chance. In one word, we grant plenty of what the King, grown more mature, has described as the 'giddiness' of his younger years."

When Frederick, pleading that in shipwreck each must save himself, forsook his allies in the summer of 1742, he did so with certain definite intentions. He wished to give Prussia time to digest Silesia, and Europe time to accustom herself to Prussia. "The only question now," he wrote to Podewils, "is to accustom the cabinets of Europe to see us in the position which this war has given us, and I believe that much moderation and much good temper towards all our neighbours will lead to that result." The words breathe peace, but peace only so long as it was both safe and profitable for Prussia. "The safety of our new possessions," he had just pointed out, "rests on a large and efficient army, a full treasury, powerful fortresses and showy alliances which easily impose upon the world." For a time, it is clear, the King intended to revert to the old policy of drilling men and saving money. But it seems equally clear that if all went well the question which Frederick propounded in 1740 would in due course present itself again. "When one has an advantage is he to use it or not?" Is it reasonable to suppose that the conqueror of Silesia would in future answer No?

For the present, however, while the Prussian system of government was being established in Silesia, Frederick scanned every rise and fall of the political barometer. What he saw made him at first congratulate himself on having forsaken a losing cause before it was too late. Early in September, 1742, the Saxons quitted the war empty-handed, and it was evident that France repented of her share in it.

Before the end of the year her troops had been driven out of almost all Bohemia, and in January, 1743, the death of Fleury deprived her of what unity in policy and administration she still possessed. Worse than all else, the Sea Powers now entered vigorously into the war. George II. was anxious to protect Hanover; Carteret and the English people longed to strike a blow at their natural enemy, France; and the importunity of England at length induced the Dutch to move.

Frederick, though he had arranged affairs in Russia to his liking, had, therefore, every reason to fear lest Austria should grow strong enough to turn against himself. He was annoyed beyond measure by the news of King George's lucky victory over the French at Dettingen on June 27, 1743. "The devil fly away with my uncle," he wrote to Podewils. He declared that he would never hear the name of France again. "Noailles is beaten, and by whom? By people who do not understand how to draw up a line of battle, and who, in fact, did not draw one up." Frederick's disgust was only increased by the fact that his military criticism was well founded. Owing to George's want of skill, Noailles had caught his army in a trap, from which it escaped only by calm courage and desperate fighting hand to hand. "I have tolerably well foreseen everything that has passed in Europe hitherto," wrote the King of Prussia, "but for this blow I was not prepared."

Dettingen and the fear of worse to follow impelled Frederick to take up arms anew. Early in September, 1743, he visited Wilhelmina at Baireuth and endeavoured in vain to organise a league of German princes to rescue the Emperor. The Austrian diplomats were more successful. In the same month, by a treaty made at Worms, they secured the definite alliance of England and Sardinia. Frederick noticed with some alarm that the Treaty of Berlin, which gave him Silesia, was not treated at Worms as indispensable to the future of Germany. In December a compact more distinctly menacing to Prussia, should she again interfere in the war, was concluded between Austria and Saxony.

Early in the new year (1744), therefore, Frederick turned unabashed to France. He offered to join her in a war which both parties should pledge themselves to continue until Bohemia should have been wrested from the Queen. The Emperor was to receive the greater part of the kingdom, but Prussia, as in 1742, claimed the four Bohemian circles east of the Elbe and also that fringe of Silesia which the Treaty of Berlin had left in Austrian hands. Early in June all was arranged. By the so-called Union of Frankfort some share in the undertaking was promised by the Elector Palatine and the Landgrave of Hesse-Cassel. But the substantial allies were, as in the earlier war, France, Prussia, and Bavaria. The general plan agreed upon was that France should cripple the Sea Powers by attacking the Netherlands and Hanover. If the result was to bring an Austrian army into Alsace, Frederick promised in his turn to cripple Austria by flinging eighty thousand men into Bohemia. In that case the French undertook to make another campaign in the East.

The motives which inspired Frederick to take action are so clear that there is no need to seek them in the solemn accusation against Austria which he gave to the world in August. He deemed it expedient to take up the attitude of a German patriot, who, after exhausting the resources of negotiation, was driven to repel by force the conspiracy of the Queen of Hungary against the constitution of the Empire.

"The race of those Germans of old, who for so many centuries defended their fatherland and their liberties against all the majesty of the Roman Empire, still survives, and will make the same defence to-day against those who dare to conspire against them. . . . In one word, the King asks for nothing and with him there is no question whatever of personal interests. His Majesty has recourse to arms only to restore liberty to the Empire, the sceptre to the Emperor and peace to Europe."

Such was the Prussian account of the origin of the Second Silesian War.

Frederick again resorted to the method of simultaneous parley and stroke which had served so well when he seized Silesia. On the same day (August 7, 1744) that his ambassador at Vienna announced his crusade to rescue the Emperor, he himself astonished the Saxons by showing them the Emperor's order to permit the passage of Prussian troops. It is characteristic of the tangled politics of the time that Prussia and Saxony remained technically at peace with each other while Frederick, as the Emperor's servant, led sixty thousand men up the Elbe into Bohemia and Augustus, as the ally of the Queen of Hungary, sent twenty thousand men to act against him. For the moment Frederick profited by his speed. At the beginning of September he lay before Prague and joined forces with twenty thousand men whom Schwerin had brought from Silesia. Eighty thousand Prussians were thus assembled in the heart of Bohemia, and on September 16th they took the capital.

The appearance of success was, however, delusive. Far from being panic-stricken by Frederick's sudden spring, the scrupulous Queen rejoiced to see him break the treaty which gave him a title to Silesia. From every point of the compass she summoned forces to defend Bohemia. The army of Alsace recrossed the Rhine with great skill and marched eastwards. They were undisturbed by the French, among whom Frederick's treacheries were passing into a proverb:—*se battre pour le roi de Prusse,* to fight without reward. Clouds of irregular horse issued from Hungary. The Saxons were marching southwards. The people of Bohemia showed themselves hostile to the Prussians and assisted an Austrian army to maintain itself in the kingdom. What course, we may ask, was the wisest for a commander surrounded by so many dangers?

After the fall of Prague Frederick lay in the centre of Bohemia, a kingdom walled in by a quadrilateral of mountains. He held the north-eastern gates which led into Silesia. The south-western led into Bavaria, and through them the army of Alsace was soon to enter. But at the head of nearly

80,000 men the King was vastly stronger than any single force that could be brought against him and his communications with Prussia were safe. There was therefore much to be said for a simple defensive policy. North-eastern Bohemia was the prize that Frederick hoped to gain by the war, and this he could have held like a second Silesia. Such a desertion of his allies would, however, have shocked public opinion, particularly in France, and Frederick admits that he shrank from it on that account.

The next best course, if some offensive movement must be made, would have been first to crush the army of Bohemia and then to hold the south-western gate against the army of Alsace. This course was advised by Schwerin and favoured by the King. But the fatal influence of Belleisle proved stronger than the promptings of common-sense. France was avenged for the treacheries of Klein Schnellendorf and Berlin when Frederick allowed himself to be persuaded to strike due south, in the hope of conquering Bohemia, opening communications with Bavaria, and cowing Vienna.

At first the plan prospered. Several towns were captured for the Emperor, and by October 4, 1744, the Prussians had almost reached the frontier of Austria proper. Then they began to realise that they were the dupes of a mirage. The armies of Bohemia and of Alsace had united in their rear and lay between them and Prague. They found themselves isolated, ill fed, and worse informed. Swarms of light horse enveloped them, cutting off convoys, scouts, and messengers. Schwerin opened a line of retreat, but their recent conquests were lost with the garrisons which held them. The Austrians had found a soldier, Field-marshal Traun, and at his hands Frederick received painful lessons in the art of war. The King had already begun to negotiate. He thirsted for French co-operation and a pitched battle, but could obtain neither boon. Traun, who was now superior in numbers, had no need to fight. He occupied unassailable positions to the north of Frederick's force and left hunger, disease, and irregulars to do their work upon the enemy. Thus harassed, the Prussian rank and file deserted by thousands, and many offered their services to Traun. Schwerin again took umbrage and withdrew from the campaign.

Step by step the reluctant King was driven towards Silesia. Before the end of November it was plain that his whole enterprise must be abandoned. It was mid-December before the last detachments of some 40,000 men, the remnant of his 80,000, straggled across the mountains to the friendly walls of Glatz. Thanks to the determination of Maria Theresa, a postscript had yet to be added to the history of the campaign. In the spirit of her own Hungarians, who scorned to provide a commissariat because their forefathers had journeyed from Asia to the Land of the Five Rivers without one, the Queen dictated a winter assault upon Silesia. The Old Dessauer, whom Frederick had left in command, at length succeeded in clearing the province of anything like an Austrian army, but it was not till February that the Prussians were able

FREDERICK THE SECOND, KING OF PRUSSIA.
AFTER THE PAINTING BY F. BOCK.

to go into winter quarters. Thus a campaign which
had begun with the conquest of Bohemia came to an
end to the sound of *Te Deums* sung at Berlin for the
deliverance of Silesia. Europe began to suspect
that the sword of Traun had pricked the Prussian
bubble.

The anxiety with which Frederick awaited the
spring of 1745, when he must expect to have to
fight in earnest for Silesia, was rendered more intense by a sudden change in the attitude of his
allies. He had joined in the struggle with the expectation that Austria would be attacked by the
French and hampered both by the war in Italy and
by the forces of the Emperor. On January 20th,
however, Charles Albert died, and the youth who
succeeded him was soon beaten to his knees. By
the Treaty of Füssen, in April, Austria and Bavaria
agreed to ignore the past ; and the latter for the first
time guaranteed the Pragmatic Sanction and promised to vote for the husband of Maria Theresa at the
imperial election. The effect of this treaty upon
Frederick's position will be appreciated when it is
borne in mind that the road from France to Austria
passed through Bavaria, while the Austrian Netherlands, which France coveted, lay at her very door.
Thus it was easy to suspect that in the coming campaign Prussia would receive little effective help from
France. Suspicion passed into certainty when Louis
XV. elected to accompany his army in person.

The campaign of 1745 might therefore be expected
to fall into two separate halves. In the Netherlands,
France would be pitted against the Sea Powers and an

Austrian contingent, while in Silesia Austria would make a great effort against Prussia. At the same time the secondary struggle of Austria with Spain and France would go on in Italy, while French and Austrian corps would guard the Rhine. It is evident at a glance that the withdrawal of the French and Bavarians must greatly improve the prospects of Austria with regard to Silesia. And when (May, 1745) she was joined by Saxony, whose help all parties desired, in an undertaking to make no peace until Frederick should resign Silesia and Glatz to the one and part of his hereditary dominions to the other, the Queen might well be sanguine. Much of her advantage was, however, thrown away by an error common to Hapsburg rulers, who are wont to believe that no family is so fitted as their own for command. The invasion of Silesia was entrusted to Prince Charles of Lorraine, the nominal leader of the army in the previous year, while Traun, the real author of the Austrian success, was sent to watch the Imperial election at Frankfort. The consequence was that the Austrians did not move till May, and that they were worse generalled than the Prussians.

Meanwhile Frederick had been assiduous in preparing for war and in negotiating to avoid it. He was ready to put 80,000 foot and 30,000 horse into the field : but he had sued in vain for the alliance of Saxony and the aid of England and of Russia. The King, who in 1740 had offered millions to Maria Theresa and planned a partition of her dominions, must in 1745 implore Louis XV. for a subsidy to avert the partition of his own. But the danger to Prussia, though real, was not yet as overwhelming as her enemies believed. "Excellent bearskin to be slit into straps," chuckles Frederick's admirer, "only the bear is still on his feet."

The King could still count upon two mighty allies, —upon his army, whose spirit had been restored by the successes of the Old Dessauer in the defence of Silesia, and upon himself. Both grew year by year more valuable. At this crisis, as events were soon to prove, Frederick's spirit was worthy of the Queen herself. "I have made it a point of honour," he wrote to Podewils on April 27, 1745, "to contribute more than any other to the aggrandisement of my House. I have played a leading part among the crowned heads of Europe. These are so many personal engagements which I have taken and which I am resolved to fulfil even at the cost of my fortune and my life." Since the middle of March he had been making ready in Silesia, and in April he sent home directions for carrying on the government if Berlin should be in danger.

Next month he learned that his French allies, who were bent on capturing Tournay, had gained a great victory at Fontenoy (11th May, 1745). He received the news with mixed feelings. He had been striving to find words which might force into the mind of Louis XV. the truth that victories in the Netherlands would do nothing for the common cause in Germany. "We beg the King of France," he wrote, "not to imagine that any efforts of his in Flanders can procure the least relief for the King of Prussia. If the Spaniards land in the Canary Islands, if the King of France takes Tournay, or if Thamas Kuli-Chan besieges Babylon it is all one," since such feats could not influence the war in Bohemia and Moravia. Yet it was not disheartening to know that Dettingen had been avenged and that other foes of Austria could more than hold their own. With renewed hope, Frederick bent all his energies to the task of holding Silesia.

The King had learned much from Traun, and he was no longer compelled to consult the interests of his allies. He therefore avoided the mistakes of the former year. In 1745 his clear gaze penetrated the heart of the problem which he had to solve, and he followed the right course with the coolest daring. Silesia, he knew, was divided from the country of the enemy by a mountain rampart more than three hundred miles in length and pierced by many roads. Veiled by clouds of light horse, Prince Charles might choose any of these roads without betraying his choice to the army of defence. What Neipperg had accomplished when he entered Silesia in 1741 might be repeated by Prince Charles on a greater scale, and with less favour from fortune the Prussians might this time be crushed in detail. Frederick therefore drove sentiment from his breast, abandoned south-eastern Silesia to the Hungarians, and concentrated all his force in the neighbourhood of Neisse, a stronghold which the Prussians had made impregnable. His design was to admit the invaders to Silesia in the hope of catching them at a disadvantage and of destroying their enterprise at a blow.

The result was that, when the allies came, they came in the highest spirits. Their progress had been as fortunate as they could have hoped. First, as usual, troops of wild riders poured into Silesia from the south-east. They enjoyed the success which Frederick's plan assured to them, and treason among his soldiers gave them Cosel, a fortress on the upper Oder. Then Prince Charles moved northward from Königgrätz into the mountains and 30,000 Saxons joined him on the way. On June 3, 1745, the combined army marched proudly down into the plain. Breslau lay little more than two days' march to the north-east of them.

The fixed idea of Prince Charles was that Frederick would behave in 1745 as he had behaved in 1744; that is to say, that he would retreat. This delusion had been carefully fostered by the King. Discovering that one of the spies whom he kept in the Austrian camp was in fact selling Prussian secrets to the enemy, Frederick cleverly hinted to him that he was afraid of being cut off from Breslau. The spy informed Prince Charles, who readily gave credit to information which confirmed his previous belief. Frederick then ordered some repairs on the roads leading to the capital and supplied further proof of his intention, if any were needed, by leaving the passes unguarded. Prince Charles therefore emerged from the mountains in entire ignorance of the fact that he was to be attacked by a force of 70,000 men. The invaders encamped upon a plain some five miles broad and as flat as the field of Mollwitz, with the little town of Hohenfriedberg on the edge of the mountains to their rear, and Striegau, a place of greater size, on the hills before them. The Saxon vanguard, which had already been in contact with the enemy, was instructed to seize Striegau next morning, if the Prussians still ventured to hold it. "There can be no God in heaven," said Prince Charles, " if we do not win this battle."

Frederick's camp lay almost at right angles to the line of the allies between Hohenfriedberg and Striegau. That night (June 3–4, 1745) the Prussians stole silently from their stations, crossed a stream which separated them from the enemy, and ranged themselves before him in line of battle. At dawn they began a general attack as furious as it was unexpected. The Saxons, always unfortunate in war, were the first to suffer, and their dogged resistance only increased their loss. The Austrian infantry stood firm, but their cavalry could no longer face the Prussians. Thus the Austrian centre and right wing, though favoured by the ground, could gain no advantage sufficient to compensate for the disasters of the Saxons on the left. Hohenfriedberg was a soldiers' battle, and the decisive stroke was an irresponsible charge of the Baireuth dragoons, who dashed at the enemy through a dangerous gap in the Prussian line. The shock carried all before it. More than sixty standards were captured by this regiment alone. By eight o'clock in the morning the Austrians were in retreat towards the mountains and the invasion of Silesia was at an end.

The allied army fled so quickly, writes the historian of the Evangelical church at Hohenfriedberg, that little damage was done in the place, and the inhabitants were soon able to bear what succour they could to the wounded, who lay in thousands on the plain below. In about four hours' fighting the victors had lost more than 4000 men killed or wounded, and the vanquished about 10,000. These figures do not, however, represent one tithe of the advantage which Frederick gained at Hohenfriedberg. He had reduced the allied army by some 25,000 men, of whom 7000 were prisoners and many more deserters. Every German army at that time included thousands of professional soldiers who fought for either side indifferently and preferred the victors' pay to their pursuit. Thousands more fought against their will, and the retreat through mountains gave them an opportunity to slip away. For a month the Prussians hung in the rear of the allies and drove them as far as Königgrätz. Instead of his defensive attitude in Silesia, Frederick now took up a defensive-offensive in Bohemia, a plan which was as creditable to his strategy as the battle had been to his tactics. Above all other advantages he had gained this at Hohenfriedberg—that he could henceforth trust his cavalry. Worthless at Mollwitz, respectable at Chotusitz, at Hohenfriedberg they proved themselves superb. The panel which commemorates the victory in the Prussian Hall of Fame portrays the dragoons swooping down upon the white-clad infantry of Austria.

The triumph of Frederick the Warrior on this bloody fourth of June revealed interesting glimpses of Frederick the man. In his first transports of

delight he hugged the French ambassador and astonished him by owning gratitude to God. "So decisive
a defeat," he informed his mother, "has not been
since Blenheim."   He believed that the Queen would
now come to terms, and wrote to Podewils that it
must have softened the heart of Pharaoh.   His delight found vent in music, and he composed his
March of Hohenfriedberg. But soon the statesman reappeared.   None of these ebullitions clouded
his insight into the situation of affairs. He saw
clearly that his aims of the year before were still
impracticable, that what he needed was peace, and
that his victory must have brought peace nearer
by discouraging the enemy.

It is true that now, as so often before, Frederick
underrated the firmness of the Queen. He was
further disappointed by the unyielding attitude of
Augustus, who possessed a dangerous patron in
the Czarina. But England, the paymaster of the
coalition, had no stomach for a war of vengeance
against Prussia. To her the Austrian alliance was
merely an investment. It would be profitable only
if it produced hard fighting against her real foes,
the French. Fontenoy, where the Sea Powers had
been left to do their own fighting, shook her faith
in her Hapsburg ally, and the conduct of the
Eastern campaign showed that the Queen's thoughts
centred on the recovery of the province which
England had induced her to give up. At this
juncture England herself was attacked. The invasion of the Pretender compelled her to recall her
troops from the Continent and favoured the conven-

tion which was concluded at Hanover towards the end of August. By the Convention of Hanover, signed on the 26th August, 1745, Frederick a third time deserted the French. He promised to vote for Francis at the Imperial election on condition that Silesia should be guaranteed to him by all Europe, while George II. undertook to induce Austria to renew the Treaty of Berlin within six weeks.

The good offices of England, which as usual consisted in pressing the Queen to buy off her enemies, were entirely useless. At the end of August Austria and Saxony drew closer together, and on September 13th the House of Hapsburg regained its old prestige by the election of Francis as Emperor. Soon afterwards Frederick perceived that he had exhausted the supplies of north-eastern Bohemia and began to retire towards Silesia. By the end of September he had crossed the Elbe and encamped with 18,000 men at the foot of the mountains near the village of Soor. There something like his own manœuvre of Hohenfriedberg was practised upon him by Prince Charles with an army almost double the size of Frederick's. Under cover of darkness the Austrians took up positions commanding the Prussian camp. Only the King's swift grasp of the situation and the wonderful skill and speed of his troops averted a great disaster. In a five hours' fight the Austrians were driven off, leaving more than 4000 men on the field and more than 3000 in the enemy's hands. The number of Prussian casualties exceeded 3000—a heavy price to pay for bad scouting. Frederick was, moreover, put to great inconvenience by the sack of his camp and the capture of his secretary, the silent, assiduous Eichel.

At Soor, Frederick gained a safe retreat to Silesia and a lesson to be careful in the future. But victory made him inattentive to the lesson. The behaviour of his men had been beyond all praise. They formed under fire; the cavalry charged up-hill and routed the enemy, and the infantry, though unsupported, attacked superior numbers and captured batteries. The King, not unnaturally, began to believe that there was nothing which he and his soldiers could not accomplish. The result, in a future as yet far distant, was great glory mingled with great disaster.

During the winter months the Prussian rank and file gathered fresh laurels. Once more Frederick believed that he had tamed the Queen and once more he found himself mistaken. As in every previous year of the Silesian wars, Maria Theresa ordered an attack upon her enemy in the winter. This of 1745 was threefold and the goal was not Breslau but Berlin. Prince Charles's army was to march from Bohemia into Saxony and to join with the Saxons in a march to Frankfurt-on-Oder, while 10,000 men detached by Traun crossed Germany and seized Berlin. Enough of this elaborate plan was blabbed to the Swedish ambassador by the Saxon Premier, Count Brühl, to put Frederick upon his guard. His own army had gone into winter quarters. A force under the Old Dessauer, which had been stationed for some time at Halle in readiness to spring at the throat of Saxony, was likewise laid up for the winter. Podewils and the Old Des-

sauer refused to credit a scheme at once so grandiose and so dangerous to the Saxons, who in case
of failure would be left at the mercy of Prussia.
The King, however, overruled them, rushed into
Silesia, collected 35,000 men, marched for some days
parallel with the unsuspecting Prince Charles, and
on November 23, 1745, crushed his Saxon vanguard
at Hennersdorf. At this blow the whole enterprise
collapsed. The Austrians retired into Bohemia, followed by Augustus and Count Brühl, who stub-
bornly rejected the Prussian overtures for peace.

Meanwhile the Old Dessauer, who had captured
Leipzig, was making for Dresden under urgent orders to attack the Saxon force wherever he might
find it. Four armies were at this time converging
upon the capital. The Saxons under Count Rutowski, with whom were the Austrian contingent
from the West, formed a force of 35,000 men and lay
to the westward of the Elbe and of the city. The
Old Dessauer, having secured Meissen, had provided
a bridge across the river by which Frederick marching from the East could join him in case of need.
But Prince Charles with 46,000 men was advancing
towards Dresden from the side of Bohemia, and
Frederick feverishly urged his veteran lieutenant to
strike a speedy blow. If the allies were to join
forces the war might be prolonged and it seemed
likely that Russia would attack Prussia in the
spring.

Prince Charles was in fact only five miles distant
when, on December 15th, the Old Dessauer came
upon Rutowski strongly posted at Kesselsdorf.

"Heavenly Father," prayed the old man in the hearing of his devoted soldiers, "graciously aid me this day : but if Thou shouldest not be so disposed, at least lend not Thy aid to those scoundrels the enemy, but passively await the issue." The task of the infantry was even harder than that of capturing the batteries at Soor. Twice they were repulsed with a loss of nearly 1500 men out of 3600. But the usual impetuosity of armies not perfectly trained came to their aid. The Saxons in the intoxication of victory charged from the entrenchments, only to be routed by the Prussian horse. This proved the turning-point in a battle which cost Rutowski 3000 men killed and wounded and twice as many taken prisoner.

The Prussians lost some 4600 men, but they gained peace. Prince Charles fled once more into Bohemia and Dresden made no resistance. In the hour of triumph Frederick's bearing was admirable. All through the winter campaign he had showered insults upon the Old Dessauer, a prince born the year after Fehrbellin and hero of well-nigh half a hundred battles and sieges. " My field-marshal is the only person who either cannot or will not understand my plain commands." " You go as slowly as though you were determined to deprive me of my advantage." Such were the royal words which had goaded the old man into attempting the impossible at Kessels-dorf, where he exposed himself recklessly and received three balls through his clothing. Now he enjoyed as ample amends as Frederick's conception of the royal dignity permitted him to bestow. On the day after the battle the King sprang from his horse at sight of him, advanced to meet him with doffed hat, embraced him, and accepted his guidance over the field.

At Dresden Frederick stayed eight days and showed himself anxious to please. He entered the city, it is true, as a conqueror, in a carriage drawn by eight horses, and he exacted a million thalers from the land. But he visited and honoured the children of Augustus, played a leading part in the society of the place, attended church and opera on Sunday, and in general acted with the utmost moderation.

In the existing political situation, such conduct was no less politic than humane. In spite of his triumph over the Saxons, Frederick's position was far from secure. Augustus was only a recent recruit in the phalanx of kings arrayed against Prussia. Russia, his patron, had yet to be reckoned with The army of Prince Charles was unbroken. Southern Silesia was flooded with Hungarians. Traun might yet leave the Rhine and revive the painful memories of 1744. In face of all these dangers Frederick had no reserves. His treasury was empty and the anger of the French at the Convention of Hanover forbade him to expect assistance from them. These considerations made him willing to name a low price for peace. Even when fleeing from Traun in 1744 he had demanded a part of Bohemia. Now after four victories he stipulated only that Austria should renew the Treaty of Berlin. Maria Theresa was thus confronted with the painful choice between abandoning, at least for the present, all hope of recovering Silesia and resigning the help of the Sea Powers, on which her hope of retaining Italy depended. The Saxon alliance had broken down, a negotiation with France was unsuccessful, and the Queen wisely consented to accept Frederick's terms. At Dresden on Christmas Day, 1745, treaties were signed which restored peace to a great part of Germany and closed the Second Silesian War.

CHAPTER VI

TWO Silesian wars, episodes in the eight years of general turmoil produced by the Austrian Succession question, had now been brought by Frederick to a fortunate end. The Hapsburgs once more possessed the Imperial crown, but the Hohenzollerns were masters of Silesia and their days of vassalage were over.

The course of history has shown that by gaining Silesia Prussia enabled herself to become in time the principal German state. From this time onward, the Teutonic elements in the Hapsburg realm became more and more outweighed by the rest, until in 1866 Austria, as a Power whose political centre was Buda-Pest, was finally expelled from Germany. In 1745, it is true, the full significance of the transfer of Silesia was felt rather than understood. But it was felt strongly enough to prevent Frederick from deluding himself with the vain belief that Austria would be easily reconciled to her loss, or that she regarded the Peace of Dresden as more sacred than the Peace of Berlin. The Queen, it was said, could not behold a Silesian without tears. Her

155

spirit was so high that she is believed to have thought seriously of becoming her own commander-in-chief, and her resources grew greater with every year of peace.

Frederick's task of holding what he had so lightly seized in 1740 therefore grew no less difficult as time went on. He had good reason for remaining constant to the principle which he professed at Dresden : " I would not henceforth attack a cat, except to defend myself." His policy, as he wrote in his Testament of 1752, was to maintain peace as long as might be possible without lowering the dignity of Prussia. " We have drawn upon ourselves the envy of Europe by the acquisition of Silesia," he confessed. " It has put all our neighbours on the alert ; there is none who does not distrust us." The ink of the Treaty of Dresden was hardly dry ere new plans were mooted to blot it out. The attitude of Russia towards the victor was menacing, that of Poland defiant, and it was easy to see that Austria and Saxony had an understanding with the Northern Powers which boded him no good.

Frederick was, however, no longer a novice in diplomacy and he knew his own mind. Evading all efforts to tempt him back into the whirlpool of war, he watched its successive phases till the Peace of 1748. He saw the Queen turn her energies to Italy, while the Sea Powers, who could not maintain themselves in the Netherlands without her aid, hired troops in the only market open to them and brought 35,000 Russians to the Rhine. But the value of this new factor in the politics of Western

Europe had not been tested when the Peace of Aix-
la-Chapelle was patched up.   Then the exhausted
combatants entered upon the task of reconstruction,
in which Frederick had more than two years' start of
them.   To him the peace brought a guarantee by
all Europe of the treaty by which he held Silesia.

Imperfect as it was, for it settled no great question, the Peace of Aix-la-Chapelle gave pause to the
armed strife of Europe for eight years.   Prussia
therefore enjoyed a full decade of rest before 1756,
when the third and greatest of her struggles for
Silesia began.   She dared not put off her harness,
but she stood at ease.   After the peace her army
still numbered 135,000 men.   But the crowned commander-in-chief had now a leisure unattainable in time
of war.   His excuse for deserting his ally at Dresden was that he wished to enjoy life and to labour
for the good of his subjects.   Now his opportunity
had come.   It would be strange if a reign of less
than six years had destroyed the ideal which Frederick championed in his early treatise on kingcraft.
Prussia and Europe might well expect that he would
be, like the great-grandfather of whom he wrote the
words, " as great in peace as in the bosom of victory,"
and that he would apply his untrammelled power
to remedy whatever defects his enlightened insight
might still discover in the Prussian State.   Frederick
the Warrior had cleared the way for Frederick the
Reformer.   Ought not Prussian history in the fifties
to be a story of regeneration ?

The King himself, however, practically omits the
record of this decade from his history of the reign.

He assigns as the reason that "political intrigues which lead to nothing deserve no more notice than teasing in society, and the particulars of the internal administration do not afford sufficient material for history." His great English admirer holds that this routine work in itself was eminent, that "one day these things will deserve to be studied to the bottom ; and to be set forth, by writing hands that are competent, for the instruction and example of Workers," but that "of Frederick's success in his Law-Reforms, in his Husbandries, Commerces and Furtherances, conspicuously great as it was, there is no possibility of making careless readers cognisant at this day." Carlyle then explains that the visit of Voltaire to Frederick and their quarrel is one of the few things perfectly knowable in this period and the only thing which the populations care to hear.

The following chapter of this book is written in the belief that readers of the story of Frederick may well demand, above all else, whether he is justly termed "The Great," and if so, in virtue of what achievements? Unless we are willing to answer that the title is his of right because he seized Silesia and held it against great odds, these questions compel us to enquire into his home administration. We know well that the ruler is strong only because he wields the collective strength of his nation, and that his chief task is to render the nation stronger and to improve the machinery by which its strength is collected and exerted. A great ruler is one who, when the difficulties which he had to contend with are taken into account, is perceived to have accom-

plished much more in the performance of this task
than could be expected from an ordinary man. If
we find that Frederick improved the lot of his subjects in a remarkable degree, or that he invented
beneficial institutions, or devised a system by which
the future of government in Prussia was assured and
progress made easy, then we shall have to concede
to him a right to the title of Great other than that
which conquest may confer.

It is of high importance to ascertain at the outset
of the enquiry how far Frederick was free to act as
he pleased and to what extent he was fettered by
constitutional or social ties. His whole manner of
life, indeed, was such as to suggest the most complete freedom. From the moment of his father's
death he was master of his people and of his policy
as few European potentates have ever been. Autocracy as well as diligence is stamped upon even the
externals of his everyday existence. Though his
stature was not quite five feet seven inches, his ablu-
tions, when performed at all, slight and few, and his
dress of the shabbiest, no one ever suggested that
his presence lacked kingliness. He usually wore an
old grey hat of soft felt, a faded blue uniform smeared
with the snuff in which he indulged immoderately,
and boots which through neglect were of a reddish
colour. But his bearing, stern and caressing by
turns, his clarion voice, and his glance which, as a
contemporary owned, nothing could resist, made him
the cynosure of whatever company he was in. The
absence of the customary trappings of royalty rendered the King of Prussia less formidable to the

poor, whom he patronised, while it marked his contempt for the official and middle classes, whom he sometimes allowed to kiss the skirts of his dirty coat.

Frederick, it need hardly be said, was fully conscious of his own superiority to his subjects in birth, address, and talent. During his incognito visit to Strasburg in 1740, Marshal Broglie remarked the contrast between Frederick and Algarotti on the one hand and the awkward Germans of the party on the other. The vivacity of the King's circle was almost all imported from abroad. Many years later the French philosopher d'Alembert stated that Frederick himself was the only man in Prussia with whom it was possible to hold conversation as the word was understood in France. The man who by right of birth was absolute ruler of Prussia had some reason to believe that he was also the greatest poet, historian, philosopher, critic, administrator, legislator, statesman, captain, and general in his dominions.

There is perhaps no more conclusive proof of his wisdom than that his consciousness of this unique endowment did not cause his home policy to become tyrannical and his foreign policy grandiose. From the second fault he was saved by his keen eye for realities, which taught him that, as he confessed, Prussia was playing a part among the Great Powers without being in fact the equal of the rest. That he never became a tyrant, was probably due in part to natural humanity and in part to the philosophy which was his pride. He was often harsh towards his subjects, but he proclaimed that his duty was to make them happy and he never shed their blood.

SANS-SOUCI. CARYTID FRONT.

His threats to execute his ministers were mere insults. But philosophy did not check one evil to
which he was inclined by nature and impelled by
situation. Nothing short of human sympathy could
have mitigated his contempt for the populace, which
gathered strength with years. " My dear Sulzer,"
he replied to an educational theorist who urged that
men were naturally inclined to good, "you do not
know that curséd race as I do." "It is more probable," he held, "that we sprang from evil spirits, if
such things could exist, than from a Being whose
nature is good." As he rode through the streets of
his capital on one famous occasion, he came upon
a group of the discontented staring at a seditious
cartoon. "Hang it lower down," was his scornful
order, "so that they need not strain their necks to
see it."

To the service of those whom he termed the
rabble, none the less, Frederick devoted a great
share of a life of incessant labour. Every day, Sunday and week-day alike, was parcelled out so as to
contain the greatest possible amount of work. "It
is not necessary that I should live," wrote the King,
"but it is necessary that I should act." He toiled
for the State and for himself, and, with the exception
of regular visits to his mother and Madame de Camas,
he admitted few social claims upon his time. His
Queen never even saw his favourite home, Sans
Souci, which he built in the park at Potsdam in
1747. She knew so little of his affairs that she gave
a party at Schönhausen while he was lying *in ex-
tremis*. The consideration which he denied to her

he did not give to others whose title to it was less strong. As he grew older, he curtailed even the short time that he had been wont to spend in his capital, and divided the bulk of the year between seclusion at Potsdam and the inspection of his provinces.

His habit was to rise at dawn or earlier. The first three or four hours of the morning were allotted to toilet, correspondence, a desultory breakfast of strong coffee and fruit, preceded by a deep draught of cold water flavoured with fennel leaves, and flute-playing as an accompaniment to meditation on business. Then came one or two hours of rapid work with his secretaries, followed by parade, audiences, and perhaps a little exercise. Punctually at noon Frederick sat down to dinner, which was always the chief social event of the day and in later life became his only solid meal. He supervised his kitchen like a department of State. He considered and often amended the bill of fare, which contained the names of the cooks responsible for every dish. After dinner he marked with a cross the courses which had merited his approval. He inspected his household accounts with minute care and proved himself a master of domestic economy. The result was a dinner that Voltaire considered fairly good for a country in which there was no game, no decent meat, and no spring chickens.

Two hours, sometimes even four, were spent at table. Occasionally the time was devoted to the discussion of important business with high officials, but in general Frederick used it to refresh himself after his six or seven hours of toil. He ate freely, preferring highly spiced dishes, drank claret mixed with water, and talked incessantly. He was a skilful and agreeable host, putting his guests instantly at their ease, and, by Voltaire's account, calling forth wit in others. After dismissing the company he returned to his flute, and then put the final touches to the morning's business. After this he drank coffee and passed some two hours in seclusion. During this period he nerved himself for fresh grappling with affairs by plunging into literature. In the year 1749 he produced no less than forty works. About six o'clock he was ready to receive his lector or to converse with artists and learned men. At seven began a small concert, in which Frederick himself used often to perform. Supper followed, but was brief, unless the conversation was of unusual interest. Otherwise the King went to bed at about nine o'clock and slept five or six hours. In later life he gave up suppers, but continued to invite a few friends for conversation. He then allowed himself rather more sleep. In his last years he lost the power to play his flute and with it, apparently, the desire to hear music.

The sketch which has been given of Frederick's daily life suggests that whatever his power might be, it was not subjected to the interference of others. At Potsdam there was no place for the ordinary influences which were brought to bear upon Kings. Frederick would not endure the presence of any woman, and, strictly speaking, he had no courtiers. His intimates were not politicians, but wits and men of letters, for the most part of foreign birth. Even those who accused him of hideous vices admitted that he never suffered his accomplices to have the smallest influence over him. Eichel and the two other secretaries who worked with the King every day were slaves rather than counsellors. They lived in such seclusion that, according to the French ambassador, Eichel was never seen by any human being. During Frederick's last illness, he forced their successors to attend him at four o'clock in the morning, so that the few weeks that might yet remain to him should be serviceable to the State. One of them fell to the ground in a fit, but the King merely summoned another, and went on with the business. Through their hands passed Frederick's correspondence with his ministers, whom he rarely saw. "In his orders of two lines," grumbled a subordinate, "he announced no reasons." He was of course obliged to listen to the ambassadors of foreign Powers. As though to avenge himself for this, he tolerated no suggestions from his own. He desired spies rather than advisers, and often chose men of inferior intelligence to fill high diplomatic posts. On every hand we find tokens that Frederick looked to his own breast alone for inspiration in the exercise of his power.

To realise how unfettered was the authority that Frederick wielded we must consider the peculiar structure of the society over which he ruled and of the machinery by which he ruled it. Frederick's

Prussia was a state which just a century of strong monarchical rule had manufactured out of a number of Hohenzollern fiefs. Its basis still remained feudal. There were few social classes, and strong barriers separated class from class. The career open to a Prussian was strictly limited by his birth. Between town and country the law reared a dividing wall, unseen but impassable. Townsmen alone were allowed to become manufacturers, merchants, and civil servants. They paid a special tax, the " Excise," levied on the articles which they consumed. They had magistrates of their own choosing, a relic of the municipal independence which the Great Elector had broken down.

To the countryfolk, on the other hand, the King looked for his army. They were divided into two great classes ; the nobles, who alone might become officers, and the peasants, who were still serfs tied to the estates of their lords. The nobles enjoyed exemption from ordinary taxes and paid only a small feudal rent to the Crown. Upon the shoulders of the peasants fell the heavy burden of the " Contribution," a direct payment in money. Neither they nor the nobles might become craftsmen or engage in commerce. The barrier which separated the two classes of countryfolk was as firm as that which separated both from the dwellers in towns. New patents of nobility were rarely granted by the King, but all the children of a noble were nobles. Even the soil was divided into noble-lands and peasant-lands, and neither class might acquire the portion of the other.

It is easy to see that this system of rigid class division was unlikely to ensure to every Prussian the career for which he was best fitted. In Frederick's eyes, however, it possessed two supreme merits, and for the sake of these he was willing to make it eternal. It provided a gigantic army and it contained no germ of opposition to the Crown.

Prussia under Frederick was practically one vast camp. Every social class had a military function to perform. The King was commander-in-chief and paymaster-general. The nobles formed the corps of officers. Some of the peasants were called on to bear arms while the rest laboured in the fields to produce the necessary supplies of food. The burghers, who have been styled the commissariat department of the army, armed and clothed the troops, and helped to provide funds with which to hire the foreigners of whom half the army was composed.

It was possible to entrust to foreigners so great a share in Prussian wars because the framework of the army was of iron. The native half of each regiment was drawn from a particular locality. It consisted of peasants led by the lords whom they had been accustomed from infancy to obey. The regiment was ruled in a fashion almost patriarchal by a commander who gave it his own name. Under this system *esprit de corps* became a passion, and none knew better than Frederick how to turn it to good account. To the army " Prussia " was a name which within the memory of their fathers had been arbitrarily assigned to the dominions of the elder branch of the House of Hohenzollern. Where national

patriotism was in its infancy, local patriotism was all
the more intense, and it was by playing upon this
that Frederick, the Father of all his lands, called
forth many marvellous feats of arms.

But the King, though he fostered profitable sentiment, was far too wary to trust to it over much. He
had other expedients for attracting nobles to the
colours and for keeping the ranks full. He withdrew his royal favour from those of noble birth who
were so unpatriotic as either to avoid his service
or to leave it in a few years. The social arrangements which have been outlined above were yet
more powerful in securing a supply of officers. The
nobles were numerous, poor, and brave. They must
find some career, and what other lay open to them?
When Frederick's father began to impress cadets,
many parents even tried to prove that they were not
of noble birth. But with them, as with many other
classes of the discontented, firm government in the
long run brought cheerful obedience. " The King's
bread is the best," became their maxim. Frederick
marked his appreciation of their worth by rarely giving commissions to men of lower rank. It was not
the least of his gains that he thus acquired military
authority over the most influential class in his
dominions.

He made sure of the common man by stern discipline. Although the Prussian members of each
regiment were bound together by social and local
bonds, by no means all of them were willing to fight
for the King. They were conscripts, not volunteers,
and they were released only when they became unfit

to serve.   Not a few deserted to the enemy under
stress of war.   The foreigners who were their comrades under arms were a varied host.   Some were
mercenaries, some deserters from the enemy, some
keen fighting men who were glad to serve in the
finest army in the world.   Many had been kidnapped or pressed or tempted into the Prussian service by false promises or admitted when their own
countries were too hot to hold them.   Frederick's
directions to Prussian commanders for the march are
based on the assumption that many of the men will
desire to run away.   When in time of war some of
the peasants volunteered, the astonished King asked
what finer deed the Romans of old had performed.

His standing remedy against disintegration was
"to make the discipline so stern and the punishments so severe that the men would learn to fear
their own superiors more than the enemy."

"The punishments were barbarous," writes Professor
Martin Philippson.   "Thrashing was customary.   Imprisonment, sharpened by all kinds of chastisement and
torment, was not rare.   The most terrible of all was running the gauntlet, in which the offender was stripped to
the waist and forced to run from twenty to thirty times
through a living lane of hundreds of soldiers armed with
rods, while the officers looked to it that every man laid
on lustily.   Hundreds of wretched men gave up the
ghost under these tortures."

Yet of the rank and file it may be said with more
confidence than of any other section of Frederick's
subjects that they loved the King.

Enough, perhaps, has been said to suggest that where classes were so sharply divided there was little likelihood of any national resistance to the Crown and that the Prussian military system gave Frederick a peculiar authority over two great sections of his people. A further source of power consisted in his enormous wealth. In every province the Crown possessed vast domains amounting in all to nearly one-third of the soil of Prussia. The result was that Frederick was lord of innumerable peasants and by far the greatest capitalist in his dominions. To him the nobles looked for help in time of dearth, while the townsmen expected him to bear the initial loss of new industrial enterprises. His domestic policy was directed towards the maintenance of this position. For him the notion of taxes fructifying in the pockets of the people had no charm. His ideal was that of subjects paying the greatest possible amount of taxes to be administered by the head of the State. Under his father's rule the limit of profitable taxation had already been reached, but Frederick was able to make the collectors stricter than before. Though no spot in the Mark or Pomerania or Magdeburg was more than twenty miles from a border, the frontiers of his straggling dominions were watched with a vigilance which became proverbial. An Italian priest, whom he begged to smuggle him through the gate of heaven under his cassock, professed that he would be charmed to do so, provided that the search for contraband were not so keen as in Prussia. Liberty of commerce and remission of taxes were not among the ideals of a

King who claimed to direct all the economic activities of his people.

The Prussian clergy had less power than the moneyed interest, and less desire than the landed interest, to oppose or influence the will of the King. His absolutism was favoured by the fact that in his dominions several jealous churches existed side by side, and that he alone could be the umpire in their disputes. His own point of view was perfectly clear. He valued pastors because they taught their people to obey their superiors and not to rob and murder, as, in the King's opinion, they would do if unrestrained. If the pastors accomplished this duty with reasonable success they might, without fear of his displeasure use any ritual or proclaim any doctrine of which their congregations approved.

Frederick regarded the Protestant teaching as far more useful than the Romanist, but was determined to protect each in the enjoyment of its rights and privileges. He professed himself willing to build mosques for Turks and heathen if they would people the land. He was the official head of the Lutheran Church, whose clergy then, as always, preached the divine right of Kings. The King for his part usually jeered at their faith only in private. At times, however, he allowed his contempt for their observances to appear. When several congregations appealed to him to condemn a new hymn-book he despatched a refusal, and added with his own hand, " Everyone is free to sing ' Now all the woods are resting ' and more of such stupid nonsense." In the same spirit he answered the clergy of Potsdam who begged him not to block out the light from their church, "Blessed are they which have not seen and yet have believed."

Frederick's relations with his many papist subjects ran all the smoother because the contemporary Popes were as a rule too much engrossed by troubles within their own flock to engage in unnecessary aggressions. His treatment of the papists in his hereditary dominions was always carried out in the spirit of his answer to the monks of Cleves. Though hardly meritorious in the eyes of the Holy Father, it was too upright to give reasonable cause of offence. Near the royal palace in Berlin rose the Hedwigs-Kirche, a temple modelled on the Pantheon at Rome and built by the heretic King for the use of Romanists.

In the conquered provinces, however, a more difficult problem confronted him. The Romanists, who formed the bulk of the population of Upper Silesia and were powerful even in Breslau, could not be expected to accept with pleasure the head of an alien church as their supreme lord. The Prussian confiscation of one-half the net revenues of the conventual houses and at a later date the disgrace of Cardinal Schaffgotsch were measures dictated by needs of State, but not on that account less unwelcome to the Church. The papists of Silesia, particularly the clergy and the Jesuits, long continued to hope for the restoration of Hapsburg rule.

Even in Silesia, however, Frederick's policy of impartial firmness disarmed his religious opponents in the end. While his neighbours were expelling the

Jesuits from their dominions and confiscating the estates of the Church, his doors stood open to the fugitives and the original settlement of the relations
between Church and State remained unvaried. It
must not be forgotten, too, that the King of Prussia
was the patron and paymaster of a vast number of
ecclesiastics of all creeds. This fact finds illustration
in one of the practical jokes which he played upon
his needy friend Pöllnitz. Although he had already
changed his religion in hope of a lucrative marriage,
Frederick tempted him by hinting that a rich canonry
in Silesia was vacant. Next day, as he expected,
Pöllnitz came to tell him that he had again recanted
and was now eligible for the post. The King replied that the appointment was already made, but
that he had still a place of Rabbi to dispose of—
"Turn Jew and you shall have it." With the same
cynicism he exhorted and often compelled the clergy
to practise apostolic poverty. "We free them from
the cares of this world," he wrote to Voltaire after
a sweeping measure of confiscation, "so that they
may labour without distraction to win the Heavenly
Jerusalem which is their true home." It is not surprising if Carlyle is justified in stating that under
Frederick "the reverend men feel themselves to be
a body of Spiritual Sergeants, Corporals and Captains, to whom obedience is the rule and discontent
a thing not to be indulged in by any means."

If, then, it is vain to look either to any class of society or to the military or ecclesiastical organisations
for a possible check upon Frederick's absolutism, the
remainder of our quest must be confined within two

fields—the Judiciary and the Executive. It is idle
to imagine parliaments in Frederick's Prussia. His
ancestors had freed themselves from the privileged
assemblies which grew up in the several provinces
under the feudal system. To this day his successors
upon the Prussian throne reject the claims of their
subjects to what William II. stigmatised as "the freedom to govern themselves badly according to their
own desires." Nor was the absence of parliament
atoned for by the influence of public opinion. Society at Berlin occasionally ventured to mark its dis-
approval of the King's action. It was, however, a
narrow caste, which lacked even the wit to temper
despotism by epigram. The King, though he endowed his capital with many handsome buildings,
took little pains to conciliate its inhabitants by living
in their midst, and on occasion did not scruple to
play upon their stupidity. " In 1767, the King found
the public at Berlin inclined to tattle on the chance
of another war. To turn their attention he immediately composed and sent to the newspapers a full
account of a wonderful hail-storm stated, though
without the smallest foundation in fact, to have
taken place in Potsdam on the 27th of February in
that year. Not only did this imaginary narrative
engross for some time, as he desired, the public conversation, but it gave rise to some grave philo-
sophical treatises on the supposed phenomenon."
(Mahon.)

Many despotisms have, however, been tempered
by the judicial system of the nation or by the established machinery of administration. We, therefore,

turn finally to the judges and civil officers of Prussia for some check upon Frederick's power. But we find that in the department of law he was as absolute as in any other. His subjects were no longer entitled to carry their suits to the Imperial courts, and the King at once supplied the deficiency, and kept his judges under by making himself in person an accessible and swift tribunal of final appeal (1744).

In this connexion the case of Miller Arnold is of world-wide celebrity. A miller living near the Polish border was condemned by his lord to be evicted for persistent non-payment of rent. He appealed to the chief court of the province for restitution, alleging that another noble, who afterwards bought the mill, had deprived him of water by restoring a fish-pond higher up the stream. When the court decided against him, he availed himself of the privilege of petition which Frederick accorded to all his subjects. The King deputed one of his colonels to investigate the matter in company with a member of the provincial court. The colonel reported in favour of Arnold, but his colleague upheld the previous decision. The King, convinced that his colonel was in the right and that a poor man was being robbed of his livelihood by a legal quibble, ordered the provincial court to make a fresh enquiry. This second investigation only served to confirm their previous view of the case, though an expert in drainage was of opinion that the fish-pond really restricted the flow of water to the mill. They declined to alter their verdict and Frederick ordered the judges at Berlin to revise it.

The judges obeyed and revised the depositions with great care. Once more sentence was pronounced against Arnold. Thereupon the King determined to make an example of those who in his name oppressed the poor under form of law. He summoned before him the Chancellor and the three judges at whose door he supposed the guilt to lie. To the Chancellor he addressed six words only: "March, thy place is filled already." The three judges were first rated like malefactors and then flung into the common gaol.

It would be tedious to recite all the items of the King's vengeance. His hand fell as heavily upon the provincial court as upon the judges at Berlin. When the Minister of Justice refused to pronounce sentence against them, Frederick himself condemned them to loss of office, a year's imprisonment, and the payment of all that Arnold had lost. Thus the miller triumphed, though he had in truth suffered no loss of water power. Not till the succeeding reign was his knavery exposed and the royal decree reversed.

These proceedings, which took place in the later years of the reign, serve to show that Frederick was strong enough to trample the law and its ministers underfoot. In general, however, he proved himself practical, impartial, and firm in all that pertained to the judicial system. The story that a miller of Potsdam refused to sell his wind-mill to the King and answered his threats with a reference to the courts, has been destroyed by modern criticism. "The laws must speak and the sovereign be silent," was, however, one of his maxims. The distrust of lawyers which caused him to prefer the verdict of one colonel to that of many judges did much to inspire the sweeping changes for which the years following the Peace of Dresden are illustrious.

Frederick's law-reforms were in great part achieved by the aged jurist Cocceji, who, with the King's support, triumphed over all the interested opposition of lawyers and of his rivals. In the course of the years 1747 and 1748, he abolished superfluous courts, raised the fees for litigation, quickened the procedure, established satisfactory tests for judges and advocates, reduced the numbers of these functionaries, and did away at one stroke with the whole class of solicitors. The violence of these reforms is a fresh proof of the King's omnipotence. He might by a stroke of the pen have given binding force to the *Codex Fridericianus*, a famous code of law which Cocceji drew up on principles of his own choosing.

It is evident that in Prussia the judges were forced to be "lions under the throne." The civil service gave less proof of courage and was equally impotent to oppose the will of the King. Its structure might have been designed for the very purpose of preventing any official save the King from enjoying any substantial power or prominence. The lower agents, who could not be dangerous, had no colleagues, but all the higher functions were performed by boards. The villages were governed by the bailiffs of their lords, and thus a vast number of petty local officers were directly responsible to the representative of the Crown. Above the bailiffs stood the Sheriff (*Land-*

rat), who was nominated by the local nobles, but appointed by the King and acted as his factotum. One young *Landrat* strove to convince Frederick that there were locusts in his country by sending him some live specimens in a box. They escaped in the palace, and the angry King straightway altered the conditions of the office, decreeing that in future no one should be eligible who was under thirty-five years of age.

In the towns royal commissioners were charged with the collection of the " Excise " and with duties of general supervision. But at the next stage collegiate administration begins. *Landrat* and commissioner alike were responsible to the Provincial Chamber for War and Domains—a body such as that on which Frederick had served while a prisoner at Cüstrin. The individual members of the Chamber served the Crown as inspectors in their province and as special commissioners to carry out the public works which the King constantly initiated. The Chamber as a whole reviewed the work of the lower officials and reported to the General Directory, a clumsy corporation of ministers, which in its turn reported to the King. It is hardly necessary to observe that Frederick conceded to no person or body in this hierarchy the right to stand between himself and any business with which he chose to interfere. He, like his father, often preferred the evidence of his own eyes and of his soldiers to the statements of his civil servants.

The General Directory had been created by Frederick William in 1723.

"We wish," he frankly stated, "that any odium, however undeserved, should fall not on us . . . but on the *General-Ober-Finanz-Kriegs-und-Domänen-Directorium* [General Supreme Financial War and Domains Directory] or on one or other of the members of the same, unless it shall prove possible to make the public change its bad opinion."

The members were instructed to give such a turn to the business that this aim might be realised, "because," as the King expressed it, "we wish to be frugal as regards the love and affection of our subjects and of the friendship of our neighbours."

The new body, as its name implies, was primarily concerned with finance, which lay at the root of all Prussian government. It was called into being at the moment when Frederick William amalgamated two machines for collecting and expending revenue. It presided over the administration of the old feudal revenue which came from the Domains and over that of the new national revenue which came from the Contribution and Excise,—taxes imposed for the support of the apparatus of war. Foreign affairs and justice, each of which formed the charge of two or three other ministers, lay outside the sphere of the General Directory.

This consisted of four departments, each of which supervised the general administration on one great section of the soil of Prussia. The North-east, the Centre, the West, and the districts lying between the Centre and the West formed four distinct spheres of government, each of which was the special charge of a chief minister and several assistants. To these sectional departments, however, were assigned various minor charges extending over the whole kingdom. Thus the second department, which governed the Electoral Mark and Magdeburg, at one time also fulfilled the functions of commissary-general for all Prussia. It had in addition oversight over questions of salt, millstones, cards, and stamps, in whatever locality they might arise. If the chief of the department had four or five assistants a certain specialisation was possible, but he was obliged to reckon with the contingency that one or more of them might be commissioned to spend part of their time in another department.

The General Directory, as Frederick found it, contained four departments, but five chief ministers. The fifth, whose functions were the general supervision of justice and of finance, was in Frederick William's conception a royal spy upon his colleagues. If they were idle, deceitful, or inharmonious, it was his duty to report the facts to the King, "that His Majesty may get no short measure anywhere and may not be tricked."

It is easy to see that this machine of government, however cumbrous, was admirably designed to serve a despotic king. An army of clerks and inspectors was always at his disposal. If he desired to know what was passing in the furthest corner of his dominions, a curt note of enquiry to the General Directory sufficed to set the machine in motion. The Directory met five times a week, with no vacations. At its bidding, commissioners were appointed by the Provincial Chamber to ascertain the facts. In due

course the Chamber received, digested, and anno-
tated their report, and supplied the necessary information to the Directory.   There, in the department
which presided over the province in question, the
papers were again sifted and abstracted.

The Directory could not often be hoodwinked by
its subordinates, for Frederick William had furnished
it with an army of local spies.   Check after check
was applied.   When the member of the department
before whom the affair was brought had satisfied
himself, he procured the assent of his colleagues.
The department procured the assent of the Directory as a whole.   The Directory then reported to the
confidential servants of the King.   Eventually the
most concise and accurate information obtainable,
together with a table of arguments for and against a
given course of action, was laid before the King by
Eichel and his colleagues in the Cabinet.   Frederick
had only to glance at the paper and scrawl a few
words upon it in the morning and in the afternoon
to sign a royal order embodying his decision.   Then
General Directory, Provincial Chamber, Sheriff, and
Bailiff set to work in turn to procure the execution
of his commands.

It was objected that little Prussia had thirteen or
fourteen ministers when France required no more
than five.   But the multiplication of high officials
had this advantage—that it prevented them from
leaving the real conduct of affairs in the hands of
obscure subordinates.   Not only must every State
paper be signed by one or more ministers, but every
signature implied actual knowledge of its contents.

The system, too, prevented the rise of any single man or board that could challenge comparison with the King by reason of its ascendancy in any great function of government. Even Cocceji appeared to the people merely as a royal commissioner appointed to accomplish a definite mission.

Corruption on any great scale was impossible. The public accounts passed under so many eyes that the King of Prussia could never, like Charles VI., be deprived of three-fourths of his revenue before it reached the exchequer. It was useless to bribe Frederick's ministers to betray him, for they had not the power. They were there to give him information and to obey his behests. He seldom asked them for advice. " Good counsel does not come from a great number," was his maxim. Newton, he maintained, could not have discovered the law of gravitation if he had been collaborating with Leibnitz and Descartes. As Minerva sprang armed from the head of Jupiter, so must a policy spring from the head of the prince.

Frederick, therefore, admitted no man or body of men as his colleague, in the work of government. The officers of the Directory, Justice, and Foreign Affairs were not allowed to form a conclave which might meddle with questions of general welfare. As a body they were wont to appear before the King only once a year. As individuals they seldom communicated with him save in writing. The ministers of Foreign Affairs had not even the privilege of writing about all of the important matters which fell within the scope of their department. Their master kept the conduct of weighty

negotiations within his own Cabinet and corresponded with his ambassadors direct. Eichel was
his sole familiar. Secrecy, which the King termed
the soul of public business, was thus preserved inviolable. " To pry into my secrets," he boasted,
"they must first corrupt me."

This is not the place to marshal the disadvantages
to the State which the Prussian system of administration involved. At this stage it is sufficient to
note that it placed absolute power in Frederick's
hands and that he regarded it as a monument of
the highest wisdom. " If you depart from the
principles and the system that our father has introduced," ran his warning to his brother and heir,
" you will be the first to suffer by it."

The ten years of peace were therefore not devoted
to structural reform. In the first year of his reign
Frederick had created a fifth department of the
General Directory. To it he entrusted first the
trade and manufactures of the whole kingdom and
later the posts and the settlement of immigrants
from other lands. In 1746 he established in like
manner a sixth department, that of Military Affairs.
These changes merely developed the system of
Frederick William a little further. By a new departure, however, the Government of Silesia was
made independent of the General Directory. For
reasons which the King never stated, Münchow became the only minister for the province, and he was
responsible to Frederick alone. With this addition
the whole framework of government was stereotyped by an ordinance of 1748.

The years 1746–1756 are notable for Frederick's use of his machine rather than for the changes which he made in it. He now displayed in action the principles of domestic policy which were the fruit of his early training and the guide of his later years. His ideal is as simple to understand as it was difficult to realise in practice. He allowed his subjects to think as they pleased on condition that they acted as he pleased. Neither in home nor in foreign policy did the King recognise any bounds to the assistance that he might demand from the dwellers within his dominions.

The main object of his foreign policy was to extend the borders of Prussia to the utmost limit consistent with the safety of the State. His home policy was to bring within those borders the greatest possible number of men, to prevent them from falling below a certain moderate level of righteousness, comfort, and knowledge, to organise a huge army, to collect a vast revenue, and to enable Prussia as far as possible to supply all the needs of every one of her people. Other states were useful to her because they supplied recruits to her army, teachers for her artisans, and gold and silver in exchange for her surplus manufactures. The gold and silver were drawn into the treasury by taxation and used to build villages, to establish new manufactures, to hire more soldiers, and to fill Frederick's war-chest. Then, by war or a display of force which made war superfluous, a new province would be joined to Prussia and the routine of development, taxation, armament, and acquisition could begin anew.

It does not appear that Frederick regarded any single part of this programme as weightier than the rest. In spite of all his economies and accumulations he was no miser, cherishing money for its own sake. He hoarded treasure so that his army might be sure of pay in time of war and his subjects sure of help in case of devastating calamity. On the same principle he maintained and added to the huge Government granaries, which bought in years of plenty and sold, at high but not exorbitant prices, in years of dearth. Frederick did not refuse to make some profit from the institution, but his main object was to confer upon the State the inestimable boon of freedom from famine. The establishment of public warehouses for wool, silk, and cotton was similarly designed to guard against glut and shortage. It was merely a new adaptation of the policy of the Staple, which England had discarded at the end of the Middle Ages. But it secured a market to the Prussian producer and an unfailing source of supply to the Prussian manufacturer and placed the whole traffic in raw materials under the supervision and control of the State.

Frederick is as little open to the charge of megalomania as to that of avarice. He was singularly free from foibles. He frankly admits that the adventure of 1740 was partly inspired by the desire to make himself a name. But before the Peace of Dresden his lust of mere conquest seems to have been extinguished. Thenceforward his armaments and acquisitions were strictly regulated by reasons of State, and in his conception of statecraft domestic policy stood on a par with foreign. He likened the Finances, Foreign Policy, and the Army to three steeds harnessed abreast to the car of State, and himself to the charioteer who directed them and urged them on.

Frederick's most striking innovations in the department of home affairs were made during his later years. It will therefore be necessary in a subsequent chapter to give further illustrations of the working of his principles and to calculate the results which he accomplished. All through his reign, however, the process of internal improvement and interference was carried on in conformity with these ideas. Agriculture, as the basis of all, had the first claim upon the King's attention, and he made unceasing efforts to render every acre of the land productive and to provide it with a cultivator. If in the course of his innumerable journeys he observed a waste place that seemed capable of improvement he would commend it to the Provincial Chamber as a site for a certain number of new villages of a given size. If the suggestion proved feasible it was carried out at the expense of the State, which reaped its profit in course of time from the new taxpayers, producers, and recruits, who were thus included in the commonwealth.

The most signal of these victories in time of peace was the reclaiming of huge swamps lying along the Oder below Frankfurt. In July, 1747, the King appointed commissioners, including the famous mathematician Euler, and placed troops at their disposal. The task demanded not only dams and drainage works, but also in parts excavation of a new bed for the great river. It was urged forward by Frederick with all speed. He often inspected the works and exacted a report of their progress week by week. Boats were commandeered by force from the reluctant villagers. Some of those whose fishing rights were done away conjured the King, " falling at his feet," so ran their petition, " most submiss- ively in deepest woe and dejection as a most terri- fied band fearing the fatal stroke," that he would lay to heart the ruin which his measures would inevitably bring upon them. The King drily an- swered that they might let him know when they had suffered any actual harm and compensated them with reclaimed land.

Early in 1753 Frederick was able to make ar- rangements to people the new province which he had thus conquered from the domain of Chaos. The landowners, who had shared in the general opposi- tion to the enterprise, were compelled to resign to the State their claim to a large percentage of the reclaimed land and to provide a prescribed number of peasants for the remainder. Born Prussians were as a rule declared ineligible, for here was an oppor- tunity of tempting valuable fresh blood into the State. Freedom from military service to the third genera- tion, exemption from taxes for some years, and at first actual assistance were the terms offered to many immigrants. The result was that Frederick secured an influx of new subjects from far and wide. The Rhineland, Würtemburg, Mecklenburg, Swed- ish Pomerania, Saxony, Bohemia, Poland, and the mountains of Austria—all sent contingents. He laid

out more than 500,000 thalers in all and secured a
rental of 20,000. More than 250 villages were created. Thanks in great part to this policy of internal
colonisation, the numbers of the people steadily
rose. At his accession Frederick had ruled over
rather more than 2,200,000 people. Thirteen years
later the number in the old provinces had become
more than one-sixth greater, while East Frisia added
90,000 souls and Silesia some 1,200,000 more. In
1756 the total exceeded 4,000,000.

The decade which followed the Peace of Dresden,
though uneventful in comparison with the periods
of seven years which it divides, was thus by no
means barren. For Frederick it was indeed a period
of manifold activity. It was signalised by the establishment of Sans Souci and by the memorable
visit of Voltaire. For three years (1750-1753) the
King enjoyed the constant exchange of homage
with the cynosure of the world of letters, who described his new home, Potsdam, as "Sparta and
Athens joined in one, nothing but reviewing and
poetry day by day." Each of the two friends revered the genius and despised the character of the
other. The sequel was a desperate quarrel, and the
flight and arrest of Voltaire. When he was suffered
to pass beyond the reach of Frederick's sceptre he
strove to avenge himself with the pen which had
lavished exquisite flattery upon the King for many
years and which was often to resume the old style
in the future.

Literary effort and witty company were, however,
only the King's solace in a life of labour. Day by

day he scanned the political horizon, resolved to take no action which would not serve the State, and to shrink from nothing if Prussian interests were threatened. Day by day, too, he urged forward the labours of peace and the preparations for war. While Silesia was being gradually assimilated and the old Prussia developed, Frederick was making use of his new possession, East Frisia, in a tardy and only moderately successful endeavour to further commerce overseas. Commerce in Frederick's opinion ranked far below agriculture and manufactures in value to a state with ideals such as those which he had chosen for Prussia. He therefore devoted far more of his energy to the task of forwarding Prussian industry, which he argued gave employment to a thousand times as many men, brought more gold and silver into the country, and remained more amenable to State control. At the same time he was steadily accumulating treasure and perfecting his military force. In the fateful year 1756 he had upwards of 14,000,000 thalers stored up for war. The standing army then numbered more than 150,-000 men.

CHAPTER VII

THE SEVEN. YEARS' WAR TO THE BATTLE OF LEUTHEN

ALL the world knows that in 1756 the King of Prussia embarked upon a struggle in comparison with which his previous wars might almost be called sham-fights. This was the Third Silesian War, commonly known as the Seven Years' War, which Macaulay's lurid prose depicts as setting almost the whole globe on fire. The true cause of Austria's new struggle, not merely to regain Silesia, but also to curb the dangerous power of Prussia, will be patent to all who have followed the story of Frederick's life. It was the memory of past wrong quickened by apprehensions of worse to come. Maria Theresa could not believe that Heaven would suffer her despoiler to go unchastised, and she watched the political horizon for signs that the day of vengeance upon him was at hand. At the same time all the neighbours of Prussia perceived with that instinct which is the surest guide of states that the system to which they belonged was jeopardised by an intruding Power whose conduct had been such as to justify a crusade against her.

In that age of unstable alliances and easy wars it was certain that a conviction shared by so many states would sooner or later lead to action. It was equally certain that, while Frederick was king, Prussia would strike back. Hence we may regard with some indifference nice balancings of moral judgment upon the great fact of 1756, when Frederick suddenly made war upon Austria and treated Saxony with almost greater violence. It seems idle to maintain that because Austria had yielded up Silesia by treaty she was debarred for ever from retaliating upon Frederick in the fashion which he had set. Who would apply such a rule to the problems of the present? If it be lawful, in our own day, for France to hope to recover Alsace and Lorraine, or for Spain to hope to recover Gibraltar, it is not easy to understand why, in 1756, Maria Theresa might not lawfully hope to reverse the verdict of 1742 and 1745. And if she and her neighbours contemplated something more than a recovery of lands actually lost, if they sought to reduce the King of Prussia to the harmless level of a Margrave of Brandenburg, who can be indignant or even surprised? A new coalition against Frederick would be merely the Austrian answer to his own riddle, " If I have an advantage, am I to use it or not? "

But if, as seems undeniable, Austria and her neighbours had good grounds for hoping to attack Prussia, and if, as Frederick had reason to believe, the danger was becoming imminent in 1756, what could be more futile than the statement that none the less he was not justified in striking the first blow? It

THE EQUESTRIAN STATUE OF MARIA THERESA IN THE VIENNA HOFFBURG.

is true that for reasons of current politics the Austrian Chancellor, Kaunitz, schemed with success to shape events so as to make Prussia seem the aggressor, and that he thus established the conditions under which Austria could claim the fulfilment of a treaty of defensive alliance. At a distance of a century and a half, however, such subtleties can be appraised at their true value. Though in 1756 war emerges from as dense a cloud of diplomacy as ever befogged the path of European history, our generation may regard the Third Silesian War as the natural result of the original aggression of Frederick and of the abiding interests of other Powers.

Those interests, however, demand a brief explanation, for they determined the time and the form of a war which at some time and in some form was inevitable from the very moment at which Austria and Prussia laid down their arms at Dresden. In an age when the true course of states was steered by kings and statesmen of whom some were lazy, some self-seeking, some timid, some honestly mistaken in their designs, it was not to be expected that many should, like Prussia, make straight for a definite goal. Since the Peace of Utrecht, Europe had lived in an atmosphere of general uncertainty. Nations formed countless short-lived comradeships for the pursuit of objects often transient. It was almost impossible to forecast who, if war broke out, would be ranged on one side or the other, and hardly less difficult to forecast the side upon which those who had entered the war as allies of one of the combatants would be found at the end of it. What might, however, be

anticipated with confidence was that few Powers
would neglect the chance of profit which war
afforded. Walpole's famous boast, " There are fifty
thousand men slain in Europe this year and not
one Englishman," was called forth by his triumph in
keeping clear of the War of the Polish Succession,
which was not too remote to embroil every other
Great Power.

While there was then a tendency for every Power
to share in every war as an auxiliary if not as
a principal, two alliances had become traditional.
Ever since the undue predominance of France first
imperilled the liberties of Europe, England had
steadily supported Austria against her. And so
soon as the Great Elector showed that Prussia might
be a serviceable ally, France strove to employ her
with a view to the humiliation of Austria. Though
only occasionally successful in engaging Prussia, she
continued to regard her as a natural ally. Thus
each of the maritime and commercial rivals of the
West had its *liaison* with one of the German Land
Powers of the East.

More to be reckoned on than these connexions
were, however, three great antipathies which the
course of history had revealed. The clash of interest between Austria and Prussia seemed destined
to distract Germany until one or other proved
supreme, and, so long as Maria Theresa confronted
Frederick, it would be made harsher by a duel
between the sovereigns. Russia, while Elizabeth
ruled, would go with Austria. The giant State
whose westward path had been marked out by Peter

the Great already discerned in Prussia the athlete braced to dispute the way. Ost-Preussen was always a tempting bait, and long ere this an ambassador at Frederick's Court reported that the King feared Russia more than his God. None the less Frederick had permitted his sharp tongue to goad the luxurious Czarina into a fury which surpassed that of the Queen whom he had robbed of Silesia. In April, 1756, the Austrian ambassador at St. Petersburg was informed that Russia was ready to co-operate in an immediate attack upon Prussia by sending 80,000 men, and that she would not lay down her arms until Maria Theresa had recovered Silesia and Glatz.

The jealousy of the rival states in Germany and the wrath of the despot who swayed the policy of Russia would count for much in the coming war. Weightier still was the struggle between France and England for the primacy in three continents and on the seas. This great national duel had been begun by William III. and brilliantly continued by Marlborough. During the pacific rule of Walpole, when the two countries were nominally in alliance, England was gaining strength and taking up a position in America and India which her rival could not witness unmoved. The close league formed by France with Spain, the monopolist of the New World, rendered lasting peace with England impossible and even Walpole was forced into war. This war, known as the War of Jenkins' Ear, began with an attack on the Spaniards in 1739, and developed into a world-wide struggle with the French in which

Dettingen and Fontenoy were incidents. The settlement at Aix-la-Chapelle in 1748, which put an end
to it, was obviously a mere breathing-space. In the
early fifties hostilities broke out anew between the
English and French in India and North America,
and it could hardly be doubted that Europe would
soon catch fire.

In 1756, therefore, war between France and England had already begun, and war between Frederick
and his two Imperial neighbours was imminent. The
custom of Europe and the precedent of the former
struggle made it in the highest degree unlikely that
these wars would be kept apart. What would be
the connexion between them? The answer was
determined by three accidents. The King of England happened to be Elector of Hanover, the ruling
spirit at Vienna happened to be Kaunitz, and the
mistress of Louis XV. happened to be Madame de
Pompadour.

Hanover, argued George II., will certainly be attacked by the French. It must be defended at all
costs. The only possible defenders are Austria,
Russia, and Prussia. Austria, the old patron of
Hanover, would be preferable. But the Queen has
grievances against England and is bent on attacking
Prussia. Alliance with her would therefore expose
Hanover to the Prussians as well as to the French,
and must therefore be regarded as out of the question. Russia and Prussia remained to be considered.
Russia actually made a convention to hire out troops
for the defence of Hanover. But Russia, the King
found, also desired to attack Prussia, and was there-

fore as ineligible an ally as Austria. Only the Prussian alliance remained possible. In January, 1756, by the Convention of Westminster, it was secured.

The Convention of Westminster, by which Frederick bound himself to defend Hanover against attack, helped on the far more difficult task of Kaunitz. This was no less than to reverse the secular policy of France and Austria and to bring Bourbon and Hapsburg into alliance. Kaunitz based his calculations on the assumption that France might help Austria to recover Silesia, but that England never would. This view of the political situation was urged for seven years with great ability by a statesman in whom the Queen reposed a confidence greater than that with which our own Elizabeth honoured Burleigh, and who treated her in return with a haughtiness such as Essex would never have dared to show. Kaunitz, whose life was spent in the endeavour to exalt the power of his mistress, forced her to shut her windows to humour his prejudice against fresh air, and stalked out of her Council when she interrupted him with a question. At another meeting, it is said, she remonstrated with him on his riotous living. He replied that he had come there to discuss her affairs, not his own.

But the great, it is said, are known to the great, and Maria Theresa's confidence in Kaunitz seemed to be justified when his visionary scheme proved feasible. It was easy to form a league to despoil Prussia. Kaunitz tempted Russia with parts of Poland, Poland with an indemnity in Ost-Preussen, Saxony with Magdeburg, Sweden with Prussian

Pomerania, the princes of the Empire with the favours which the Emperor alone could bestow. But it required great powers of imagination to conceive that France might quit the beaten track of history, which was at the same time plainly the path of self-interest, in order to assist her hereditary foe in a great land-war at a time when she needed all her strength to meet England upon the seas.

Kaunitz had not only the strength to see this vision, but also the fortune to realise it in fact. The circumstance that favoured him the most was that the Pompadour was now at the height of her influence in France. The mistress of Louis XV. furthered the plan of Kaunitz for selfish reasons, but in the expectation that its result would be the exact reverse of what it was. She desired to keep the peace in Europe in order that she might continue to live quietly at Versailles. The Minister of Marine, moreover, was her friend ; the minister who might profit by a land-war was her enemy. She therefore favoured a covenant of neutrality with Austria in the hope that the two wars would thus be kept apart.

The Convention of Westminster, however, made it impossible that the affair should rest here. The fact that Prussia had bound herself to resist a French invasion of Hanover frustrated all Frederick's efforts to propitiate the Pompadour and to throw dust in the eyes of the French.

"If the ministry of France will consider it well," wrote Frederick on January 24th, ". . . it should find nothing to say in reason if I undertake such a convention, by which, moreover, I flatter myself that I render an essential service to France, seeing that I shall certainly arrest 50,000 Russians by it, and shall hold in check another 50,000 Austrians at least, who but for that would all have acted against France."

He further endeavoured to discount his alliance with George II. by turning a sympathetic ear to the French plans for assisting the Young Pretender, and by advising her to strike in Ireland and on the south coast of England at the same time. It was beyond his art, however, to disguise what he had done, and Kaunitz knew how to profit by it.

The labours of the diplomatists were immense, but at last they were successful. On May 1, 1756, by the Treaty of Versailles, both France and Austria undertook for the future to defend the European possessions of the other with 24,000 men. In the war with England, Austria was to remain neutral, but if in the course of it any province of France in Europe were to be attacked by any ally or auxiliary of England, Austria promised by a secret article to provide the stipulated assistance and France offered a similar guarantee. This might be interpreted as binding Austria to join in the war if the French were masters of Hanover and the Prussians marched against them. It thus deprived the Convention of Westminster of half its value, and at the same time threatened to connect the war against England, which France had begun brilliantly at Minorca, with the war against Prussia, for which Elizabeth was clamouring. Negotiations for a still closer union between Austria and France were pressed on, and Kaunitz hoped that in 1757 all would be ready.

Too much was, however, in the wind for Frederick's keen scent to be entirely baffled. Austria, indeed, sincerely desired peace for the present. The published articles of the Treaty of Versailles were innocent. The English ministry disingenuously tried to lull the protector of Hanover into false security by assurances that they could answer for Russia. But the King of Prussia had his own sources of information as well as the most perfect faith in the malevolence of his fellow-men. For three years and a half one Menzel, a clerk in the Saxon Foreign Office, had been furnishing him with copies of the secret state-papers of Augustus. The whole truth about the negotiations against Prussia was not known at Dresden, but enough reached Frederick from this source to impress upon him the desirability of anticipating his foes. So early as June 23, 1756, he sent to General Lehwaldt, in Königsberg, three sets of instructions, military, economic, and secret, for dealing with the anticipated Russian invasion, and even for negotiations with a view to peace.

"You know already," wrote the King, "how I have allied myself with England, and that thereupon the Austrian court, from hatred of my successful convention with England, took the course of allying itself with France. It is true that Russia has concluded a subsidy-treaty with England, but I have every reason to believe that it will be broken by Russia and that she has joined the Austrian party and concerted with her a threatening plan. But all this would not have caused me to move if it had not been brought to my notice through many channels and also by the march of Russian and Austrian troops that this concert is directed against myself."

Frederick probably told the truth to his commander-in-chief in Ost-Preussen. On the same day Sir Andrew Mitchell, the shrewd and honest Scotchman who then represented England at the court of Prussia, had an audience with the King. He reported that, notwithstanding the great number of enemies, the King seemed in no wise disconcerted, and had already given orders everywhere. "In a fortnight's time he will be ready to act. His troops, as I am informed, are complete, and the artillery in excellent order."

On the eve of war, then, Frederick's sword was as sharp as of old and his courage as high. He soon showed that his pen had not lost its cunning. At the end of June he indicted his enemy before the judgment-seat of England. Austria regarded her new connexions, so stated his clever memoir, as the triumvirate of Augustus, Antony, and Lepidus. The three courts, like the three Romans of old, had sacrificed their friends to each other.

"The Empress abandoned England and Holland to the resentment of France, and the court of Versailles sacrificed Prussia to the ambition of the Empress. The latter proposes to imitate the conduct of Augustus, who used the power of his colleagues to aggrandise himself and then overthrew them one by one. The court of Vienna has three designs towards which her present steps are tending—to establish her despotism in the Empire, to ruin the Protestant cause, and to reconquer

Silesia. She regards the King of Prussia as the great obstacle to her vast designs."

Thus Frederick claimed to be the champion of the balance of power and of Protestantism, and proposed to solicit not only Denmark and Holland, but even the Turk and the Empire for aid. His appeal to England concluded with the assurance that Prussia was not cast down. " Three things can restore the equilibrium of Europe—a close and intimate connexion between our two courts, earnest efforts to form new alliances and to foil the schemes of the enemy, and boldness to face the greatest dangers."

A paper of this kind, brilliant, concise, astute, and even eloquent, is worth many thousand lines of the rhymed platitudes by which the author set greater store. We might expect to hear that it was followed at once by a spring at the throat of the enemy. It is true that Kaunitz, who was not yet ready for war, and who wished that if war must come Frederick should be the aggressor, held the Russians back. But he was pressing forward warlike preparations in Bohemia and Moravia, and Frederick was not likely to ignore the advantage of striking swiftly and of waging war outside his own borders. The military men, when they saw the evidence in the King's hands, were all for action. "Schwerin," says Carlyle, "much a Cincinnatus since we last saw him, has laid down his plough again, a fervid ' little Marlborough' of seventy-two." He urged the immediate seizure of Saxony, as a base of operations against Bohemia.

Cooler heads, indeed, counselled Frederick to have

patience. On behalf of England, a Power always singularly dispassionate when the interests of a German ally were at stake, Mitchell urged that many chances of war and politics might swiftly change the face of affairs, and that to attack Austria would give unnecessary provocation to France. The faithful Podewils ventured to spend a summer afternoon at Potsdam in labouring to turn the King from his purpose. In his letter of July 22, 1756, to Eichel, he speaks of the "respectful freedom" with which he begged the King not to drive France and Russia to do what they had no desire to do that year if Austria were not attacked. Let him rather use the ten months' grace before the next campaign in securing allies within and without the Empire, in trying to reconcile France and England, and in preparing an imposing defence.

"But all this," says the poor man, "was completely rejected as arising from far too great timidity, and at last I was dismissed coldly enough with the words, '*Adieu, Monsieur de la timide politique.*'" His concluding phrases, however, have in them so much of prophecy that they may be cited here.

"That it was not doubtful that progress and success might at first be brilliant, but that the complication of enemies, at a time when the King was isolated and deprived of all foreign help, which had never happened to him yet, at least in regard to the diversions which had been made in his favour in the two preceding wars, would, perhaps, make him remember one day what I took the respectful liberty of representing to him for *the last time.*"

Such is the literal rendering of the French into which Podewils, who writes the bulk of his letter in a jargon of German, French, and Latin, forces his tortuous German thoughts.

Frederick, indeed, seems already to have passed the stage at which he could be influenced by argument. An agile rather than a deep thinker, he reached at times a point at which calculation became agony and the only remedy was action. Now, as in his earlier adventure, " pressed with many doubts, he wakes the drumming guns that have no doubts." That a mere Prussian minister should combat his plans seemed to him little short of *lèse-majesté*. Nor could he be moved by those who were not so tightly bound to the car of Prussia. Mitchell followed Podewils with arguments, and Valori, the French ambassador, followed Mitchell with threats. Frederick's answer was a series of blunt questions pressed home twice over at Vienna—Have you a treaty with Russia against me? Why are you arming? Will you solemnly declare that you do not intend to attack me this year or next? The final answer was received on August 25, 1756. Next day the Prussians invaded Saxony.

The Seven Years' War had begun. Needless to say, every movement of the Prussians had been planned out long before. The army was under orders which enforced the most perfect mobility. A hundred supernumeraries had been added to every regiment. On the 13th to 15th August Frederick issued directions that the secret of their destination was to be strictly kept from the troops. They were to take with them provisions for nine days, every cavalryman carrying three days' supply of hay, and every infantryman three days' supply of bread, while bread for six days was placed in the single baggage-cart allowed to each company. None of this reserve of food was, however, to be broken into save in the utmost need, and no officer of any rank whatever might have table utensils of nobler metal than tin.

A word would set all in swift motion, but the machine had to be arrested until it should be known that the Prussian ultimatum was rejected. Klinggräffen, Frederick's ambassador at Vienna, caused some delay by asking for instructions. On the 24th the King wrote to General Winterfeldt, the most impatient advocate of war: "The cursed courier is not yet here, so I have been compelled to stop the regiments till the 28th. Klinggräffen deserves to be made a porter by way of punishment. Such stupid tricks are unpardonable and the prolonged uncertainty is unbearable." On the 26th, however, after hearing from Vienna, the King was able to set all in motion anew.

"The answer," he wrote to his brother, the Prince of Prussia, "is impertinent, high, and contemptuous, and as for the assurances that I asked of them, not a word, so that the sword alone can cut this Gordian knot. . . . At present, we must think only of making war in such a fashion as to deprive our enemies of the desire to break the peace too soon."

While one royal messenger was bearing this message from Potsdam to Berlin, others were on their way to Vienna, to Dresden, and to every division of the Prussian army. Klinggräffen was instructed to return a third time to the charge, with the final offer that if the Empress-Queen would declare definitely that she would not attack Frederick that year or the next, the troops now moving should be recalled. More profit was, however, expected from the message to the Saxon Court. King Augustus, or Count Brühl, was to be informed, " with every expression of my affection and of your respect that good breeding can supply," that Frederick was compelled by the Court of Vienna to enter Saxony with his army in order to pass into Bohemia.

" The estates of the King of Saxony," continued the royal missive, " will be spared as far as present circumstances allow. My troops will behave there with perfect order and discipline, but I am obliged to take precautions so as not to fall again into the position in which the Saxon Court placed me during the years 1744 and 1745. . . . I desire nothing more ardently than to behold the happy moment of peace, so that I may prove to this Prince the full extent of my friendship, and place him once more in the tranquil possession of all his estates, against which I have never had any hostile design."

This declaration was addressed to a ruler who had made no engagements hostile to Frederick, and who now offered to observe perfect neutrality and to allow his troops to pass. A commentary upon it is supplied by a document which was probably drawn up several days earlier, and which was soon to be put in force. By this " instruction " for the administration of Saxony during the war, "in order that His Majesty may not leave a highly dangerous enemy in his rear," the Prussian minister von Borcke is directed to suspend the native administration of the land and to substitute a Prussian Directory of War. The Saxon royal revenue, it is said, amounts to about six million thalers, but Frederick "will be contented with five million, so that the inhabitants may be solaced thereby." In other respects the order and temperance which distinguished the Prussian Government were to be applied to the subjects of Augustus. Such was Frederick's plan for the future of Saxony, a would-be neutral, during the war.

The problem which the King set himself was to cripple Austria before Russia or France could come to her assistance. Austria had assembled forces in Moravia and in Bohemia. If Frederick attacked the former the Bohemian army might cut off his retreat. He therefore directed Schwerin to guard Silesia while he himself converted Saxony into a base for the invasion of Bohemia. From the Saxons he expected little or no opposition. He therefore proposed to march in three columns upon Pirna, a fortress situated at the point at which the Elbe bursts through the mountain-wall of Bohemia to enter the fertile plains of Saxony. Then, with a granary and a highway behind him, he would follow the river into Bohemia as far as Melnik, less than twenty miles north of Prague, where it ceases to be navigable. He would thus at the very least have gained a commanding position on the further side of the mountains.

"As he does not think that the Austrians will soon be ready to attack him," wrote Mitchell on August 27th. "he imagines they will throw in a strong garrison into Prague, that [*sic*] as the winter approaches, he can have good quarters in Bohemia, which will disorder the finances at Vienna and perhaps render that court more reasonable."

To the ambassador of England Frederick made light of his enterprise and insisted that it would permit him, if necessary, to defend Hanover. But it is difficult not to surmise that he looked for a great campaign. The capture of Prague, the rout of the army of Bohemia, and the seizure of its magazines—all this would be a fitting sequel to the coercion of Saxony. It was not too grave a task for the main host of Prussia.

Even the lesser scheme failed, however, because Augustus, though a weakling, was a man of honour. His army was less than twenty thousand strong, but it sufficed to hold Pirna and to block the highway of the Elbe. On September 9, 1756, Frederick entered Dresden, but Augustus had fled to the army and lay safe in the impregnable rock-fortress of Königstein. While the invader was rifling his archives for proofs of a great conspiracy against Prussia, he offered to observe the most benevolent neutrality and begged for an exact statement of what more could be expected from him. He received the answer on September 14th from the lips of Frederick's favourite, Winterfeldt. It was nothing less than that he should join Prussia in attacking Maria Theresa.

"How can I turn my arms against a Princess who

has given me no cause for complaint, and to whom, in virtue of an old defensive alliance of which Your Majesty is aware, I ought to furnish 6000 auxiliaries, only that it is doubtful whether the present war is a case of aggression?" Such was the old King's reply to the Prussian tempter, and he coupled with it renewed assurances of neutrality. Frederick reiterated his demands and expressed regret that he could not extend complaisance further. By no effort of diplomacy could he shake the honourable firmness of Augustus, and it was therefore necessary to gain the highroad into Bohemia by force.

Frederick had surrounded Pirna, but he did not venture to assault it, though Napoleon declared at first sight that there were nine points of attack. It was clear, however, that hunger must soon force the Saxons to move and that their only hope lay in succour from the Austrians. Browne, the Irishman who had proved himself to be one of the Queen's best generals, therefore led an army northward to the foot of the mountains and was confronted by Frederick in person at Lobositz. On October 1, 1756, a fierce fight of seven hours proved indecisive. Early in the day the King sent twenty squadrons of horse to meet disaster at the hands of the Austrian gunners, and later the Prussian infantry showed that they were still the men of Mollwitz and of Soor. The Prussians kept the field of battle, but of nearly 6400 killed and wounded more than half were theirs.

The relief of Pirna was checked but not frustrated. Lobositz is, however, chiefly memorable as the day on which the Austrians first encountered the

Prussians at their best and were not beaten. It is no more than Frederick's due to remark that the troops whom he had now to face were men who had learned what his father's army had to teach. They had adopted the Old Dessauer's iron ramrod, and the swiftness of their fire was no longer less than the half of their opponents'. Their artillery, thanks to the labours of Prince Lichtenstein, was always good and not seldom superior to the Prussian.

In little more than a fortnight after Lobositz the campaign of 1756 was at an end. On October 11th, Browne reached Schandau, on the right bank of the Elbe, where he expected the starving Saxons to join him. They were not ready, and after waiting two days he was compelled to retreat. The failure of the relieving expedition sealed the fate of Augustus's army. On October 17th, the rank and file laid down their arms—only to be compelled, in defiance of the terms of surrender, to take them up again as soldiers of the King of Prussia.

Augustus, however, did not suffer martyrdom in vain. He lost his army and his Electorate, but his "ovine obstinacy" ruined the attack upon the Queen. In the hour of triumph Frederick wrote to Schwerin: "As for our stay in Bohemia, it is impossible for either of us to establish a sure footing there this year, for we have entered the province too late. We must confine ourselves to covering Silesia and Saxony." Both Prussians and Austrians tacitly agreed to postpone the decisive blow till the new campaign.

To balance the gain and loss which Frederick owed to his preference of his own plan to the "timid policy" of Podewils we must take into account wider considerations of war and politics. By treating Saxony in Hohenzollern fashion, without scruple and without riot, the King undoubtedly gained some advantages. He found in the archives at Dresden the material for yet another manifesto to Europe. He tested and inspired his army, which only knew that under his leadership it had won a battle, captured an army, and conquered a state. He even increased its numbers by forcing the vanquished Saxons into the ranks. Above all, he won security for the western flank of Silesia and a safe base from which to attack Bohemia.

But all this was purchased at a great price in material and moral strength. Prussia was still a Power which had to ask herself whether she could bear a second or a third campaign. To raise new taxes was difficult if not impossible. Frederick, it might almost be said, paid for the war out of his own pocket with the help of his allies and of the enemy. Already he showed some signs of being pressed for money. In the middle of September he made secret arrangements for borrowing 300,000 thalers from a house of business in Berlin. Soon the Saxon officials were told that their pay must fall into arrear and Frederick observes with some brutality that Augustus, who had retired to his second capital at Warsaw, could support his queen and her household in Saxony from the French and Austrian subsidies. He thus denied to the victim that courtesy for his family which he had ostentatiously promised from the first.

It may be doubted whether 14,000 pressed men, even though some of them might otherwise have found their way to the enemy, compensated Prussia for the loyal veterans who fell at Lobositz. Throughout the war Frederick found no servants less reliable than the Saxons whom he had impressed and no foes more bitter than their countrymen who escaped. As for Saxony itself, it is true that if war must come, which Podewils regarded as dubious, Prussia derived much strength from her possession of it. But Frederick's treatment of Saxony removed all possibility of escaping not only from a war, but from war upon the scale that he professed to expect. The spectacle of the suffering King inflamed all his enemies. As an exile in Warsaw Augustus was a more valuable ally to Austria than he could have been in Dresden. He made it absurd for Frederick to pose as the defender of German princes against the Hapsburg. In January, 1757, a majority of those princes, assembled in Diet at Ratisbon, solemnly commissioned the Hapsburg to marshal their corporate might against the Prussian aggressor.

Frederick had treated the defensive alliance between the two Empresses as a conspiracy against himself. Early in February it became such; save that what he might once have termed a conspiracy now wore the aspect of a crusade. All the North was summoned to unite with Austria in curbing Prussia for ever, and Russia bound herself to keep 80,000 men in the field until the lost provinces had been regained. Frederick had even performed

what Kaunitz and the Pompadour could not completely accomplish. France now gave in her whole-
hearted adhesion to the league for the recovery
of Silesia and Glatz. She pledged herself to pay
Austria a heavy annual subsidy, to place 105,000
French troops in the field, and to enlist 10,000
Germans. The history of the negotiations, which
were prolonged till May 1, 1757, shows how real
were the difficulties to be overcome before Bourbon
and Hapsburg could unite.

In May, 1757, when the new campaign began,
Frederick thus stood face to face with what it is
hardly an exaggeration to term a world in arms.
He, and no other, had brought Prussia to this pass.
A coalition unprecedented in history was the result
of the aggressions of 1740 and 1756. All the world
believed that the hour of reckoning had struck and
that the Third Silesian War would bring the punishment from which chance had delivered the King
who made the First.

To the biographer of Frederick, 1757 is welcome,
for Frederick now begins to be a hero. Had a chance
bullet at Lobositz struck him down, the world would
have known only a king who promised to bring in a
new era of government, but who owed to his father's
work and methods the chief part of whatever success
he achieved. For creative power he would have
taken rank below the Great Elector and Frederick
William, for military renown below the Old Dessauer and Schwerin; for the aggrandisement of his
House, who knows? for who can calculate what
havoc the Coalition of 1757 would have wrought

with his dominions? The Frederick who had bequeathed to Prussia several volumes of prose and
verse in French and the memory of sixteen years'
tenure of Silesia would hardly be known to fame
as Frederick the Great.

In 1757, however, he takes his stand for the existence of Prussia. At the moment that the military
balance turns against him the moral balance turns
in his favour. Courage, energy, resource, determination, all displayed through a score of lifetimes,
if sensations rather than moments make up life,—
Frederick is the embodiment of these things during
the next six years. At first it is his daring that
seems to eclipse all else. If Frederick feared not
God, neither did he regard man. Far from being
dazzled by the array of sceptres marshalled against
him, he determined to strike before his foes could
form.

With the first breath of spring he despatched
three royal princes and the Duke of Bevern against
four several points in Bohemia. " If those false
attacks have so far succeeded as to cover the King
of Prussia's real intention," writes Mitchell on April
18th, " I may venture to say that His Prussian
Majesty is upon the point of executing one of the
boldest and one of the greatest designs that ever was
attempted by man." Just at this juncture a plot
against his life was discovered. " I think upon the
whole His Prussian Majesty has had a very narrow
escape, which however seems to have made no
impression at all upon him, nor to have created
in him the least diffidence whatever of anybody."

Such is his Scotch friend's account of the King at the outset of the chequered campaign to which he owes the immensity of his fame.

Frederick's courage was not foolhardiness, for the very reason that he was one, and his enemies were many. Every coalition must encounter the difficulty of concerting a plan of campaign acceptable to all and the still greater difficulty of securing honest and punctual co-operation. The coalition against Frederick had the advantage that several of its members could serve the common cause by following the course most profitable to themselves. The Russians might be expected to overrun Ost-Preussen and the Swedes to attack Prussian Pomerania with the best will in the world, while the Austrians had every incentive to be vigorous in the conquest of Silesia. But France consented to help to make Silesia and Glatz Austrian chiefly in order that she might secure Austrian help nearer to her own borders. The motley forces of the Empire had little interest in the quarrel, and the activity of Russia depended upon a czarina whose health was bad. Speed and secrecy were alike unattainable by a machine which could be set in motion only after debate between the Board of War at Vienna, the corrupt and factious Court at St. Petersburg, and the inharmonious ministers of France. Once set in motion, however, the gigantic machine seemed irresistible. Kaunitz could launch battalions against Prussia from every point of the compass. Although a new English minister, William Pitt, seemed disposed to stand by Frederick, it might well be thought incredible that Prussia could escape destruction at the hands of such a multitude.

Frederick's plain course was to make use of the speed and secrecy for which the Prussian movements were famous. The Queen was massing troops in Bohemia. She had determined to raise 150,000 men, but with sisterly partiality she halved their effectiveness by appointing Prince Charles to the command. This appointment favoured the plan which Mitchell admired so highly. Frederick was devising a new form of the manœuvre by which he decoyed the Austrians to Hohenfriedberg. He was so successful that everyone on the Austrian side believed that his one object was to maintain himself in Saxony. To them the four sham-invasions of Bohemia seemed to be designed to conceal the King's defensive operations and to paralyse their own attack. The illusion was strengthened because at the same time they learned that Torgau and Dresden were being fortified in all haste and that barricades were rising on the roads from Bohemia into Saxony. The last thing that they could suspect was that Frederick was on the eve of attacking.

The result was that the movement planned for the previous autumn was now carried out in the face of 133,000 Austrians. Frederick's three columns issued from Saxony, Schwerin came from Silesia, and before the end of April 117,000 Prussians were encamped in Bohemia. In the face of such a force the astonished Austrians abandoned the magazines which they had stored for the conquest of Saxony

LEOPOLD, COUNT VON DAUN.
FROM A COPPER PRINT.

and fell back on Prague. Having occupied a strong position to the east of the city, Prince Charles awaited the arrival of Field-Marshal Daun, who was advancing from the south.

Now the Prussians were to learn that a royal command has drawbacks. Frederick was burning to attack the enemy. He had staked the success of the campaign on the chance of a pitched battle, and the timid tactics of Prince Charles filled him with impatience. At his back was the finest army in the world. He was opposed by cavalry who had never beaten their Prussian opponents since Moll-witz, by infantry who had never beaten them at all, and by a general whom he despised. Preferring, as usual, the boldest course, he crossed to the eastern side of the river Moldau, which runs through Prague, and signalled to Schwerin to join him.

Prince Charles did not venture to oppose a move-ment by which the enemy's force was made almost equal in number to his own. Such inertness could be justified only if he believed either that he was very weak or that his situation was impregnable and that Daun's arrival would make him sure of victory. His position indeed was strong enough to have given pause to a general less impatient than the King of Prussia. All Frederick's royal authority had to be exerted before Schwerin would consent that 64,000 men, of whom the half had been marching since midnight, should attack a strongly fortified position held by 60,000 of the enemy. But the vanguard of Daun's 30,000 was within ten miles of the capital and Frederick had his way.

His forlorn hope at Prague on May 6, 1757, was
to cost more blood than had been spilled on any
field in Europe for nearly fifty years. The Prussians
began by marching with great skill round the Austrian right. Browne, however, suggested an effective
counter-manœuvre, so that when Schwerin assailed
the flank at ten o'clock he did so under unsuspected
disadvantages of ground. "The cavalry began the
encounter, and after several fruitless attacks Zieten
with the reserve overthrew the Austrian cavalry.
In the pursuit, however, his troops came upon one
of the enemy's camps and drank so deep that they
were of no more use that day." Such is the statement of Schäfer, the Prussian historian of the war.
At the same time the infantry of the first line
pressed forward, but found that the way to the
enemy lay through the treacherous slime of fish-
ponds coated with green, which Frederick in his
haste had taken to be meadow-land. They struggled across unharmed, but the well-served Austrian
batteries began to destroy them at a range of 400
paces. Then their onslaught was shattered by the
Austrian grenadiers, and Schwerin, as he seized the
colours to rally his men, was slain by a blast of
grape-shot. The Austrian grenadiers began a triumphant counter-charge, but they were unsupported,
for their army had now no leader. Browne had fallen
early in the charge, and Prince Charles collapsed
in wrestling with problems too great for his powers.
The Prussian second line was therefore able to repair the disaster of the first, and, after a terrible
struggle at close quarters, they stormed the heights

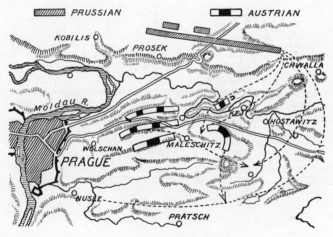

PLAN OF PRAGUE, MAY 6, 1757.

and won the battle. Many of the Austrians fled southwards across the river Sazawa, but the greater number took refuge behind the walls of Prague.

In the battle itself Frederick played the part of a brave and skilful leader. His first impression was that he had gained a decisive victory. In the evening he wrote to his mother :

"My brothers and I are well. The Austrians are in danger of losing the whole campaign and I find myself free with 150,000 men, and that we are masters of a kingdom which must provide us with troops and money. The Austrians are scattered like chaff before the wind. I am going to send part of my troops to compliment *Messieurs les Français* and to pursue the Austrians with the rest."

He informed Wilhelmina that about 5000 men had been killed and wounded. To his ally, George II., he sent word that the battle had been "as decisive as possible," and to his Scotch friend, Field-Marshal Keith, that he believed that the capture of Prague would finish the war. Fuller knowledge showed that these ideas were ill-conceived. The King's impatience had caused an attack across treacherous ground with weary men. The pursuit therefore failed, and the Austrian casualties did not greatly exceed the Prussian. Frederick himself later computed his loss at 18,000 men, "without counting Marshal Schwerin, who alone was worth above 10,000." The most moderate estimate states it at 12,500. The Austrians lost some 13,000, including prisoners, but nearly 11,000 more fled across the

Sazawa, and the Prussians made an unwonted haul of baggage and artillery. One of the musketeers wrote home that 186,000 Prussians had beaten 295,-000 Austrians and captured 200 guns. The army and the people were jubilant, but the price was great. "Schwerin's death," said the King, long after, " withered the laurels of victory, which was bought with too much precious blood. On this day fell the pillars of the Prussian infantry . . . and a bloody and terrible war gave no time to rear them anew."

The success of the campaign now hung on the fate of Prague. If the capital and its defenders fell into his hands without delay, the King might still execute the remainder of his daring scheme. He might sweep away Daun, enter Moravia, and dictate peace at Vienna. Thence he might lead his army to the western scene of war, to crush the forces of the Empire, and drive the French across the Rhine. A strong reinforcement, he believed, would enable Lehwaldt to grapple with the Russians, whose soldierly qualities he had not yet learned to appreciate. The moral effect of his victory was felt by all Europe. Frederick became the hero of the English nation. At Vienna depression reigned, and Kaunitz grew loud in his appeals to France and Russia. Roving bands of Prussians spread terror through the Empire by pretending to be the vanguard of the King, and demanding contributions from the magistrates of hostile towns with threats of stern measures if their demands were not complied with. Austria could not protect her German allies, and Louis XV. feared that she might now desert him as

Prussia had deserted him in 1742 and 1745. If Prague fell the coalition would be shaken if not destroyed.

But however great the profit to be gained by the fall of Prague, Frederick realised that he could not hope to carry by storm a city which Browne had previously undertaken to hold with 8000 men and which now contained a garrison of 44,000. He therefore detached the Duke of Bevern with a force of 17,500 to observe Daun in the south, while he himself set to work to reduce Prague by starvation. In the hope of destroying the magazines he maintained a severe bombardment, which put the inhabitants to great suffering but brought little military advantage. He even brought a notorious burglar out of gaol to break into the city and procure information. Prince Charles, who had plenty of meal though little meat, did not risk his army in a sally *en masse*, but with the approval of his Government simply waited for Daun to set him free. This was an afflicting policy for the impatient King. On May 24th, Frederick hoped " at present more than ever that all this race of Austrian princes and beggars will be obliged to lay down their arms." On May 29th, he informed Wilhelmina that a week ought to see the end, but before the week was over he began to admit the possibility of failure. On June 11th he wrote to Lehwaldt that it might be three or four weeks before he would be free to move. Next day, after hearing from Bevern that Daun could no longer be kept at bay, he sounded the knell of the whole enterprise :

"Who loses time in war," runs Frederick's broken German, "cannot make it good again. Had you pressed forward at once towards Czaslau, Daun would have retreated further . . . and I wager that if one flies at his throat he will do it. To get together 10 battalions now is impossible, but perhaps I will come myself to make an end of the matter, so that what has been gained by bravery be not lost by hesitation. . . . Daun must be driven into Moravia be he weak or strong, else we do not win Prague and cannot resist the other enemies who come on, and the whole campaign, however well begun, is lost."

The cause of this note to Bevern was that with less than 10,000 men he had at last fallen back before the enemy. Daun, whose caution was to earn him the nickname "*Fabius Cunctator*," had assembled an army some 54,000 strong and was advancing under strict orders to venture a battle for the relief of Prague. Frederick felt that the crisis called for his own presence. For the issue he had no fear. In order to risk nothing during his absence, he took with him only some 14,000 men, so that by strict count of heads he would attack against odds of more than five to three. But if Schwerin were worth 10,000 men, the King may well have believed that his own value was far greater. On June 16th he wrote to his representative in London that he had joined Bevern,

"in order to march straight on Field-Marshal Daun, to fight him, and to drive him altogether out of Bohemia into Moravia. I flatter myself that in a few days I shall be able to give you good news of our success; and when this expedition is happily over, I believe that the town of Prague will fall of its own accord, and that then with hands more free, I shall be able to send a detachment against the French."

The King's confidence was in great part warranted by what he had already seen in the present war. It seemed that only a Browne would dare to attack Prussian troops led by their King. Had not Prince Charles been overruled by his generals, he would have abandoned Prague to avoid a battle. Daun had retreated before Bevern till he became overwhelmingly superior in force, and he advanced only when his Queen promised him gratitude for a victory and her continued favour if he were beaten. The most that could be expected from such commanders as these was that they would stand on the defensive in a strong position.

This very fact made the tactics of the Prussians doubly formidable. Drilled to the last degree of perfection, they could change their formation with a speed which their enemies admired but could not rival. Frederick could therefore veil his movement till the last moment. Having chosen the enemy's most vulnerable wing, he could strengthen the wing opposed to it without fear that the enemy would either accomplish the countermove in time or attack the section which he had weakened. It was therefore of little consequence that the Austrians greatly outnumbered the Prussians in the part of the field where no fighting was likely to take place. The battle was gained because the

Prussians swiftly overcame all that nature and art could oppose to them at the spot selected by the King for contact. The doomed wing would be broken, the centre laid bare, and then the cautious Austrian would make off, rejoicing that it was not dishonourable to be beaten by the King of Prussia, and that the attack demanded so much preliminary marching that the weary victors were not often terrible in pursuit.

Such were the tactics attempted in the battle of June 18, 1757, when Frederick attacked Daun in his camp overlooking the highroad between Vienna and Prague, within sight of the town of Kolin. The country undulates sufficiently to make it impossible for the King to have ascertained every detail of the problem with which he was confronted. But from many points, and with especial clearness from an isolated height across the highway, he could see that the Austrian right wing held the crest of a gentle slope south of the road and parallel with it, and that it was at the further extremity of this wing that the ground seemed most favourable to the attack.

The morning of the stifling summer's day was spent in marching along the line of the highroad towards Kolin, and it was after midday that the Prussian left turned upon the enemy. Zieten, the terrible hussar, put to flight the Austrian horse, but an oak-wood gave them shelter behind which to rally, and meanwhile Daun made all haste to move up supports to his right. But though the Austrians fought doggedly and poured in a deadly artillery fire, the matchless Prussian infantry pressed on. They captured point

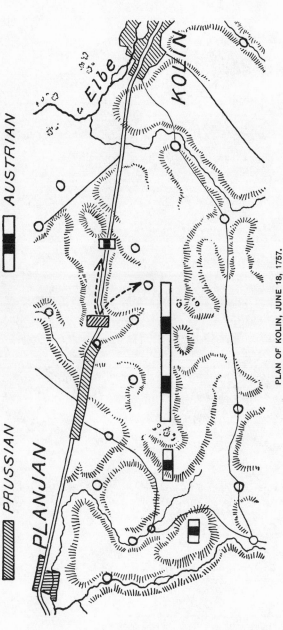

PLAN OF KOLIN, JUNE 18, 1757.

PRUSSIAN

AUSTRIAN

PLANJAN

Elbe

KOLIN

after point of Daun's position until the moment came at which, although their cavalry had turned tail, they needed only reinforcements to crush his right. It was the duty of Prince Maurice, the son of the Old Dessauer, to bring help from the centre. The moment was critical. The Austrian musketeers, seven times charged by the Prussians, had shot away their last cartridge. "Four fresh battalions," wrote the King four days after, "and the battle was won." Daun had already begun to withdraw his heavy guns and to issue orders for retreat. But by a fatal misunderstanding, due, it is hinted, to the impatience of the King in giving orders, Maurice was attacking the enemy more than half a mile further down the line. Still nearer to the Prussian right General Manstein defied orders and dashed at the enemy.

The Prussians were therefore involved in a frontal attack, and their inferiority in numbers at once began to tell against them. Yet still, though Frederick had only the reserves of cavalry in hand and these, even when he put himself at their head, refused to pass through the fire to aid them, the dauntless Prussian left achieved fresh triumphs. When the deadly wrestle reached its fourth hour they still maintained their hold upon the heights. Daun hurled his light Saxon cavalry upon them, but with a heroism worthy of Mollwitz field they formed into groups and drove back the foe. But at this moment the Count de Thiennes, colonel of a regiment of young dragoons from the Netherlands, begged for leave to attack. He won a grudging assent, at first refused, "but," said Daun, "you won't do much good with your beardless boys." "You will see," answered Thiennes and galloped back to his regiment. "Boys," he cried, after repeating the field-marshal's taunt, "show that though you are beardless you can bite." Uniting with the Saxons, the "boys" swept the enemy's horse from the field, then flung themselves on the grim square of tattered heroes, broke it, and drove it from the heights. This was the prelude to a general flight of the exhausted remnants of the Prussian infantry. Almost beside himself with rage and disappointment, Frederick collected some forty men and led them against the foe. But even the King could not persuade them to suicide. One by one they slunk away till at last his adjutant put the question, "Will your Majesty take the battery alone?" Frederick once more gazed at the enemy through his glass, then rode to Bevern on the right and ordered retreat.

Of 31,000 Prussians little more than 17,000 were left. As at Prague, it was the infantry whose loss was the greatest. Of 18,000, more than two-thirds were killed or captured. It was true that they had inflicted upon the enemy a loss of more than 8000 men, and that Daun, "like a good Christian who would not suffer the sun to go down on his wrath," did nothing by way of pursuit. But Frederick saw at a glance that the conquest of Bohemia was now beyond his strength. On June 20, 1757, the very day on which Prince Charles had announced that he would be compelled to surrender, the besiegers quitted Prague.

Frederick's plan was to retreat slowly through north-eastern Bohemia into Saxony, exhausting the country as he went. "My heart is torn in pieces," he wrote to Prince Maurice two days after the battle, "but I am not cast down and will try on the first opportunity to wipe out this disgrace." Perhaps because, in hi.. own phrase, "a certain Hungarian rabble has taken kennel on the highways," his letter to his sister makes light of Kolin. "I attacked Daun on the 18th. In spite of all our efforts, we found the country so difficult that I believed myself bound to abandon the enterprise in order not to lose my army." For the information of Berlin, Eichel magnified the gentle slopes which are all that the battle-field can show into "a steep mountain, cut by many ravines and defiles at its base." But to London the King sent a franker statement.

"After winning eight battles in succession, we have for the first time been beaten, and that because the enemy had three posts on a tolerably high hill fortified by strong batteries one behind another. After taking two of them, the attacking battalions and their supports had suffered so much that they were too few to force the third post, and so the battle ended for lack of combatants."

The transports of the Queen and the exaggerated caution with which Daun and Prince Charles neglected to follow up their advantage attested the truth of Frederick's assurance that his situation was by no means desperate.

From day to day however, it altered for the worse.

Disaster in the field was followed by affliction in the home. Within a fortnight of Kolin, Frederick suddenly learned that his mother was no more. The crushing news was blurted out by a letter from his wife, whose thoughtless use of a red seal in place of a black one frustrated the kindly machinery which Podewils and Eichel had devised for preparing the mind of the King. He had just written to Wilhelmina a letter full of confidence.

"You have nothing to fear on my account, dear sister, men are always in the hands of what is called destiny. . . Germany is passing through a terrible crisis. I am obliged to stand alone in defending her liberties and her faith. If I fall, there will be an end of them. But I have good hope. However great may be the number of my enemies, I trust in the goodness of my cause, in the admirable courage of my troops and in the goodwill which exists from the marshals down to the humblest soldier."

Then the blow fell and for two days, even at such a crisis, the flow of political correspondence is checked. His grief finds utterance in an agonised note to his sister Amelia.

"All kinds of misfortune are overwhelming me at once. . . . I am more dead than alive. . . . Perhaps Heaven has taken away our dear Mother that she may not see the misfortunes of our House." "Yesterday and the day before," writes Eichel on July 3d, "His Majesty's grief has been very great and violent, but to-day it is somewhat lessened, because his Majesty has taken into consideration his duty to his state, his army and his faithful subjects at the present crisis, and the necessary orders have somewhat relieved his depression, though there is no lack of gloomy moments and intervals."

On the same day the King began to pour out his soul to Mitchell, who owns himself " most sensibly affected to see him indulging his grief and giving way to the warmest filial affections."

Calamity was, however, as impotent as success to teach Frederick good faith towards his allies. Mitchell had reported on June 30, 1757, that " he renewed to me on this occasion his firm resolution to hearken to no terms of peace without His Majesty's privity and approbation." On July 9th he describes a further interview in which " His Prussian Majesty said that, as he resolved to continue firmly united with His Majesty, it would be for their mutual interests to think of terms of peace, honourable and safe for both, and to concert together what terms they would adopt, if a favourable opportunity occurred to propose them." Yet between these assurances of fidelity to England Frederick accepted with enthusiasm an offer made by Wilhelmina to send an envoy to procure peace with France by bribing the Pompadour.

" I will willingly charge myself with his expenses," he writes on July 7th. " He may offer the favourite anything up to 500,000 crowns for peace, and he may raise his offers far higher if at the same time they would promise to procure us some advantages. You see all the nicety of which I have need in this affair and how little I must be seen in it. If England should have the least wind of it all would be lost."

Job's tidings continued to pour in upon the King. In the sunshine of Kolin the crop sown by Kaunitz was ripening fast. Before July was half over Frederick learned that the French had seized East Frisia and were striking east, that the Swedes were sending 17,000 men into Pomerania, and that the Russians were likely to destroy Lehwaldt in Ost-Preussen. Thus all his northern frontier was on fire and the army of the Empire was about to join the Austrians in kindling new conflagrations in the south. Bohemia, of course, must soon be abandoned, and how would it be possible to hold Saxony, Silesia, or even Brandenburg against such a host of foes? Men said that in Voltaire the King of Prussia had lost his pen and in Schwerin his sword.

In the latter half of the month the situation altered still further for the worse. While Frederick lay motionless at Leitmeritz on the Elbe, intent on devouring Bohemia till the last moment, but keeping open his retreat into Saxony, his eldest brother, Augustus William, was out-manœuvred by the Austrians further east. Prince Charles, with inferior numbers, seized one of his posts, outpaced him to Zittau, burnt the magazine there, and finally compelled him to flee far into Saxony. Nothing remained but for the indignant King to rescue the heir to the throne, who had thus opened to the enemy the Lusatian door into both Saxony and Silesia. On his way Frederick paused to garrison

Pirna, and there, on July 27, 1757, he received what Mitchell terms "a draught of comfort to one who has not had a single drop since the 18th June."

So serious was the crisis that the King had sent orders to Berlin that at the first news of further disaster in Lusatia the archives and treasure should be removed to Cüstrin. That very day he had written a plain account of the situation to convince his ally of England how desperate was his plight. "If I except Spain, Denmark, Holland, and the King of Sardinia, I have all Europe against me. Even so, I fear not for the places where I can set armies against them, but for those where he who comes will find no one to oppose him."

Such was the King's mood when his friend, the ambassador of England, laid before him with delight the contents of as considerate a despatch as was ever penned in Whitehall. Sympathy for Kolin, approval of the new plan of campaign, "entire reliance upon the King of Prussia's great military abilities," a cheerful review of the forces still at his disposal—all this might be expected from the ministers of George II. But what followed might well have heaped coals of fire upon Frederick's head. His ally, little suspecting the overtures to the Pompadour, persisted in treating him as a man of honour.

"The hint his Prussian Majesty threw out to you, of an inclination to peace, is agreeable to the language that Prince has held from the very beginning of the present troubles in Germany. . . . The King will at all times be glad to contribute to a general pacification, whenever equitable conditions can be had for himself, the King of Prussia, and their allies . . . the King being determined to take no steps in an affair of this consequence without his Prussian Majesty's concurrence and approbation."

Then follow solid offers of co-operation with ships and above all with gold, the latter " only meant as the convenient and proper contingent of England to her allies."

Frederick, by Mitchell's account, received the message

"with a flow of gratitude not to be described. After a short pause, he said, ' I am deeply sensible of the King's and your nation's generosity, but I do not wish to be a burden to my allies; I would have you delay answering this letter till affairs are ended in Lusatia; if I succeed, I will then consult with you upon the different points suggested in the letter and give my opinion freely upon them. If I am beat, there will be no occasion to answer it at all; it will be out of your power to save me, and I would not willingly abuse the generosity of my allies by drawing them into unnecessary and expensive engagements that can answer no valuable purpose.' I was pleased, but not surprised," the report continues, " with the noble dignity of this answer, for I have seen the King of Prussia great in prosperity but greater still in adversity."

There was, however, little of dignity or greatness in the King's treatment of his unlucky brother and heir, whom he met on the road to Bautzen two days later. It was in the early hours of the morning, according to the narrative of an eye-witness, the son of one of the chief delinquents, that Augustus William saw the King and beside him Winterfeldt and Goltz, two of his own generals, for whom he had waited a full hour in vain. Each of the royal brothers rode at the head of his staff, and in Frederick's train were Prince Henry and Ferdinand of Brunswick. At a distance of about three hundred paces the King stopped. Augustus William did the like, and he and his party doffed hats. The King's party bowed to them, but Frederick turned his horse round, dismounted, and lay down upon the ground as though awaiting his vanguard. He made Winterfeldt and Goltz sit by him. All his officers dismounted, as did the Prince and his party. Soon Goltz crossed over to the Prince and said a few words to him, whereupon the Prince called his officers together and requested him to repeat the King's message in their presence. This he did in the following words:

" His Majesty bids me tell Your Royal Highness that he has cause to be very dissatisfied with you. You deserve that a court-martial should be held over you, and then you and all the generals with you would lose your heads. But His Majesty is not willing to carry the matter so far, because in the General he would not forget the Brother."

Augustus William made answer like a brave man, exculpating his generals, and requesting a strict enquiry into his own conduct. But the King replied only by putting himself at the head of his vanguard, which had now come up, and riding on with his staff past the Prince, always keeping from three to four hundred paces away from him. At Bautzen he encamped, but still kept at a distance from the fugitives, lest, suggests Eichel, their fear should contaminate his own officers. Augustus William, treated like a leper, applied for permission to go to Dresden. "The Prince may go where he will," said Frederick to the lieutenant who bore the letter. He went to Berlin and died of a broken heart.

If anything could palliate brutality to the merely unfortunate it would have been the situation in which Frederick was placed by his brother's blunder. Despite all his efforts, the Austrians remained masters of the pass into Lusatia. With French, Swedes, Russians, and Imperialists all pressing on, it became imperative to dispose of the Austrians by a second Hohenfriedberg. But Prince Charles was not to be tempted from the strong position which Daun had chosen with his wonted skill. After three impatient weeks Frederick decided that the peril from the French was too acute to permit of further delay in trying to force the Austrians to give battle. Early in August he received the news of Cumberland's downfall at Hastenbeck. Hanover lay at the mercy of the French under Richelieu, and when on August 25, 1757, the King turned his face towards the west, Soubise with a second French force and the army of the Empire was already at Erfurt. Frederick was determined to maintain his hold on Saxony. Bevern, he decided, must watch the Austrians, distance and fortune must account for the Russians and Swedes, while he himself undertook a march of two hundred miles to muster 20,000 men and lead them against Soubise.

It seemed at first as though the King did wrong to trust in fortune. On August 30, 1757, the army of Ost-Preussen was vanquished by the Russians at Gross-Jägersdorf. Frederick, however, kept on his way. In the middle of September he reached the scene of action, only to suffer from the caution of Soubise a month of the same torture that Prince Charles had inflicted in Lusatia. Then he was suddenly called upon to hurry a hundred miles towards the north-east to drive the Austrians from his capital. In his absence Prince Charles had moved eastwards into Silesia and his rearguard of light cavalry, 15,000 strong, seized a favourable moment for a foray on Berlin. They exacted a ransom of 200,000 thalers from the town, and then made off by forced marches. Frederick, who feared an invasion in force, was greatly relieved at the news, which reached him on October 18th. Next day, despairing of bringing the French to book, he informed Prince Maurice that it was time to think of chasing the Austrians from Silesia, but on the 23rd he sent him word that Soubise was after all leaving the hills and marching straight for Leipzig.

"Here very much is altered in a day," he added with his own hand. It was in fact the turning-point of the most marvellous and chequered year of Frederick's life. Full of hope, he ordered a concentration between his own command and those of Ferdinand, Keith, and Maurice. The sum-total was not great, but the quality and temper of the troops were incomparable. They were face to face with Frenchmen, of old the scorners of the German race, which they were wont to conquer by their arms and to corrupt by their example. Now these invaders were laden with the spoils of Thuringia. Insolent and infatuated, they were too proud to see among themselves defects which were patent to Prussian eyes. It was little wonder that Frederick's veterans shared the ardour of their King. " The spirit of the soldiers was remarkable," noted Mitchell when they came to Leipzig. "They did not complain of fatigue, notwithstanding of the long marches, but desired to be led out immediately, and murmured on being ordered to quarters."

Three days later their desire was gratified. On the last day of October, 1757, Frederick was at Weissenfels on the Saale, checked for the moment because the enemy burned the bridge in his face and held the line of the river against him. His road from Leipzig had led him across the dismal plain where Charles XII. held for a moment the fate of Europe in his hand, past the granite slab which marks the spot where a greater King of Sweden fell at the head of his men. The region is memorable in history, but the deed which would have been most notable of all was averted. At Weissenfels, tradition says, Frederick owed his life to the chivalry of a French officer who forbade an artilleryman to pick him off.

The French and Imperialists gave up the line of the Saale, joined forces, and took up a strong position in the undulating country to the west. On

FREDERICK VIEWING THE BURNING BRIDGE AT WEISSENFELS.

FROM A RELIEF ON HIS STATUE AT WEISSENFELS.

November 3rd, Frederick crossed the river and expected that next day the intolerable tension would be at an end. When, however, he came to reconnoitre the enemy's position in force he found that to attack it against odds of two to one would be to invite a second Kolin. To the exultation of the allies, he drew back under a heavy cannonade and encamped with his left wing resting on Rossbach. On November 5th, Eichel, who was lodged at a safe distance, sent word of this fiasco to the Government, which had taken refuge in Magdeburg. "The whole war," wrote this most submissive of Frederick's slaves, "is of no avail. May Your Excellency soon make a good peace." He added a postscript: "At the moment of closing this, about 2 o'clock in the afternoon, we hear a very loud cannon-fire and, as it seems, musketry also." Frederick was being delivered from his troubles by a game of hide-and-seek.

The King's object in encamping near Rossbach was to turn the allies' position, or, failing this, to hang upon their rear when hunger should compel them to retreat. By the enemy, however, the movement was attributed to fear. Hot-headed Frenchmen, full of the martial traditions of their race, urged Soubise to crush a foe whose stroke they had yet to learn lest his little army should escape them. Vengeful Saxon voices joined with theirs, while shivering Imperialists, who for five days had subsisted on what food they could pick up among the peasants, clamoured for the break-up of the camp. Soubise at last gave way and planned a second Soor, to be done this time in broad daylight. Screened by the low

hills, the allies were to march round Frederick's left
and to take him in flank and rear.   Believing themselves to be four times as strong as the King, they
feared only lest he should flee to Merseburg in time.

After a march of some three hours the allies
reached a point due south of Rossbach.   With a
salutary access of caution, the French proposed to
encamp there, right on Frederick's flank.   But this
proposal was angrily resisted by the Imperialists
and Saxons, and at the critical moment the news
came that the Prussians were retreating.   It was
evident that they could delay no longer without
permitting Frederick to escape.   If, however, they
hastened round the eastern end of the long, low
ridge which hid his army from view, they might still
take it in flank as it fled along the road to Merseburg.   With this plan in mind, Soubise and his colleagues cast prudence to the winds.   From the first
they had omitted to name a place of retreat or a
formation to be adopted in case they should be attacked.   Now their army hurried along pell-mell,
with three generals at the head of the cavalry, the
infantry straggling after as best they might, the
French reserves pressing between the marching columns and the artillery, and the whole flank exposed
on the left, where the low ridge still screened the
enemy from their sight.

Behind that ridge Frederick was ranking his men
for battle.   He, too, had believed his opponents to
be in retreat and received with coarse taunts and
disbelief the report of a lieutenant that they were
trying to outflank him.   The sight of their infantry,

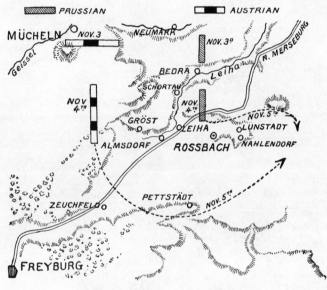

PLAN OF ROSSBACH, NOVEMBER 5, 1757.

however, convinced him that they meant even more than a reconnoissance. At a glance he saw his opportunity. "In less than two minutes," writes an onlooker, "all the tents lay on the ground, as though someone had pulled a string behind the scenes, and the army was in full march." At first, by great luck, the heads of the Prussian columns pointed north-east towards Merseburg, and thus the allies were deluded into the belief that they were in retreat. Then, hidden by the ridge, they moved east and finally south-east, converging towards the enemy. In the waning November afternoon they formed line and waited unseen, cannon massed on the right, Prince Henry with the infantry in the centre, on the extreme left Seydlitz, the prince of dragoons, smoking his short clay pipe till the King should order the charge.

Little more than an hour after the Prussians struck their tents they were dashing at the open flank of the allies, and ere another hour had passed Frederick's western frontier was saved. The so-called battle of Rossbach would be better named the drove of Reichartswerben. But for the slaughter inevitable when the best troops in the world swooped down upon a mob, the encounter would have been a pure farce. First Seydlitz by repeated charges drove the cavalry of the allies off the field. Then, to the accompaniment of a heavy cannonade, Prince Henry led the infantry down the slope and poured swift volleys into the medley out of which Soubise was vainly struggling to form a line of battle. Some of the French, Swiss, and West-German troops showed fight, the rest fled. Finally Seydlitz fell upon their rear and the butchery was checked only by darkness. At the cost of about five hundred men Frederick destroyed an army of nearly fifty thousand and made himself the hero of the Teutonic race. He jeered at the vanquished enemy in blasphemous French verses and set to work to reap the fruits of victory.

Everywhere save in Silesia the aspect of affairs was changing in his favour. A report that Elizabeth was dying caused the Russians to withdraw from Ost-Preussen just when their victory had placed it at their mercy. Lehwaldt was therefore set free to undertake the defence of Pomerania against the Swedes. England, inspired by Pitt, was proving herself a worthy ally against France. A new army was formed for the defence of Hanover. The command was offered to Prince Ferdinand, and British soldiers were to serve under him. For the present year at least, the North and West might be accounted safe. But from the Eastern theatre of war the news was bad. Prince Charles had followed Bevern into Silesia and now stood between him and Schweidnitz. Not a moment was to be lost if the King would save this important fortress.

Once more, however, Prussian speed was equal to all demands. Two days after Rossbach Frederick was already on his way. " I will leave you as strong a corps as I can on this side," he writes to Keith, "and march unceasingly for Silesia. A toilsome year for me!" In good heart after Rossbach, he strongly approved of Bevern's resolve to attack the Austrians.

" For God's sake have no fear of a weak enemy," he wrote, " but trust to your own insight and experience." But the days of Schwerin and the Old Dessauer were over. Except Henry and Ferdinand, Frederick had now no general from whom he could expect victories like his own. While he strode swiftly through Saxony Silesia was lost. On November 18, 1757, at Königsbrück, he learned that Schweidnitz had fallen without a blow. The confused reproaches and threats which he poured out upon Bevern and his generals were futile, for on the 22nd Prince Charles drove the Prussians from Breslau across the Oder, and within the week the capital was Austrian once more.

Before the news of Breslau reached him Frederick had declared to Bevern that he was firmly resolved to attack the enemy, but that it must be with their united forces, " else I am too weak and not much over 12,000 strong." Next day, November 24th, at Naumburg on the Queiss the report reached him that Bevern had gained a victory. He therefore planned to catch Prince Charles in a net at Neumarkt by marching from Liegnitz to meet Bevern sallying forth from Breslau. He even hinted that Keith might surprise Prague, and wrote to Ferdinand : "With good fortune I flatter myself that I shall finish this business in a fortnight." " The Almighty shows us one great mercy after another," wrote Eichel. Next day they learned part of the truth, though rumour multiplied fourfold the Austrian loss of 6000. " Defend Breslau to the last man—on peril of your head," was the sum of Frederick's orders to his brother-in-law, accompanied by much military counsel and a promise of speedy aid. But soon the news came that Bevern was a prisoner, that his army had fled to Glogau, worst of all, that Breslau had capitulated without firing a shot. Thousands of the garrison volunteered to serve Maria Theresa. It is said that one battalion quitted the capital in a strength of nine officers and four men. After sixteen years Silesia seemed to be welcoming home its Queen.

For a fortnight Frederick's army had struggled along bad roads at the astonishing rate of nearly sixteen miles a day. They drew rein at Parchwitz, within two marches of Breslau. There on November 28th the King composed a short testament. " I will be buried at Sans-Souci without pomp or ceremony—and by night," was his decree. ". . . If the battle be won, my brother must none the less send a messenger to France with full powers to negotiate for peace." The words show how completely he identified himself with Prussia amid circumstances so gloomy that Eichel forbore, ever after, to mention the document lest he should recall them to the mind of the King. Yet on the same day Frederick wrote one of his most characteristic letters to Wilhelmina, who had expressed her fear that the army vanquished at Rossbach would afflict Germany anew. " This is now our task," ran his reply:

" to put the Austrians to flight and to recover all that we have lost ; and it is no trifle. However, I am undertaking it at the risk of what may follow. Neither Soubise nor the Imperialists will come back this year: as for the future, we must hope for peace, for indeed it seems as though our enemies had determined to destroy the human race. . . . I beg you to await the issue in these parts with patience ; neither our anxiety nor our care make any difference to it, and nothing will happen except what pleases His Sacred Majesty Chance. . . . If I reach winter quarters, I shall have the honour of sending you a prodigious quantity of verse of every kind."

Needless to say, Frederick's fatalism did not abate his energy, nor against such odds did his courage degenerate into rashness. He gave the command of Bevern's ruined army to Zieten, who had defeated the enemy's right in the battle of Breslau, and bade him bring men and guns from Glogau. Then he and his weary 14,000 waited four full days at Parchwitz, with Prince Charles's victorious army to their front, the garrison of Liegnitz on their flank, and Austrian slowness letting slip the opportunity to attack.

On December 2nd, Zieten arrived at Parchwitz, having rallied some 18,000 men. Frederick had now an army about 32,000 strong, well furnished with cavalry and artillery. His plan had from the first been as clear as the task before him. He was resolved to perish rather than abandon Silesia. The Austrians held the province by means of an army and two strong places, Breslau and Schweidnitz. He must therefore first beat the army and then capture the strong places. The advent of December forbade long manœuvring in the hope of catching Prince Charles at a disadvantage. To save

Silesia this year and Prussia next, he must lead his
army straight to the enemy. The problem that he
expected to find resembled the problem of Prague
and of Kolin — to destroy an army not inferior in
numbers posted in ground of its own choosing.
Prince Charles, he believed, had his back to Breslau
and his front protected by a stream of some size.
" He is in an advantageous camp," wrote Eichel on
December 1st, " well furnished with artillery ; he
lives on our magazines, and the possession of Breslau gives him liberty to retire in any case across the
Oder, from which God preserve us ! " The ejacula-
tion reminds us that if the Austrian force remained
in being, Frederick would be foiled.

The King was determined to venture all upon a
battle. That he appreciated the odds against him
is not entirely clear. Writing to his brother Henry
on November 30th, he declares himself hopeful of
pitting 36,000 men against the 39,000 at which he
estimates the Austrian force. Next day he alters
the former number to 39,000, and Eichel states that

" According to many letters from his officers which
we have intercepted, the enemy has lost more than
24,000 men, as well as 8000 at the siege of Schweidnitz ;
he has suffered much from sickness ; half of his cavalry
is ruined ; yet notwithstanding all this he must be equal
if not superior in numbers to ourselves."

On the other hand, Prussian tradition represents the
King as declaring on December 3rd that, contrary to
all the rules of war, he would attack Prince Charles's
army wherever he found it, though it was nearly

thrice as strong as his own. But whatever be the truth,—whether or no he would have done what he had declined to do on the day before Rossbach, whether or no he knew or guessed the truth that Prince Charles had 80,000 men,—Frederick spared no effort to fill every soldier with his own spirit. Rest and food and drink, the story of Rossbach to chase away the memory of Breslau, all these were showered upon an army which since adversity had purged it of its foreign elements responded with eager loyalty to the touch of the Prussian King.

Stripping off his cherished French manners, he was for a brief space the Father of his people. The news flew round the army that the King had bandied rough pleasantries with his grenadiers, that veterans had called him "Thou" and "Fritz," that he had told the Pomeranians that without them he would not dare to give battle. The effect was magical, and the rank and file caught the glow which warmed the breasts of their superiors. For Frederick had done what he had perhaps never yet deigned to do, save when he quitted his capital in 1740 to grasp Silesia. He had called his officers together and appealed in impassioned phrases to their honour, their loyalty, and their patriotism. "Gentlemen," he cried, "the enemy stand in their entrenchments armed to the teeth. We must attack them there, and conquer, or remain every one of us on the field. If any of you is unwilling, he may have his discharge at once and go home." Then he paused. The devoted men were silent, many in tears, only one major cried out: "High time for such wretched scoundrels to be off." Fred-

erick smiled and declared that he was sure of their
faithful service and of victory.　He then denounced
stern threats against the man or regiment who
should fail in the hour of battle.　" Farewell, gentlemen," were his concluding words; " soon we beat the
enemy or we see one another no more."　More than
twenty years later the rough soldiers wept like children as they told the tale, and those who heard it
could not keep back their tears.

On Sunday, December 4, 1757, King and army
set out for Breslau.　From Parchwitz to the walls of
the city the distance is some thirty-two miles as the
crow flies.　The road runs through Neumarkt, about
twenty-three miles from Breslau, and Lissa, a little
more than nine.　That evening Neumarkt was in
Prussian hands, and besides the little town 80,000
Austrian rations of bread, welcome in themselves,
but far more welcome for the news which they con-
veyed.　" The fox," cried Frederick, " has crept out
of his hole, now I will punish his presumption."

On December 2nd, the day of Zieten's junction
with the King, the Austrians had indeed determined
to attack.　The reason for this fatal decision was by
no means over-confidence born of success.　Prince
Charles was very far from despising the adversary
who had defeated him on four stricken fields.　With
almost nervous anxiety, in spite of his 80,000 men,
he sought to be informed of every movement in Frederick's camp at Parchwitz.　It is true that Austrian
policy would be best served if the Queen were to
regain Silesia without the armies of her allies.　It is
false that she ordered the army of Silesia to give

battle at any cost. Before and after the fight Prince Charles stated expressly that his generals were unanimous in favour of marching on Neumarkt. The object was to save Liegnitz from Frederick and to prevent him from making his position too strong.

Both combatants, therefore, made for Neumarkt on the same day, and the forward movement of the Austrians was only quickened when they learned that the Prussians had chased their vanguard from the town. On the night of December 4th the armies lay within a few miles of each other. The Prussians were exulting in the news that Prince Charles had crossed the two streams which rendered his old position so formidable that Frederick had enrolled 800 volunteers for the first attack.

With an army tuned to the highest pitch and a King who knew every rood of the ground on the road to Breslau, the Prussians advanced to give battle. Before five o'clock on the dismal morning of December 5, 1757, they were on the march, Frederick in the van, and only a single battalion left in Neumarkt with the baggage. The exact position of the Austrians was not known to them as they hastened through the broken country east of Neumarkt towards the champaign west of Leuthen. If the enemy had placed this champaign at their back, the attack would still be hampered by the ground.

The Prussians had espied watch-fires on a height to the south of the great road a few miles east of Neumarkt—a height from which in daylight both the towers of Neumarkt and the farms and cottages of Leuthen may be seen. Was this an Austrian wing?

To their delight it proved to be only a vanguard. Three regiments of Saxon light horse, heroes of Kolin, had been placed there with two of Imperial hussars to collect the wreck of the Neumarkt garrison and to watch the road to Breslau. They clung too closely to their task and were crushed by the Prussian vanguard. Eleven officers and 540 men were taken prisoner, many fell, and the rest fled wildly to alarm the Austrian right. Frederick could with difficulty check the mad pursuit of his hussars, who drew bridle almost within cannon-shot of the enemy.

The King's spirits rose yet higher when he learned from the prisoners that Prince Charles had left most of his heavy guns in Breslau. He indulged his advancing columns with the sight of the captured troopers filing past them to Neumarkt and again condescended to repartee. " Why did you forsake me?" he asked a Frenchman who had previously deserted from the Prussian army. "Indeed, your Majesty," the man replied, " our position is too hope-less." "Well," said the King, "let us strike one more blow to-day, and if I am beaten we will both desert to-morrow."

As the gathering daylight revealed Prince Charles's army Frederick's confidence was more than ever justified. The Austrian position, chosen perhaps to cover three routes to Breslau, was far too extensive. Their line, which stretched from Nippern due south across the highroad, then on behind Leuthen village as far as Sagschütz and the pine-clad hill beyond, was not less than five miles long and unpro-

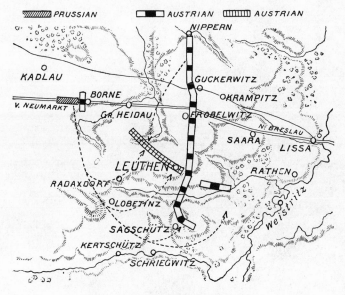

NIPPERN

KADLAU

BORNE
V. NEUMARKT

GUCKERWITZ

KRAMPITZ

GR. HEIDAU

FROBELWITZ

N. BRESLAU

SAARA

LISSA

LEUTHEN

RATHEN

RADAXDORF

OLOBETINZ

SAGSCHÜTZ

Weistritz

KERTSCHÜTZ

SCHRIEGWITZ

PLAN OF LEUTHEN, DECEMBER 5, 1757.

tected for the most part by the ground. Only the right wing, where the Italian Luchesi was in command, was defended in front and flank by hills and woods and marshes. These made it practically impossible for the Prussians to attack at any point between Nippern and the highroad, and if they fell upon the centre Luchesi might advance through the wood and take them in flank.

Prince Charles, who knew something of Frederick's methods, would have done well to strengthen his left. But on the day of Leuthen, Fortune seemed resolved to favour the side which trusted most to her help. By design or by accident, Frederick's movements were such as to convince Luchesi that the Prussians were about to hurl all their strength upon him. While the King reconnoitred, the heads of his columns remained pointing in the direction of their line of march and thus seemed to threaten the Austrian right. In each of the great battles of this year, at Prague, at Kolin, and in a sense also at Rossbach, it was the right wing of the allies upon which the Prussians fell. Now when he saw Frederick diligently inspecting his own quarter of the field Luchesi insisted on being reinforced. His clamour prevailed and, at the moment when Frederick began the movement towards Leuthen and Sagschütz, Daun was galloping with cavalry from the centre and left towards Nippern, the point most distant from the danger.

The Prussian army this day surpassed itself in the swift precision of its movements. No sooner was the King's plan formed than Maurice and Zieten

were ranking the eager veterans for their mysterious
march due south—parallel with the Austrian line of
battle and in part hidden from its view by the un-
dulations of the ground. Frederick rode along the
ridge between the armies and exulted as he marked
the mistake of Daun. For some two miles he might,
for all the Austrians knew, be in retreat. Then as
the ground sinks into a plain he drew nearer to the
enemy's left and hurled all his strength upon it.

Frederick and his 32,000 men had only some
four hours of daylight in which to overthrow a
host nearly 80,000 strong. Despite the tension
the Prussian machine worked perfectly. The complicated attack in oblique order was accomplished
as never before or after, and an invincible assault began. By steady valour, not by desperate
onrush, the infantry cleared the height near Sagschütz and in perhaps fifteen minutes they took the
battery which crowned it. The Austrians and Bavarians made furious efforts to regain what the
flight of their comrades from Würtemburg had sacrificed. Nothing, however, could now withstand the
disciplined onset of the Prussians, who swept before
them the shattered regiments and the breathless
supports who hurried to their aid. Hindered by
ditches, the Prussian cavalry had as yet been able
to give little help, but the irresistible advance of the
infantry brought them at length to better ground
and Zieten completed the ruin of the Austrian
left.

In numbers, however, Prince Charles was still
superior to his assailants. He might fairly ascribe

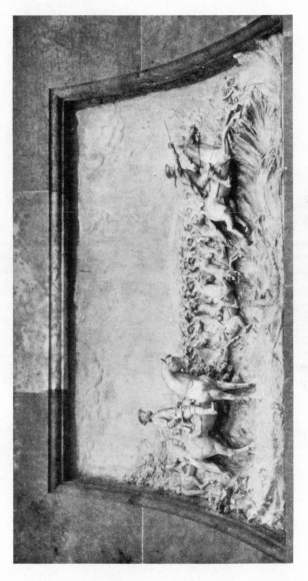

THE CHARGE OF THE WALLOON DRAGOONS AT KOLIN.

FROM A RELIEF ON THE MONUMENT OF VICTORY NEAR KŘEČHOŘ, UNVEILED 1898.

the disaster on his left to the blunder by which the Würtembergers, mere auxiliaries, were entrusted with the key of the position. Out of his unbroken centre and right he formed a new line of battle of which Leuthen village was the key. Leuthen, with a wall of men and a hasty breastwork in front of it, with its courtyards and churchyard packed with men, and behind it men in thick masses with cannon, might surely be held until Luchesi and his cavalry could come to the rescue on the right.

The advanced guard was soon driven off by the terrible fire of the Prussians, whose heavy guns now and throughout the battle tore frightful gaps in the crowded ranks of the enemy. But the village proved a formidable obstacle to their progress. House after house had to be stormed, and the churchyard was most difficult of all. At last the Prussians carried Leuthen. Then, however, they were exposed to the batteries behind and for perhaps an hour a furious conflict raged on something like equal terms. Frederick sent his left wing into action, but still the Austrians stood firm. But again, when already three of the four hours of daylight were spent, Luchesi proved to be the evil genius of his side. Coming up with his cavalry, he took the Prussian infantry in flank, only to be himself outflanked, crushed, and killed by a concealed reserve of Prussian cavalry. The panic produced by this sudden onslaught spread to the infantry, and the Prussians pressed home their advantage with a bayonet charge. At last the Austrians were beaten. They flung away their muskets, forsook their guns, and fled wildly towards Breslau.

A regiment which strove to cover their flight was reduced to one officer and eight men.

As at Rossbach, darkness robbed the victors of the full fruit of their success. The Prussian loss of one man in five proved that Leuthen was no easy triumph. But they struck down 10,000 men and captured 12,000, they put to flight an army nearly three times as great as their own, and they won Silesia and undying fame.

CHAPTER VIII

THE SEVEN YEARS' WAR (*continued*)

LEUTHEN TO MAXEN (DECEMBER, 1757, TO DECEMBER, 1759.)

W HAT profit would Leuthen bring to Prussia? was Frederick's first thought after the glorious fifth of December, and may well be ours. He himself was worn and ill. In the excitement of victory he had closed the long day of Leuthen with a jest. Pressing on to the castle of Lissa, he found it full of Austrian officers. "Bonjour, Messieurs," cried the King, suddenly appearing out of the darkness, "can you find room for me?" But reaction and depression followed the strain of 1757. "If the year upon which I am entering," he wrote on his birthday (January 24, 1758), "is to be as cruel as that which is at an end, I hope it will be my last."

Every kind of anxiety, public and private alike, pressed at the same time upon the hero of Rossbach and Leuthen. His brother, Augustus William, for whom a chance bullet might at any moment clear the throne, had not yet succumbed under the burden of disgrace, and wearied Frederick with complaints and acid congratulations. His brother-in-law, Ferdinand of Brunswick, was stricken with fever, and the King's mind was full of vague fears which he confessed but could not account for. Upon his sister, Wilhelmina, who had more need of it, he lavished sympathy and encouragement in a flood of tender messages.

"I am delighted that you are having some music and a little dissipation," he writes, early in the new year; "believe me, dear Sister, there is nothing in life that can console us but a little philosophy and the fine arts. . . . I swear to give thanks to Heaven on the day when I can descend from the tight-rope on which I am forced to dance."

If we must choose a simile from the circus to describe Frederick during this war, he might be likened to an acrobat juggling with five bomb-shells at once. Of three, the Swedes, the Russians, and the Imperialists, he had not yet felt the full weight, and with a supreme effort he had flung the French and the Austrians high into the air. What would be his task in 1758?

While he harvested the fruits of Leuthen without pause Frederick permitted himself to hope that his victory would bring peace. After the fall of Breslau on December 19, 1757, he estimated the Austrian losses and found them overwhelming. He even gave out that at a sacrifice of less than 4000 Prussians killed and wounded, he had reduced the enemy's force by 47,707 men. He was still gathering in pris-

oners and deserters every day. Before the year was
out he could assure Prince Henry that, according to
sound opinion, Prince Charles's army consisted of
no more than 13,000 foot and 9000 horse. " If this
does not lead to peace," writes Frederick on December 21st, " no success in war will ever pave the
way thither." A week later he is still hopeful, " but
even if one were sure of it, we must none the less
labour to make our position formidable, since force
is the only argument that one can use with these
dogs of Kings and Emperors." Leuthen indeed
gave Maria Theresa another opportunity to prove
her constancy and courage. Frederick made overtures to her for peace, but she refused to engage in
any negotiation apart from her allies. Early in
January, 1758, the King became aware that Austria
whatever it might cost her, was determined on another campaign.

Gradually the prospect grew clearer. Almost beyond the hopes of the Queen her alliance with France
survived the double shock of Rossbach and Leuthen.
At the beginning of February Louis promised to
send 24,000 men into Bohemia. Since his encounter
with Soubise, Frederick regarded the French as brigands rather than warriors, but their onset compelled
him to place a sturdy watch-dog in the West. This
part was played by Ferdinand of Brunswick, who
drove them across the Rhine before March was over.
Another foe, the Swedes, were even less considerable. Frederick jeered at them as " cautious people
who run away eighty miles so as not to be taken,"
and assured his sister, the Queen of Sweden, of his

willingness to grant them peace. So long as France was willing to pay subsidies, however, the Swedes were willing to provide 30,000 men. They still occupied their "bastion," Pomerania, in force, and therefore Lehwaldt must still act as the Ferdinand of the North. The King himself proposed to astonish Europe by his dealings with the Austrians and Imperialists. From his ally he might look for the same assistance as in the previous year. He laboured in vain to persuade the Sea Powers that the Protestant cause and their own interests demanded that they should attack France with their own troops. But in April Pitt undertook to furnish an annual subsidy of £670,000, and for four years the money was punctually paid.

With Silesia at his back, the French and Swedes held in check, and England in close alliance, Frederick's prospects for the campaign of 1758 might seem almost brilliant. He had some 206,000 men under arms. Ready money was not plentiful, but Frederick procured it in a thoroughly Prussian fashion—unscrupulous but practical. His own subjects he spared so far as possible. At times indeed he treated even them in the manner of his father. In January, 1758, the merchants of Breslau answered "Impossible" to a royal demand that they should advance 300,000 thalers to the Jews who had charge of the coinage. Frederick's minister reported the fact, adding that the Jews enjoyed no credit in the mercantile world. The King's annotation, scrawled in German on the back of the report, is still treasured in the archives of the General Staff at Berlin. It runs as follows:

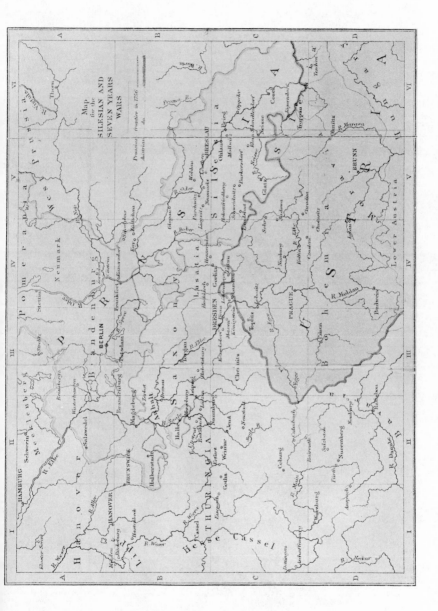

Map
for the
SILESIAN AND
SEVEN YEARS
WARS

Present frontier in 1756 ‒‒‒‒‒‒‒
do. Austrian

" I will cook something for the President if he don't get the money out of those merchants at once without arguing."

In general, however, with the exception of a few loans, no new demands were made upon the ill-lined purses of the Prussians. Indirectly, of course, they felt the burden of the war. The coin with which the State supplied them was debased and therefore purchased less goods. The pensions of those who had served the King in the past, but could serve him no longer, were left unpaid or paid only in paper. But the chief granary of the Prussian army was, whenever possible, the territory of the enemy. The second great source of supplies consisted in those countries which the fortune of war had placed in their hands. " Mark well the contributions of Mecklenburg," was Frederick's order to General Dohna. " Take hostages, and threaten the Duke's bailiffs with fire and plundering to make them pay promptly." But by far the heaviest burden fell upon the Saxons. Besides systematically draining them of cash, Frederick resorted to what he termed " reprisals " at their expense whenever " the allies of the King of Poland " pillaged any of his dominions. Men who were thus made scapegoats for the sins of half Europe betrayed with seasonable treachery the allegiance which the King of Prussia had compelled them to swear against their will.

In 1758, however, Frederick allowed the notorious disaffection of the Saxons to fetter him no more than the armies of France and Sweden. He had a great plan of campaign, and he began to execute it

with a speed and secrecy which no one in the world
could equal. On March 15th he left Breslau. Within
five weeks he had captured Schweidnitz, the sole
fortress in Silesia which remained Austrian, and was
making for Moravia in order to besiege Olmütz.
The Austrians, he argued, must relieve it and might
be vanquished in a battle in which he would have
choice of ground. Olmütz could then be taken and
Vienna threatened. This would compel the enemy
to concentrate in defence of the capital. Prince
Henry would thus be free to swoop down from
Dresden upon Bohemia and to erase the traces of
Kolin.

Frederick's idea was brilliant, and for a time success waited upon his arms. Daun, who, to the great
profit of the Austrians, had replaced Prince Charles
in the chief command, continued to fortify Bohemia
against the attack which he expected from the East.
On May 3rd Frederick reached Olmütz. Consterna-
tion reigned at Vienna, but for eight weeks the
cautious Daun did not venture to disturb the siege.
Till the last day of June all went well. Then came
what the King frankly terms a terrible *contretemps*.
At Domstädtl a convoy of some 4000 waggons from
Neisse was destroyed by General Laudon, who made
himself a great name by a victory which cost Zieten's
command at least 2400 men. The Prussians were
thus deprived of the supplies which were indispensable to their success.

Frederick recognised at once that the siege must
be abandoned, and with it his whole enterprise. He
admitted that he had lost the superiority over the

Austrians which he had gained in 1757. Threatening to imprison and cashier officers who should make
faces or say that all was lost, he slipped cleverly past
Daun's left into Bohemia, and for a month remained
there at his ease. Then he sped swiftly northward.
On August 22, 1758, he was at Cüstrin dictating a
fresh testament on the eve of the encounter with a
new and gigantic foe.

In estimating Frederick's prospects for the campaign of 1758, no account has yet been taken of
Russia. The action of the Muscovite forces was
proverbially uncertain and of necessity slow. It
was possible that they would not influence the main
struggle at all, or that Frederick's plan of aggression
in the South would be accomplished before they had
time to become formidable. Since the New Year,
however, storm-clouds had been massing to the north-
eastward. It is fortunately no part of our task to
peer behind them into the dark secrets of the Russian court. Suffice it to say that Elizabeth still
lived, and that so long as she remained on the throne
peace with Prussia was impossible. Her armies
might be ill-found and her ministers corrupt, but it
would be strange if the mistress of Russia proved
too weak to wound Frederick in his ill-guarded flank
beyond the Oder.

Fermor received the chief command of an army
34,000 strong. In January, 1758, he overran Ost-
Preussen and forced the inhabitants to swear fealty
to the Czarina. In February Königsberg was illu-
minated in honour of Russian royalty. Frederick
avenged the first offence by reprisals upon the

Saxons, the second by withdrawing his favour for ever from the polluted province. His power of self-restraint is attested by the fact that he attempted nothing by way of rescue. He calculated dispassionately that Fermor's advance would at best be slow, that a broad expanse of barren Polish territory separated the invader from the rest of the Prussian dominions, and that offensive action in the South was more likely to be profitable than defensive in the North. Königsberg had been a Russian city for more than three months when Frederick dashed into Moravia.

The danger, however, grew greater throughout the summer months. The Muscovite tide rolled slowly across Poland into Frederick's dominions east of the Oder. Europe now had an opportunity of learning something of the nature of the society which Peter the Great had brought within her pale. In the Russian army, as in the nation, the highest classes were men of honour when not too sorely tried, but the lowest were filthy savages, who made the country a desert and tortured and burned men and women alike. What the rank and file might be, Frederick had yet to learn. But that his trusted field-marshal, Keith, gave him timely warning, he might well have been pardoned for his belief that Fermor's unseasoned horde would not face the heroes of Leuthen led by himself, the foremost captain in the world.

As the King sped towards his old prison, Cüstrin, the trembling peasants came in crowds to kiss the hem of his coat. He found the fortress unharmed, but the defenceless town reduced to ashes by Fermor's bombs. The Russians, more than 40,000 strong, lay on the eastern side of the Oder, having an open road to Poland, but all others barred by swamps and rivers. Before Frederick's arrival, Dohna, with perhaps a third of their numbers, the waters of the Oder, and the walls of Cüstrin had been the only defences of Berlin. Now, however, the Prussians were some 36,000 strong and as much superior to their foes in mobility as were Drake and Hawkins to the Spanish Armada. Fermor was short of supplies. He could not go forward and had hundreds of miles of desert at his rear. Was the time at the King's disposal so scanty that he could not starve, harry, and crush the enemy without the sacrifice of more than a few hundred Prussian lives?

Frederick was, however, in no mood for a war of strategy. He had published his fixed resolve to conquer or die. He was impatient to return to Silesia, where he had left 40,000 men under Charles of Brandenburg-Schwedt. He was still more impatient to annihilate the bloody vagabonds, who, he wrote, were burning villages every day and committing horrors which made Nature groan. In the spirit of Leuthen, though perhaps without like need, he resolved to attack Fermor without an hour's delay. Knowing every inch of the dismal country-side, he swiftly planned a massacre that should avenge the past and safeguard the future. The Russians had abandoned the siege of Cüstrin and taken up a position so sheltered by the Oder and its tributary, the Mietzel, that Fermor believed it to be unassailable.

Frederick crossed the Oder some miles below Cüstrin, marched right round their camp, and prepared
to hurl them into the waters in which they trusted
for defence.

The plan seems a sound one only on the supposi-
tion that Keith's opinion was ill-founded and that
the Russians would not show fight. They had much
in their favour. They were a national army, roused
to enthusiasm by the benedictions of a mob of
orthodox popes. They outnumbered the enemy
and were far better furnished with cannon. In cavalry, it is true, Frederick had a great advantage, but
this was discounted by the Russian formation in
dense masses, which cavalry could hardly hope to
pierce. Above all, the King provided his opponents
with the best possible argument against running
away when he left them no road by which to run.
With no alternative save drowning or suffocation,
the Russians chose to die where they stood, but to
sell their lives dear.

These conditions made the battle fought near
Zorndorf on August 25, 1758, one of the bloodiest of
the whole war. It was in great part a desperate
hand-to-hand struggle, kept up with mutual fury
until the Russians were cut to pieces. According
to the Prussian histories, Seydlitz, the matchless
dragoon, refused point-blank to obey Frederick's
order to advance on the Russian guns. When and
where needed, he replied, he would be at hand with
his men. "After the battle," came the King's message, "you will answer for it with your head."
"After the battle," answered the imperturbable

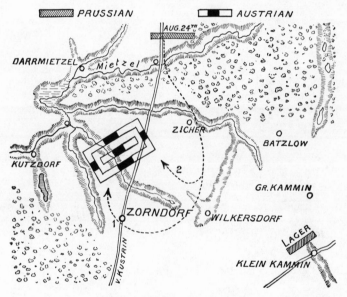

PLAN OF ZORNDORF, AUGUST 25, 1758.

general, "my head will be at the service of the
King." He justified his insubordination by twice
charging at the enemy on his own initiative. He
thereby saved the day, and, instead of being cashiered, was embraced by his delighted master. But
when the issue had once been decided by sheer rage
maintained for ten hours, some of the Prussian infantry showed themselves equally insubordinate and
less successful. It seems not the least strange feature of this chaotic death-grapple that in an attack
upon an army strongly posted the cavalry should
have formed the chief factor in Frederick's success.

Success, though much qualified, Frederick might
indeed fairly claim. Fermor, it is true, bivouacked on
the field, fought again, though languidly, next day,
sent off bulletins of victory, and retired unmolested a
week later. His troops had endured the Prussian
whirlwind with a steadfastness beyond all praise.
But of the 30,000 killed and wounded nearly two-
thirds were his, and Frederick had achieved, though
at a great cost, his prime object of securing his dominions on the eastern side.

Against a new foe the King had displayed once
more those qualities which readers of his history have
by this time learned to regard as characteristic of him.
He had been brave, secret, and masterful, swift to
plan and to carry out, tireless in body and teeming
in brain. He had at the same time proved himself
exacting, overbearing, and rash, adroit at supplying
the need of the moment rather than far-sighted and
sagacious in providing for the future. Though he
accepted victory and defeat like a philosopher, there

was too much of the despot, both in what he exacted
from his troops and in what he expected from his
foes.　In this, though in this alone, it seemed as
though the common infirmity of the overpowerful
had at last assailed a Hohenzollern, and that Frederick had lost something of his power of seeing facts
as they are.　All the torrents of Prussian blood
wasted at Prague, at Kolin, and at Zorndorf had
not swept away his belief that Prussians led by
himself could carry out any order that he chose
to give.

It is chiefly these virtues and foibles of the King
that shape the story of the remaining months of the
campaign.　While he was on the banks of the Oder
the Austrians and Imperialists had begun the reconquest of Saxony and Silesia.　Frederick by speed
and cleverness saved both, but his conceit doomed
nearly nine thousand of his army to wounds, captivity, or death.

First, by wonderful marches, he snatched Dresden
from the jaws of Daun.　The cautious general took
up a strong position, which barred Frederick's road
to Silesia, where the Austrians were besieging Neisse.
Having failed to tempt him to battle, Frederick next
stole round his army, but Daun retorted with a similar
manœuvre and encamped near Hochkirch with some
65,000 men.　On October 10th, Frederick with less
than half the number actually insisted upon occupying an untenable position hard by.　His generals,
among whom were the Young Dessauer, Seydlitz, and
Zieten, remonstrated with him in vain.　Next day
Keith arrived and spoke his mind quite frankly:

"If the Austrians leave us quiet in a position like this, they deserve to be hanged." "It is to be hoped that they fear us more than the gallows," rejoined the King, and planned a flank attack on Daun, who, he believed, was about to retreat into Bohemia. The result was that before daybreak, on October 14, 1758, the Prussian camp was surprised. Five generals, Keith among them, perished. Frederick's obstinate foolhardiness cost him more than one-fourth of his army, with more than a hundred guns and much material of war. Kolin, Domstädtl, and Hochkirch, three victories over the King of Prussia within sixteen months, formed a splendid chaplet for a general whose forte was caution. The Pope was said to have rewarded Daun with a consesecrated hat and sword.

"It may be safely reckoned," so the King informed the Berlin public a week later, "that our loss does not exceed 3000 men. . . . These disasters are sometimes inevitable in the great game of chance which we call war." The hour of disaster had again proved Frederick superior to the shrewdest blows of Fate. At the moment when the Austrians, creeping through the darkness, began to butcher his men in their tents, he proved himself once more a hero. Disdaining to order a retreat, he extricated his army from its terrible position and formed a new line only half a league to the rear. Daun, who had lost more than 6000 men, entrenched himself on the field, and was soon plying his old trade of circumspectly hanging upon the skirts of the foe. Within ten days of the battle Frederick robbed him

of the fruits of victory by marching round him once
more.   He flung himself between Daun and the besiegers of Neisse, and Silesia was saved.

Daun's counterstroke was, as was almost inevitable, an invasion of Saxony while Frederick's back
was turned.   He alarmed Dresden, but was once
more frustrated by Prussian speed.   Frederick hurried back in time to save both Saxony and its capital.   In mid-December he went into winter quarters
at Breslau, master of dominions as broad as when
he had quitted the city nine months before.

In those months he had, however, lost much that
cannot be marked upon the map.   Faithful officers
by hundreds, trained soldiers by thousands, hard-
wrung thalers by millions had been sacrificed, and
nothing but glory and a respite had been gained.
No lands outside Ost-Preussen were as yet conquered by foreign kings, but many had been wasted
by foreign armies, and some, at the dictate of urgent
need, by their own defenders.   These losses weighed
upon Frederick, whose task it was to gather men and
money for next year.   But as a man he had cause
for more poignant grief, for Death had knocked
hard at the door of his own household.   The loss of
his heir, Augustus William, once his father's favourite, now the victim of Frederick's cruelty, probably
afflicted him only because Prince Henry avenged it
by refusing to see him except on business.   But the
death of Wilhelmina, who died on the eve of Hochkirch, was the most crushing calamity of his life.
" Great God, my Sister of Baireuth ! " scrawled the
afflicted King as postscript to a brief despatch in

PLAN OF HOCHKIRCH, OCTOBER 14, 1758.

cipher to his brother Henry. The message is more
pregnant than much fine writing. "The death of
Her Highness the Margravine of Baireuth embar-
rasses me with regard to His Majesty the King
more than all war matters," wrote the faithful Eichel
from Dresden on the day after Frederick received
the news, "since I can judge how highly afflicting
and crushing it must be to him. Councillor Coeper
writes to me yesterday that although every care was
taken to prepare His Majesty gradually for sad tidings it has none the less made an indescribably
great impression upon him, and he does not believe
that deeper woe is possible." "If my head had
within it a lake of tears it would not be enough for
my grief," sighed the King to another mourner,
Keith's brother, when the hard fighting and marching came to an end.

After three campaigns the war had now, at the
close of the year 1758, reached what may be called a
chronic state. Thrice had Frederick lunged at the
heart of his enemies and each time they had parried
the thrust. At Vienna alone could the coalition receive a mortal wound. St. Petersburg, Stockholm,
and Paris were equally out of reach, and the States
of the Empire might be squeezed and harried for
ever without terminating the war. If the Prussians
failed to dictate peace at Vienna, their one hope
must be that they might defend themselves until
some of the hostile Powers should change their
minds. Their opponents, too, felt the strain of prolonged and unprofitable war. It was true that they
had not to strain themselves like the nation whose

very existence was at stake, but neither Russia nor Austria nor France knew the secret of Prussian thrift. The time might come when even Elizabeth and the Pompadour would confess that the game was no longer worth the candle. The French, in particular, were not all blind to the fact that they were losing their Empire to England in order to gratify the spite of the King's mistress against the King of Prussia. Would they hold to the Austrian alliance even for another year?

The event falsified the hopes of Frederick. With some relaxation of intimacy, the Austro-French league was renewed, and the King perceived that he must henceforward hold Prussia like a huge beleaguered fortress. Five Powers were still encamped upon his frontiers and ready to break in upon him. Like all resolute garrisons, therefore, the Prussians had recourse to sallies, and some of these met with much success. By sudden forays Henry and Ferdinand destroyed the magazines that were being formed by the Austrians and Imperialists and so retarded the invasion of Prussia, which could not proceed without them. Mere partisan inroads like these were, however, insufficient to prevent Daun from taking up a strong position at Mark-Lissa, with Bohemia at his back and Saxony and Silesia open on either hand. There he menaced Frederick while the Russian host once more drew near to the Oder, overthrowing as it came a Prussian force which had been sent into Poland to destroy its magazines and pen it in the swamps of the Vistula.

The story of this Polish campaign throws much

light on the strength and weakness of the Prussian army. Rightly neglecting the lesser danger in order to make adequate head against the greater, the King had sent against the Russians the force which usually defended the North against the Swedes. The rank and file were good, but without leadership they could accomplish nothing. "Your Polish campaign deserves to be printed as an eternal example of what every intelligent officer must avoid. You have done every silly thing which can be done in war and nothing whatever that an intelligent man can approve. I tremble to open my letters." Such were the concluding words of a long indictment which Frederick addressed to their commander, General Wobersnow.

Nothing but the royal presence, it seemed, could save the situation. The King himself was not yet free to leave Daun. He therefore invented a deputy-king, and despatched General Wedell to Poland "with the powers of a Dictator in Roman times." Twelve curt instructions were drafted for his guidance. He was "(4) to forbid lamentation and depreciatory talk among the officers on pain of dismissal. (5) To disgrace also those who cry out on every occasion that the enemy is too strong. (6) First to check the enemy by occupying a good position. (7) Then to attack in my own fashion." From the King's own lips Wedell received the order to fight the Russians whenever he should find them, and officers and men alike were commanded to obey him as though he were indeed the King. But Frederick was never sanguine that these attempts to win a

Russian Leuthen by proxy would succeed. His instructions were followed to the letter, and within four days he was condoling with the Dictator upon the disaster of Kay (July 23, 1759), where the Prussians lost more than 8000 men killed and wounded. Nothing could now hold back Soltykoff and his Russians from the Oder, and across the Oder lay Frederick's helpless capital.

But worse was yet in store. The Russians, for all their numbers and their greed, were ill-fed, irresolute, and slow. They dreaded the victor of Zorndorf and they were determined not to be the catspaw of their allies. If only they could be kept at a distance from the Austrians they might starve before they could agree upon the next step in advance. From Kay to Mark-Lissa is some ninety miles as the crow flies, and the Oder and Frederick's army lay between. To strengthen the barrier the King was prepared even to leave Saxony almost without defence. He summoned Henry to observe Daun while he himself made "cruel and terrible marches" through the burning sand towards Wedell in the North. So severe was the strain that he passed six of the torrid nights without sleep. But he was racing a fleet adversary — Laudon, the hero of Domstädtl and probably the best partisan soldier in the world. Knowing that he had served ten years in the Russian army, Daun now detached him with 36,000 men to allay Soltykoff's suspicions of the Austrians and to speed his coming. Frederick disturbed the march, but started too late to stop it altogether. When Laudon found the Russians at Frankfurt he was still master of nearly 20,000 men.

This reinforcement vastly increased the effectiveness of Soltykoff's army as a fighting force. The Russians were well furnished with guns, and their infantry had proved its toughness at Zorndorf. But their cavalry was bad and Laudon added to it some 6000 men, well-mounted and well-trained. None the less he was received with extreme discourtesy. The Russians abused him because he brought no supplies. They refused to cross the Oder unless Daun's whole army should appear. Until fresh orders from St. Petersburg produced some change of tone, Laudon felt certain that they were on the eve of retreat. Then came the news that the King of Prussia was upon them and the voice of discord was hushed.

Frederick had set himself a harder task than the destruction of Fermor on the banks of the Oder in 1758. Only overwhelming necessity made him give battle. He suspected that an Austrian detachment was threatening his capital. " I believe that Hadik means Berlin," he wrote, "and I am obliged to make haste here to parry his blow in time. A lost soul in purgatory is not in a more wretched situation than I am." In mere numbers, it is true, the disparity between the combatants was not much greater than at Zorndorf. Frederick had now nearly 50,000 men against a composite force of about 68,000, but of the enemy nearly one-quarter were light horse, who in the shock of battle counted for next to nothing.

In quality and in position, however, his army was worse off than before, while the enemy was much better. In the previous year he had led seasoned troops whose ranks had been purged by incessant marches under a scorching sun to join the army of Dohna, which was at least unbeaten and unwearied. Their meeting had provoked one of Frederick's best-remembered sayings: "Your men have made themselves wonderfully smart; mine look like grass-devils, but they can bite." Now, however, a great part of his command consisted of troops mishandled by Wobersnow and decimated by the Russians at Kay. It was unlikely that they would fight like the victors of Leuthen.

Nor was Frederick favoured by the ground. The most casual glance at the two fields is sufficient to show that Kunersdorf, the scene of the bloody drama of August 12, 1759, presented difficulties such as the assailant at Zorndorf never had to overcome. The allies were again encamped on the right bank of the Oder, and were now separated by the broad river from the town of Frankfurt. To march round their position was far more arduous than at Zorndorf. Their left wing was shielded by impassable morasses, and the right by forest. Behind them lay a fortress commanding a well-bridged river, before them a tangled mass of sand-hills, woods, and lakes which seemed to have been designed by nature to impede an attacking force and which was now made still more formidable by art. This position, even if the 16,000 irregulars be ignored, was held by some 40,000 Russians, now veterans in

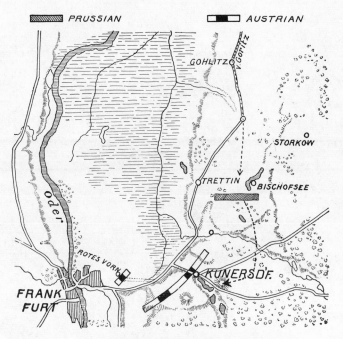

PLAN OF KUNERSDORF, AUGUST 12, 1759.

western warfare, aided by 13,000 of the flower of the Austrian army under a captain worthy to cross swords with Frederick himself.

On the other hand, the King had still Seydlitz, but such men as Wedell could ill supply the place of Schwerin, the Old Dessauer, and Keith. Some of his troops were men who had fled before the Russians every year, at Gross-Jägersdorf, at Zorndorf, and at Kay, and whom he could not even trust. Owing to the difficulties of the ground and the King's impatience, most of the Prussians went into action suffering under privations that would have well-nigh killed ordinary men. They lacked food and drink. After two nights without sleep they must drag themselves and their accoutrements through a manœuvre of nine hours' duration, now tugging cannon through pine-woods, now clambering over sand-hills under the broiling August sun. Then at noon they were ordered to attack an enemy more numerous than themselves who was resting quietly behind entrenchments in ground of his own choosing.

That they accomplished what they did proves that the Prussians were heroes. Frederick's design was, as at Zorndorf, to cross the Oder below the Russian camp, to march round it, and then to strike. But the barren waste east of Frankfurt was to him unfamiliar country. At Leuthen and at Zorndorf he had profited greatly by his knowledge of the field. But at Kunersdorf he knew neither the difficulties of the ground nor the extent to which, in one most important particular, those difficulties had been surmounted by the enemy. When he scanned their position from the north-east before completing his plan of attack, he could discern Laudon's force encamped in a seemingly isolated peninsula in the great marsh which protected the left. He was informed that Laudon and Soltykoff could communicate only by a roundabout way. Not till the issue of the day was dubious did he learn that a new causeway connected the Austrians with the main body of the enemy, and the error proved fatal. Twice in his life Frederick paid dear for imperfect information, but the price of the blunder at Prague was a trifle by the side of the price paid here.

The beginning of the fray was such as to make the end a doubly crushing blow to the King. After long and toilsome preparations it seemed as though victory was assured. When the Prussian van went into action they advanced like fresh men and turned the Russians out of their entrenchments at the point of the bayonet. A second onslaught, better supported, took the enemy in flank and by two o'clock the Russian left was beaten, with a loss of seventy guns. Frederick sent off a courier to carry the tidings of victory to Berlin. The third attack, however, made on difficult ground in the face of cannon at 800 yards and musketeers at fifty, did not succeed until the Prussian infantry had been decimated and its strength almost spent. At this point Frederick's generals cried " Enough "; but the King, as at Hochkirch, preferred his own opinion. Once more the Prussians stormed forward and for the fourth time they annihilated the Russian line. If one knoll more, the Spitzberg, and the battery upon it were taken, the victory, it seemed, would be complete.

But at this crisis Laudon intervened to save the battery and the day. His grenadiers climbed the knoll when the Prussians were still 150 paces from the top, and drove them back with a volley of case-shot. Frederick ordered up his artillery, but the heavy guns stuck fast in the sand and light field-pieces were of no avail. In the agony of the moment the King lost his head and ordered the cavalry to storm the Spitzberg. As at Zorndorf, Seydlitz declined to sacrifice his troops to a blunder, but this time Frederick was deaf to the voice of reason. He repeated the order and was obeyed. Seydlitz was wounded and his superb squadrons shattered, without the smallest gain. A crushing countercharge headed by Laudon completed the ruin of the Prussian horse, and thenceforward the allies were the attacking side.

Frederick, almost beside himself, continued to demand victory from his men, and the infantry, though it could not go forward, held its ground against the Russians. Laudon, however, contrived the *coup de grâce*. At about five o'clock he suddenly hurled a fresh Austrian host upon the heroes who had been fifteen hours under arms. The overthrow was complete. Frederick, who sought death in vain, was borne from the field by a party of his own hussars. Amid the chaos he wrote a terse note in French to inform his capital that the game was up. " My coat is riddled .with balls; two horses were killed under me; it is my misfortune to be still alive. Our loss is great ; not 3000 men out of 48,000 are with me. At this moment all are in flight and I am no longer master of my troops."

The King's first thought was that he himself was crushed and that therefore Prussia was ruined. There was indeed good reason for his despair. Even if Soltykoff should allow him to recross the Oder and to rally the remnants of his army he dared not hope to save Berlin. He had fought at Kunersdorf in the belief that an Austrian force under Hadik was advancing towards his capital from the south. If he now attacked Hadik he must expose his rear to the victors of Kunersdorf; if he stood firm against them, Hadik would take him in flank. "Only a miracle could save us," wrote the Secretary of State.

The downfall of his country seemed inevitable and Frederick was resolved not to witness it. For years he had carried poison. Before using it he spent two days in arranging his affairs. On the plea of a severe illness, he entrusted the army to General Finck and gave directions that it should swear allegiance to the son of Augustus William. He advised the well-to-do citizens of Berlin to fly to Hamburg, the Government to make Magdeburg their asylum, and Schmettau, the commandant at Dresden, to surrender on good terms if he saw no means of succour when attacked.

Frederick's life-drama, it seemed, was played out,

but the curtain did not fall. The allies, who had
bought victory dear, made no move, and on the
fourth day after the battle the King was himself
again. "All my troops have done wonders," had
been his words when he gave up hope. Now he
sent a new version to the same correspondent, Finckenstein. "The victory was ours, when suddenly my
wretched infantry lost courage. The silly fear of
being carried off to Siberia turned their head and
there was no stopping them." His loss at Kunersdorf amounted to at least 18,500 men, but he found
himself master of an army 20,000 strong. They
were, he said, not to be compared with the worst
troops of former years, but he prepared to sacrifice
them and himself for the defence of the capital, and
awaited Soltykoff on the river Spree.

A letter to Prince Henry written on August 16,
1759, shows the temper of the Prussian Leonidas.

"The moment that I sent you word of our mishap
everything seemed desperate. Do not think that the
danger is not still very great, but be assured that until
my eyes are closed I will sustain the State, as is my duty.
A case that I had in my pocket was smashed by a shot,
but saved my leg. We are all in tatters; there is hardly
anyone who has not had two or three balls through his
clothes or his hat. But we would cheerfully sacrifice
our wardrobe, if that were all."

Despite these signs of reviving courage, Frederick
felt with tenfold intensity what he expressed years
afterwards when he said that after Kunersdorf the
enemy had only to give him the finishing stroke.

Yet it is highly characteristic of him that already his thoughts ran upon another battle. To carry on defensive warfare, he argued, the support of a fortress was indispensable. But he had only Cüstrin and Spandau to choose from, and to sit down near either would be to sacrifice Berlin. Desperate evils, he held, needed desperate remedies, and he would court Fortune sword in hand. Eight days after Kunersdorf he hoped soon to have 33,000 men in his camp, but he protested that he feared them more than the enemy. "I count on the firmness and honesty of Pitt, and it is on him alone that we can at this juncture base some hope."

Frederick expected day by day the catastrophe of Prussia. Yet the only direct result of Kunersdorf was that for a time he lost a great part of Saxony. Early in September Dresden was wrested from him by the motley army of the Empire, which was accounted the most despicable member of the coalition. Schmettau had acted too mechanically in following the King's counsels of despair. But the Swedes, though their opponents had withdrawn, failed to strike south. The French, who had set out in earnest to conquer Hanover, were routed at Minden by Ferdinand of Brunswick on August 1, 1759. They were driven headlong through the narrow gorge at the spot where the Weser cleaves the bulwark of hills which guards the northern plain, and thus before the day of Kunersdorf Frederick knew that he had nothing to fear on the western side. But how, it may well be wondered, could Daun and Soltykoff, with 120,000 men at their disposal and

only half the number against them, neglect to follow
up their victory? The sequel even suggests that
Frederick's desperate measures beyond the Oder
had been superfluous. Prussia was far weaker than
before, yet she did not fall. The King was crippled,
Austrians and Russians were now massed into one
unbroken force, triumph at Dresden followed triumph
at Kunersdorf, yet they accomplished nothing.

Their opponents, it is true, were tacticians of the
first rank. Prince Henry, by wonderful marches,
evaded Daun, and Frederick, returning to the Oder,
frustrated all Soltykoff's efforts to gain Silesia. It
was, moreover, beyond the power of Daun to furnish
the Russians with supplies, and if their ally did not
supply them they refused point-blank to proceed.
But the chief cause of Prussia's salvation was that
victory, though it united the armies of her enemies,
could not unite their interests. Russians and Austrians remained as before separate armies with diverg-
ent interests to consult. At no time did Frederick
draw greater profit than after Kunersdorf from the
fact that Prussia was one and her opponents many.

Soon Berlin breathed freely and even Breslau felt
safe. Before October was at an end Soltykoff was
marching home, while Daun was struggling to save
Dresden at least from Prince Henry's reconquest of
Saxony. The *Te Deums* ceased at Vienna and dejection reigned there. Daun's sluggishness in aggressive action extinguished the renown due to his
triumphs of defence. His wife dared not show herself in public. At court the story ran that she
opened a package addressed to the Field-marshal,

and discovered that some wag had mocked his sluggishness by sending him a night-cap.

At this juncture, however, it would have been
well for Prussia if her King's activity had been less
superhuman. Flushed with the triumph of his
strategy and confident of the devotion of Pitt, he
had the audacity to demand that compensation for
Prussia should be the basis of negotiation for peace.
During the greater part of October, 1759, he was
tormented by gout and fever. He spent his enforced leisure in writing an essay on Charles XII.,
the Madman of the North, a warrior who would
have prized the bloody afternoon of Kunersdorf far
more than the strategy which drove Soltykoff empty-
handed from Silesia. Then, when the Russian peril
had vanished, Frederick set out in a litter for Saxony.
" I am very weak, but although still a cripple, I will
do all that my feebleness allows me to attempt," he
wrote on November 4th. His heart beat high with
the hope of repeating the miracles of 1757, and of
regaining, by a new Leuthen, all that had been lost
during the summer, and peace.

" I make them carry me like the relics of a saint,"
wrote the King after the first day's journey. Though
sleepless and crippled, he concocted daily bulletins
to Prince Henry in the spirit of a schoolboy. Since
it had been noised abroad that Daun had received
the papal benediction he had more than ever been
the butt of Frederick's jests. Now, to create " a favourable impression on the mind of the blessed creature and his council," he bids his brother announce
his little escort as 4000 strong, and sends a list of

the regiments of which it may be said to consist. "Daun and his Austrians shall not perceive that I have the gout," he boasted.

Two days later, on November 14th, he took over the command. Pleased that Daun paid him the compliment of retreating, he ordered Finck to pursue. All the general's objections were overruled, and he took refuge in wooden obedience to the letter of the King's orders. "In a few days," Frederick wrote on the 17th, "we shall reap the fruit of this disposition." In four the royal prophecy was fulfilled, but the harvester was Daun. Finck's command, some 15,000 strong, with seventy guns, was entangled in the hills south of Dresden. Believing themselves to be surrounded by thrice their number, the Prussians laid down their arms at Maxen (November 21, 1759).

The blow was more crushing than Kunersdorf, for the whisper now sped through the world that the Prussians were turning cowards. Eichel confessed that his heart was so full of bitterness and chagrin that it was quite out of his power that day to write anything in cipher. The King, who had boasted to Voltaire that he would despatch his next letter from Dresden, complained bitterly that ill-luck pursued him all his days. He strove to atone for his over-confidence by exertion, and for many weeks kept the field, defying the stern winter. He thereby averted an Austrian reconquest of Saxony, but the gates of Dresden never opened to him again. The Prussian cause and the Prussian King, thought the world, were failing together. "If you saw me, you

would scarcely know me again," Frederick wrote to
Voltaire. "I am old, broken, grayheaded, wrinkled.
I am losing my teeth and my gaiety." Yet this de-
jected veteran alone kept together the Prussian army.
That army was the sole bulwark of the State. If
Frederick had in truth lost health, skill, and fortune,
what hope was left to Prussia?

CHAPTER IX

THE END OF THE SEVEN YEARS' WAR (1760–1763)

BETWEEN the spring of 1760, when the weary Frederick braced himself to grapple anew with a task which four campaigns seemed only to have increased, and the moment when a sudden stroke of fortune was to give him rest, there intervenes a gap of time as great as that which separates his first plunge into the war from his overthrow at Kunersdorf. If we are compelled to be content with a swift review of these final phases of the struggle, we must by no means lose from sight the tenacity and adroitness of the hero upon whom every campaign laid a heavier burden than the last, and to whom every year seemed endless. After Kunersdorf and Maxen, we, who know that Frederick and Prussia did not perish, may be impatient to have done with their long agony. But Frederick himself enjoyed no such comfortable prescience. Hopes he had indeed in plenty. Denmark might join him, the Tartars might rise, the Turks, he was constantly assured, were on the very verge of attacking Austria. Now the French, now the Russians, he believed, were about to desert the coalition against

him.   The event testified to his courage rather than
to his insight.   Time brought only fresh disappoint-
ments and prospects ever more black, but the King
neither flinched nor paused.   Under the bludgeon-
ings of chance his head was bloody but unbowed.
"It was not the army," said Napoleon, "that defended Prussia, seven years through, against the
three greatest Powers of Europe, it was Frederick
the Great."

Till near its close the campaign of 1760 seemed to
be merely the natural sequel to that of 1759.   In
spite of all the chances of high politics, the same
combatants took the field on either side.   France,
beaten by land and sea, had tempted England with
the offer of a separate peace.   But Pitt displayed
anew the loyalty to his ally which was the consolation of Frederick's darkest hours.   The English
minister recognised that his country's triumphs over
France off Lagos, in the bay of Quiberon, and before
the walls of Quebec in the glorious campaign of
1759, had been due to the Prussian alliance almost
as directly as the victory of Minden.   He braved
the taunt that he was more Prussian than the King
of Prussia and inflexibly refused to desert him in
his hour of misfortune.   The Russians, on the other
hand, consented to serve Maria Theresa anew, but
at a high price.   Ost-Preussen, which they had conquered, was to be theirs for ever.   Thus the Hapsburg, though guardian and head of Germany, was
compelled to promise that if Prussia were crushed
the Muscovite should advance to the Vistula.

The labours of the diplomatists, from which **Fred-**

erick looked for great gains, had done nothing to
change the military situation in his favour.   The
campaign of 1760 saw once more Ferdinand confronting the French in the West, the Swedes paralysed by their own incompetence in Pomerania, Daun
striving to reconquer Saxony, Laudon striving to
reconquer Silesia, and the Russians, as usual, advancing towards the Oder.   But, whereas in 1759 Frederick's own presence had more than once caused
disaster to his armies, in 1760 he became again the
hero of the strife.   He was always most formidable
when the odds against him were heavy, and in 1760
none could doubt that the Prussians were at an overwhelming disadvantage.   Even the King regarded
the campaign as a gambler's last throw.   Failing
extraordinary good fortune, he predicted the collapse of Prussia before the autumn.

For the first time in the war the enemy began a
campaign on Prussian soil.   Laudon invaded Silesia,
and the King's friend, Fouqué, believing himself too
weak to hold Landshut, fell back on Breslau.   The
Silesians protested that they were being abandoned
to the mercy of the enemy and Frederick complained that his generals did more mischief to
him than to the enemy.   Under-estimating Laudon's
talent for war, he ordered Fouqué to recover Landshut at once, and promised to come to the rescue in
person as soon as he had beaten the enemy in Saxony.
Fouqué obeyed, but in Laudon he had an opponent
far more active than Daun.   His force of less than
11,000 men was soon in as hopeless a plight as that
of Finck at Maxen.   He, too, avenged the insults of

the King by following his orders to the letter, for the more considerate counter-orders which Frederick despatched never reached him. On June 23, 1760, near Landshut, the Prussians maintained a hopeless struggle for seven hours. It is believed that the killed and wounded numbered more than 5000 men. It is certain that only some 1500 cavalry, perhaps one-seventh of Fouqué's whole force, succeeded in cutting their way through the enemy.

At Landshut the Prussian regiments regained by their valour the repute which they had lost at Maxen, where they laid down their arms without a blow. But the fruits of Laudon's victory were great. Silesia now lay defenceless before the Austrians, and only Prince Henry's weak force screened it from the advancing Russians. Frederick, though balked of a battle, was compelled to leave his work in Saxony undone and to transfer the bulk of the Prussian army to the eastern theatre of war. His going was a proof of weakness, but the manner of it paid a signal tribute to his fame. None dared to stand in his way. The Austrians under Lacy were so determined to be on the safe side that they left Dresden bare, and Frederick was tempted by the opportunity of a brilliant triumph to turn aside.

He hoped to take the Saxon capital in two or three days, but the defenders were stout-hearted beyond his calculation. After he had wasted more than a fortnight before the walls, the news that Glatz had fallen and that Breslau was in danger compelled him to resume the dreary tramp towards Silesia. His prestige and his position had suffered alike, and his mood was more dejected than ever. Philosophy, he professed, was his only consolation. Since nothing worse could happen to him than what he looked for, he could have no occasion for disappointment. He was determined to hold fast to duty during the brief space that might still separate him from the abyss. It was no great matter, he told Finckenstein, whether they were crushed a month sooner or a month later. The death of his old servant, Podewils, affected him little, for it seemed but a small item in the general ruin of the State.

Thus began the month of August, 1760, in which Frederick and his army dispelled by their own valiant deeds some of the darkest clouds that hung over Prussia. They were escorted into Silesia, where Soltykoff's Russians and Laudon's Austrians awaited them, by the armies of Daun and Lacy, which marched, said the King, like the vanguard and rearguard of their own force. Thanks to the stout-heartedness of the Prussian general Tauentzien, Laudon had summoned Breslau in vain. Now, however, he effected a junction with Daun, and the united Austrian forces outnumbered Frederick by three to one.

At no moment of his long career, not even when he galloped from the field of Mollwitz nor when he gathered round him the wreckage after Kunersdorf, had the King's plight seemed so desperate as now. He himself upon whom all depended was in the depths of dejection. He had with him only some 30,000 men, and Kay, Kunersdorf, Maxen, Landshut, Dresden formed an unbroken series of disasters. Against him were some 90,000 Austrians, commanded by Daun, to whom his royal mistress had sent the most unequivocal instructions to fight, and by Laudon, to whom military instinct no less clearly dictated battle. They barred Frederick's path both to Breslau and to Schweidnitz, and brought his force to the verge of starvation. Across the Oder the Russians were masters of the land, waiting only for the tidings of victory to pour a new host over bridges which they had already built. To retreat was to abandon Silesia, to stand still was to be starved or crushed, to attack was beyond the imagination even of a Frederick. Prussian officers talked of a new and greater Maxen, and the British ambassador, Mitchell, burned his papers.

At last Frederick moved. Having learned from a drunken deserter that Daun was planning a surprise, he resolved to march towards the Oder, preferring the neighbourhood of the Russians on the right bank to a situation which had plainly become untenable. On the evening of August 14, 1760, the Prussians stole away from their camp and occupied a strong position to the north-east of Liegnitz. On the western side, where Daun's attack might be looked for, the ground was admirable for defence. Behind the stream of the Schwarzwasser rises a steep and sudden bank, shaped like a natural bastion. This was manned by the right wing, encamped on a champaign so level that it forms the Liegnitz drill-ground to this day. Further north-east a gentle slope descended from the lines of the Prussian left to the little village of Panten and so to the river

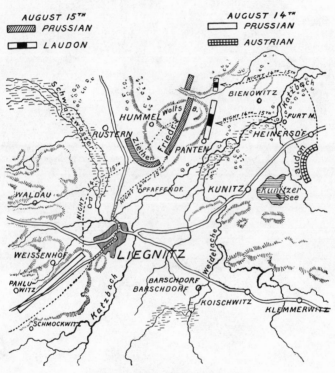

PLAN OF LIEGNITZ, AUGUST 15, 1760.

Katzbach. There through the moonlit night the
men lay under arms, forbidden to cheer themselves
with song, but filled with an expectancy that banished sleep. The King, who shared all their privations, wrapped himself in his cloak and snatched a
brief rest by a watch-fire after satisfying himself that
all was ordered aright.

Till dawn the stillness was unbroken. Then in a
moment blazed up one of the shortest and most
brilliant fights of the whole war. A breathless messenger cried that the enemy—Laudon—was attacking in force on the extreme left. Frederick hurried
off to oppose him. Had the attack been made fifteen minutes earlier, he declared, the issue would
have been far different. But the Prussians profited
much by their stealthy change of camp. Laudon's
march was a part of Daun's concerted attack upon
the position that they had quitted seven hours
before. The result of their movement was that
Daun hardly reached them, while Laudon, who expected to surprise their baggage, was himself surprised. Marching without a vanguard, he found
himself committed to an uphill fight without support from Daun. None the less he attacked with
such swing and dash that the Prussian left was well-
nigh cut in two. It was saved by the infantry, who
first valiantly held Panten and then set it on fire.
This checked the Austrian advance and enabled the
Prussians to make good use of their position. About
an hour and a half after the first onset Laudon retired across the Katzbach unpursued. The Prussians claimed to have killed or wounded 6000 men

and captured 4000 — a total loss thrice as great as their own. They had thus annihilated nearly one-third of Laudon's force, and—what was even more important—they had rent the net that was closing round them. Daun had appeared in sight of the Prussians only to learn of Laudon's disaster and to retire. Henceforward it was beyond the power of the Empress to induce her favoured field-marshal to attack.

The moral gain was perhaps the greatest of all the advantages that Frederick derived from Lieg-nitz. " A second edition of Rossbach," as he called the battle, was the best proof that Prussian valour and leadership and luck had none of them vanished from the earth. The King, who had his coat torn by one ball and his horse wounded by another, ascribed the victory to the favour of fortune and the bravery of his men. No other judge, whether Prussian, Austrian, or Russian, could fail to ascribe a great share in it to the King. The value of this renewal of prestige was apparent almost every day that the war had yet to run. However huge the masses of Austrians and Russians might be, they were usually content to watch Frederick at a respectful distance. The initiative was thus often abandoned to the weaker side and the value of Frederick's army enhanced threefold.

Yet nothing could demonstrate more clearly than their movements after Liegnitz how weak the Prussians were. Frederick's departure from the field of victory was in truth a flight, but a flight which covered the fugitives with glory. Young Lieutenant

Archenholtz, who was among the victors, tells the astounding tale of how

"this army, spent with bloody toil and girt by mighty hosts, must press on without rest and without delay, and yet must bear with it every gun and man that had been taken and all the wounded as well. These last were packed into meal-wagons and bread-wagons, into carriages and carts, no matter whose they might be. Even the King gave up his. King and generals gave up their led horses to carry the wounded who could ride. The empty meal-wagons were broken up and their horses harnessed to the captured guns. Every horseman and driver must take with him one of the enemy's muskets. Nothing was left behind, not a single wounded man, Prussian or Austrian, and at nine o'clock, four hours after the end of the battle, the army with its enormous load was in full march."

Twelve good miles were covered that day under the August sun. Frederick was still between two armies, each larger than his own. Neither Russians nor Austrians, however, dared attack him and he joined Prince Henry at Breslau without another stroke of sword.

Of his brother Henry, Frederick said at a later date, "There is but one of us that never made a mistake in war." But the King continually rejected his counsel, though the event proved it to have been wise, and his relations with the Prince often became strained. A brilliant strategist, Henry wished to husband Prussian powder and Prussian blood by manœuvring more and fighting less. The victor of Leuthen, on the other hand, was ready to take great risks if he believed that his success would be fatal to the chief army either of the Russians or of the Austrians. "If you engage in small affairs only," he maintained, "you will always remain mediocre, but if you engage in ten great undertakings and are lucky in no more than two you make your name immortal."

Frederick's habitual inclination to throw for high stakes was increased by the events of September and October, 1760. His task was to guard the Silesian fortresses against Daun, but while he—like the court of Vienna — yearned for a decisive action Berlin fell into the hands of 40,000 Russians and Austrians. The raiders occupied the city for four days and exacted a contribution of two million thalers, but the rumour of the King's approach sufficed to drive them off. Winter was drawing nigh and the Russians vanished as was their wont. There was thus less need to fear for Silesia, but the enemy still held Saxony, and Saxony was to Frederick a recruiting-ground, a treasure-house, and a home. With added reasons for a battle, but with little assurance of success, he therefore transferred thither the seat of war.

"The close of my days is poisoned," he wrote, "and the evening of my life as hideous as its morning. Never will I endure the moment that must force me to make a dishonourable peace. No persuasion, no eloquence can bring me to`sign my shame. Either I will bury myself under the ruins of my fatherland, or if this consolation seem too sweet to the Misfortune that pursues me, I will myself put an end to my woes. . . . After having sacrificed my youth to my Father, and my ripe years to my fatherland, I think I have acquired the right to dispose of my old age as I please. . . . And so I will finish this campaign, resolved to hazard all and to try the most desperate measures, to conquer or to find a glorious end."

We who have seen Frederick resign his crown after Kunersdorf are free to believe that he would have taken his life after a new Kolin. His words are in any event highly significant of the view which he took of the limits of his duty to the State, whose course he had steered according to his own will for twenty years. Five days after they were written, on November 3, 1760, he did in truth hazard all, and try the most desperate measures. Daun, who had followed him into Saxony, was encamped near Torgau in a position reputed impregnable. He had 50,000 men with an enormous park of artillery, and whatever his shortcomings in attack, none could impugn his talent for defence. Yet Frederick, with 44,000 men, determined to attack, and to attack by one of the most difficult operations in war, a simultaneous onslaught on opposite sides of the enemy's position. The King himself proposed to lead half the army through the forest, right round the Austrian camp, so as to assail it from the north. The other half was to attack from the south under Zieten, the bravest of hussars but the youngest of generals, who had commanded a wing at Liegnitz, but had never handled an army, and who did not know the ground.

It is hardly surprising, with such a plan as this,

that Torgau, like many battles, was fought not as was designed but as best it might be. The history of the day proved beyond dispute that Frederick had ventured much. The weather, their own errors, and the enemy's guns ruined the Prussian simultaneous attack. The King's contingent fought a desperate battle. Few of his attendants escaped without a wound. His own life was saved as if by miracle. Three horses were killed under him. A spent ball struck him senseless, but his pelisse saved him from serious hurt. He rallied both himself and his men, but when evening came the Austrians had the advantage. Daun felt that he might safely leave the field to dress a wound and send news of victory to Vienna.

Then, in the last hour of the fight, something like a simultaneous attack was carried out and it succeeded. After long indecision, Zieten stormed the southern heights with desperate courage and the confused struggle was taken up a third time by the King's forces on the north. By eight o'clock, thirteen hours after the Prussians had left camp, the Austrian resistance was at an end. Ere midnight Daun was fleeing across the Elbe, while Frederick, seated on the altar-step of a village church, scribbled a note to Finckenstein, promising to send details of the victory next day.

Before dawn, he was once more among his troops riding through the lines and embracing Zieten. At Torgau he had frustrated the Austrian reconquest of Saxony and reduced their forces by some 16,000 men. But when his own loss came to be counted

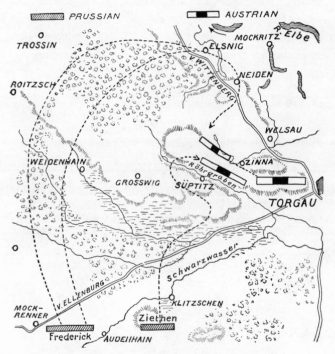

PLAN OF TORGAU, NOVEMBER 3, 1760.

he strictly forbade his adjutants to reveal the sum.
Torgau was the bloodiest battle of the war and the
Prussians had suffered most. Their casualties exceeded by nearly one thousand those of the beaten
side.

In spite of Liegnitz and Torgau the campaign of
1760 seemed to have changed Frederick's situation
but little. Dresden was still beyond his reach, but
he was able to spend a pleasant winter at Leipzig,
surrounded by books and men of letters. Diplomacy, as before, promised much and performed
little, but drilling and recruiting went on without
pause. Although the quality of the Prussian army
could not but deteriorate, the numbers were astonish-
ingly maintained. Commissions were given to mere
lads, freebooters were welcomed, and the lands of
the lesser German princes were scoured for men, till
in the spring of 1761 a hundred thousand soldiers
were ready to take the field. To furnish the necessary funds no new taxes were laid upon the Prussians, but Frederick issued great quantities of base
coin and Saxony, where the Austrians might otherwise have found support, was harried to the verge
of devastation.

It was believed at Vienna that Frederick would
resort to his plan of the preceding year by pitting
himself against the army which covered Dresden.
The Empress therefore implored Daun once more to
take command. He consented, but only on the
astounding condition that he should not be expected
to make conquests. Then the King of Prussia transferred himself to Silesia, which became the principal

scene of the events of 1761, perhaps the dreariest of all campaigns.

For the third year in succession it was beyond the power of the Prussians to prevent the armies of the Empress and Czarina from joining hands in Silesia. The King would have risked a battle against either, but battle was not vouchsafed him. Yet in face of an enemy who outnumbered his 55,000 men by more than two to one he had still a weapon at his disposal and it proved effectual. The bold offensive of his earlier campaigns had perforce given place to defensive action only. Although Ferdinand still gloriously held his own against the French, Frederick knew that he himself was too weak to meet the combined Austrian and Russian army in the field. He therefore entrenched himself and defied the allies either to destroy him where he stood or to make lasting conquests while his army remained undestroyed.

For five weeks, till near the end of September, he thus inhabited the famous camp of Bunzelwitz, resting upon Schweidnitz, the key of Lower Silesia. Then, deeming the danger past, he moved southward to seek fresh supplies. His absence woke the foe to life and the campaign closed with disaster. On October 1, 1761, Laudon astonished Europe by storming Schweidnitz. A second reverse followed. Before the year was out the Russians were masters of Colberg, the Baltic gate of Prussian Pomerania. For the first time, therefore, the armies of the enemy could winter on Prussian soil. A huge crescent of foes, French, Imperialists, Austrians, Russians, Swedes, was at last enfolding Prussia. When spring came would they not surely stifle her?

Frederick, moping through the winter at Breslau, declared once more that Fortune alone could save him. He likened himself to a fiddler from whose instrument men tore away the strings one by one till all were gone and still demanded music. Once more he declared that philosophy alone could console him in his "pilgrimage through this hell called the world." "I save myself," he wrote, "by viewing the world as though from a distant planet. Then everything seems infinitely small, and I pity my enemies for giving themselves so much trouble about such a trifle." Yet he never ceased to recruit, to drill, and to make plans for the glorious offensive campaign that he hoped to engage in with the aid of the Tartars and the Turks.

·n December, 1761, he professed indifference to the course of events in England, though two months, earlier his champion Pitt had given place to men who preferred the Austrian alliance to the Prussian, and who desired that separate peace with France which Pitt had rejected in 1758. The treaty then made between England and Prussia forbade either to make peace without the other till April 11th of the following year. In 1759, 1760, and 1761 this compact had been renewed. Now, however, Newcastle and Bute began to clamour for what Pitt had ventured only to suggest — that Frederick should purchase peace by some concession conformable to the course of the Continental war. The Prussian envoys in London dared to advise their sovereign to comply. He answered that they were in nowise permitted to give him such foolish and impertinent counsel. "Your father," he wrote to one of them, though the charge was baseless, "took bribes from France and England; has he bequeathed the habit to you?"

Frederick's inflexible resolve to make no concession was by no means the same as a resolve to make no bargain. He often played with the fancy that Saxony or a part of it might be left in his hands at the peace. For this he would gladly surrender any or all of his outlying provinces. But he would rather forfeit the English subsidy and jeopardise the very existence of the Prussian State than sue for the peace which Kaunitz was more than willing to conclude on terms of moderate profit for the allies. Two weighty reasons of policy increased his determination. The labours of the winter once again filled the ranks and the war-chest of Prussia. And Fortune, of whom the King said that she alone could extricate him, now gave with one hand more than she took away with the other. At the moment when England left him, Russia ranged herself at his side.

The cause of this marvellous revolution was the accident that the Czarina died early in January, 1762, and that her nephew and successor, Peter III., was a worshipper of the King of Prussia. Elizabeth had lived in debauchery and left upwards of 15,000 dresses to bear witness to her luxurious tastes. It is possible that her chief motive in attacking Frederick was a desire to chastise the man who had

spoken ill of her. But there can be no doubt that
her policy was suited to the interests of the State.
It was argued at a later date that her alliance with
the Queen had cost Russia countless lives and sixty
millions of money. But in 1762 it had already procured Ost-Preussen and part of Pomerania, and there
seemed to be good hope that Prussia, the only Power
which could prevent a vast extension of Russian
influence in Poland, would be permanently crippled.
If the allies dared not attack the King of Prussia,
they were at least in a fair way to exhaust his
strength.

In a moment, however, the rash young Holsteiner
who now wielded the sceptre of his great namesake,
Peter, flung away all that his troops had purchased
with their blood in five campaigns—at Gross-Jägersdorf, Zorndorf, Kay, Kunersdorf, and Colberg. In
the first hours of his reign he ordered his army to
take no step in advance. Before January was over,
Frederick knew that peace with Russia was assured.
The Czar's one desire seemed to be to gratify his
brother of Prussia. He craved investiture with the
order of the Black Eagle, and declared that he would
stand by while Turks and Tartars attacked the Austrian dominions. He resigned the Russian conquests without indemnity, undertook to promote
peace with Sweden, and even offered Frederick his alliance. Influenced by his withdrawal, the Swedes came
to terms of their own accord and concluded the Peace
of Hamburg (May 22, 1762), which re-established
the conditions of 1720. Frederick could therefore
face the remnants of the coalition without anxiety

for his rear. From Ost-Preussen he now drew 15,-000 men. By undertaking to assist Peter in his schemes for winning back the lands which the House of Holstein had lost to Denmark forty years before, he secured the immediate help of 20,000 Russians.

The situation was so completely transformed since the days when Frederick lay motionless at Bunzel-witz that in 1762 he determined once more to take the aggressive. His first aim must be the recovery of Schweidnitz. This could only be accomplished by inducing Daun to give battle, for his army, which had encamped near the fortress, was now playing the part that had fallen to the Prussians in the previous year. While the manœuvres were pursuing their tedious course the news arrived that Peter III. had been deposed. His wife, the German princess Catherine II., who was thus placed in power, at once recalled the 20,000 Russians from Silesia. Fred-erick, however, calculating on the influence which their presence would exercise upon the mind of Daun, persuaded their commander to conceal the order and to remain a few days longer as a spectator of the war. Then on July 21, 1762, the Prussians surprised Daun's right wing and gained a clever victory at Burkersdorf. At a sacrifice of some 1600 men they reduced the enemy's force by nearly 10,-000, and the retreat of the Austrians enabled them to begin the siege of Schweidnitz.

Thenceforward it was plain that the dragging war would lead to no decisive issue. Frederick was so sure of his cause that he had already sent a commis-sioner to examine the civil needs of Pomerania. But

he could only undertake formidable aggressive movements if the Turks and Tartars rose, and once again
they disappointed his hopes.   Instead of new combatants joining in the fray the old ones were quitting
it.   Bute was eager to take the step which Pitt had
scorned to take in 1760.   Before the year was out
France and England signed the preliminaries which
were embodied in the Peace of Paris in February,
1763.   Immediately after Burkersdorf, the Russians
withdrew and it was not to be expected that the
Austrians and Imperialists could accomplish by
themselves a task which had baffled the unbroken
coalition   Daun, indeed, attempted to avenge Burkersdorf by a counter-surprise.   He failed and in
October, 1762, Schweidnitz fell.   Before the month
was over Prince Henry, who was conducting the
campaign in Saxony, gained a great victory over the
Imperialist army at Freiberg.   The campaign closed
with an armistice between Frederick and the Austrians and a series of Prussian forays against the
hostile princes of the Empire.

At last the Queen realised that she had failed.
She promptly determined not to prolong a struggle
which could only add to the misery of mankind.   So
vast a legacy of hate had, however, been left by the
war that it was difficult to find a single Power whose
good offices both sides could accept with a view to
peace.   The Queen therefore brought herself to
approach "the wicked man" direct and sent an
envoy to the King of Prussia.   For nearly seven
weeks negotiations went on at Hubertusburg, a
castle of the unfortunate Saxon monarch.   Frederick

showed himself pliant in matters of etiquette and unbending where any practical advantage was at stake. He was willing to gratify Hapsburg pride by sending his envoy more than half-way to meet the envoy of the Queen, by allowing her name to precede his in the documents, and by promising to further the election of her son Joseph as Emperor. But he insisted on the restoration of Glatz by the Austrians, and on the payment by the Saxons of his grinding taxes up to the very eve of peace.

On February 15, 1763, the Peace of Hubertusburg was signed. After seven campaigns and an incalculable loss of blood and treasure, Austria and Prussia agreed to return to their situation before the outbreak of the war.

CHAPTER X

FREDERICK AND PRUSSIA AFTER THE WAR

THE monarch who had borne the burden of seven
campaigns — a burden of which his ten great
battles formed but a trifling fraction — might
well have been pardoned for appropriating to himself some share in the repose which his labours had
won for Prussia.   Even if it is difficult to couple the
thought of Frederick with that of repose, it might
at least be expected that after a triumph of defence
hardly surpassed in human history he would delight
his army by praising their achievements and his
people by accepting their plaudits.   Relaxation for
himself and courtesy towards others were, however,
equally distasteful to the King.   He slunk into his
capital by back streets and thus frustrated the preparations of the citizens to express their loyalty and
joy.   Yet in the darkest moments of the war he had
been devising plans for the improvement of Prussia
and he hardly waited for the peace to be signed before
plunging into a rapid career of reform.   After Kunersdorf, while his despair was gradually giving place
to hope and hope to confidence, he was not too ab-
sorbed in strategy to lay to heart the defects which

he observed in the schooling of the peasants near the Spree. The weeks which passed while his envoy at Hubertusburg was harvesting the fruits of the war were spent by Frederick in planning reforms for the army which had proved its matchless quality through all the seven campaigns.

His first desire was to get rid of those helpers whose services he had accepted only because of pressing need. Twenty-one free battalions had been raised and had proved immensely serviceable. Now the King bade two-thirds of them go their ways without reward. His learned friend and servant, Colonel Guichard, upon whom in consequence of a dispute about the battle of Pharsalia he had inflicted the name Quintus Icilius, appealed to him to repay to his officers part at least of the money which they had spent from their own pockets in enlisting their men. "Thy officers have stolen like ravens," replied the King; "they shall not have a farthing." Still more ungenerous was his treatment of a section of his army whose only fault was their lack of noble birth. During the long war many students and schoolboys of the citizen class entered the army as volunteers and received commissions. In the hour of triumph they were ruthlessly sacrificed to Frederick's principle that his officers, save perhaps among the garrison regiments, must belong to the caste of nobles. Prussians who had served him in his extremity must submit to be cashiered, while foreigners of rank were enlisted to atone for the dearth of natives whose pedigrees satisfied his requirements.

At the same time the army as a whole was

wounded by harsh criticism and harsh reforms. This, like much of Frederick's conduct, may be ascribed to the contempt for mankind which experience only increased, and to the almost inevitable effect upon himself of the unbridled absolutism described in the sixth chapter of this book. "Dogs, would ye live for ever?" he shrieked at his men in the crisis of one of his fights. He was forced to confess that, as his strength became less and the number of his subjects greater, he could not hope to look into all affairs of government with his own eyes. Yet he shrank more and more from creating an official or a system in anywise independent of his own immediate control. In 1763 he therefore appointed inspectors of cavalry and of infantry in every province and endowed them with wide powers of supervision of the officers and all that they did. This measure, it need hardly be said, roused the utmost bitterness among the regimental staff, which had hitherto enjoyed a great measure of independence on the sole condition that the King was satisfied with the results of its work. It was the more distasteful for the very reason which made it acceptable to Frederick—that the new inspectors were appointed at the royal pleasure without regard to seniority. The chief officer of a regiment, who had been wont to rule it like a patriarch, was now subjected to the control of a rival, perhaps his junior, who did not resign his own command and could favour it as he pleased.

The captains, too, suffered in pocket from another unpopular reform. They had hitherto received from the treasury the full wages of every man on the muster-roll of their company. In time of peace, however, the native-born soldiers spent nine or ten months of the year on furlough without pay. Each captain defrayed the cost of recruiting foreigners for his company out of what he received and pocketed the balance. Now, at the moment when war ceased, Frederick cut off this source of income. By retaining regiments of special merit on the old footing he insulted the rest, and by graduating according to his opinion of the regiment's efficiency the trifling allowances paid by way of compensation he cast a slur upon the professional honour of officers and men alike. The King paid his officers ten thalers a month and their pensions depended entirely upon his caprice. Many captains were thenceforward unable to resist the temptation to falsify the muster-rolls so as to receive pay for soldiers who did not exist.

The King's despotic power, however, enabled him to make light of military discontent in time of peace. He resolved to keep up an army of 150,000 men, to drill it as it had never been drilled before, to educate the officers, to review all the troops every year, to build new fortresses, and to establish stores of money and munitions sufficient to enable Prussia to enter at a moment's notice upon a war of eight campaigns. It is a highly significant fact that in Frederick's secret estimates for the future struggle the annual contribution of Prussia was set down at 4,700,000 thalers and the sum to be extorted from Saxony at 5,000,000. The balance of the 12,000,000 thalers, which was the price of a campaign, must come from the royal accumulations. Frederick's own expenses

were only 220,000 thalers a year. At the close of
his reign, when the total revenue of the State was
not quite 22,000,000 thalers, the treasure amounted
to more than 51,000,000, a sum fully five times as
great as that which he had inherited from his father.

Frederick was compelled by his past to stand to
arms all his life through. With advancing years he
became more lonely and more subject to disease.
In 1765 he lost his sister, the Margravine of Schwedt,
and next year the aged Madame de Camas, whom he
always called Mamma. His old friends died one by
one and the French wits had vanished. His brothers,
Henry and Ferdinand, were often estranged from
him by his bitter words. Yet to the end of his life
he prided himself on his cheerfulness between the
attacks of gout and he permitted no disease to inter-
rupt his labours. These were devoted first, as we
have seen, to making the land secure from attack by
means of the army, and also to guarding it from
famine by methods which may next be considered.
Close on the heels of these essential duties came
tasks of fresh development and reform, the acquisition of West-Preussen in 1772, and new endeavours
to uphold Prussian prestige against the House of
Hapsburg.

It is of course impossible to calculate exactly the
damage which a country suffers in time of war.
Moral gains and losses count in the long run for
more than material, and no statistics even of material
losses are truly satisfactory. As between one Prussian province and another, however, a rough comparison may be made by means of the growth or

decline of the population. Silesia and the lands east of the Oder had naturally suffered most, since, in addition to their quota of soldiers slain, they had long endured the presence of invading armies. In Silesia the numbers fell by 50,000, about one in twenty-three, but further north, in the districts in which the Russians had encamped, the proportion was nearly five times as heavy. Frederick's own estimate was that one-ninth of his subjects had perished.

The loss of property had undoubtedly been very great. The conscience of the age forbade massacre, but was lenient towards pillage and devastation. But the King surpassed himself by what Carlyle terms "the instantaneous practical alacrity with which he set about repairing that immense miscellany of ruin." So far as the material losses sustained by individual Prussians could be ascertained, they were set down by the careful hands of royal commissioners and mitigated by royal gifts. The King had at his disposal depreciated coin to the amount of nearly 30,000,000 thalers, the sum which had been accumulated to pay for the eighth and ninth campaigns. This more than sufficed for the needs of the army and the repayment of the trifling loans, less than five and a half million thalers in all, that Frederick had contracted during the war. With the residue and with the surplus revenues of the State the King set to work to prevent a single one of his subjects from falling into absolute ruin. His doles were graduated not by any standard of abstract justice, but by the rule that the minimum amount of help should be given that would serve the purpose of the State. Many towns had paid ransoms to the enemy to avoid being sacked. That of Berlin, two million thalers, was repaid out of the treasury, but Halle received less than one-sixth of what it claimed, and in the majority of cases the burghers were left to bear the loss themselves.

In the country districts, however, there was less power of recuperation than among the comparatively wealthy towns. According to Frederick's opinion, it was therefore necessary that the State should make it possible for nobles and peasants alike to resume their normal duties. The spare horses from the army, to the number of 35,000, and many rations for man and beast from the magazines were at once distributed to the most needy. Officials allotted to the peasants wood to rebuild their houses and sums of money to assist the work. Their rents were remitted for a time, and oxen, cows, sheep, meal, and seed-corn were supplied to them free of charge. The State reaped its reward in the rents and taxes which speedily flowed into the royal coffers, as well as in the rapid growth of population.

While the King was thus doling out relief to a great part of his subjects, he indulged in a singular extravagance which has been the subject of much criticism and conjecture. Though he inequitably threw upon the people the expense of restoring the coinage, though his subjects were sending him sheaves of petitions for aid, though he was of all monarchs the least addicted to pomp, none the less, three months after peace had been signed he began to build a third palace at Potsdam. The astonished Prussians believed that the cost was 22,000,000 thalers. If no more than one-tenth of this was actually expended, the King lavished on a superfluity more than one-third of the sum that he assigned to the restoration of the land.

Those who insist that he did nothing without a motive of State may find it in his desire to convince foreign Powers that it was dangerous to attack a nation which could afford luxuries while its enemies were deep in debt. Other conjectures are possible. Frederick loved to indulge the hope that the Sciences, which had visited Greece and Italy, France and England, in turn, might settle for a while in Prussia, and the new palace, like the salary paid to Voltaire, might be regarded as a sacrifice at their altar. The claims of the new Prussian industries, especially the manufacture of silk, which was largely used in adorning the interior, may have induced the King to provide an artificial market in this way. Frederick's Versailles, however, remains to this day both a monument to his absolutism and an enigma.

Absolutism and diligence are still the hall-marks of all his measures. The military reforms, the work of restoration, and the attention paid to the arts taxed him but lightly when compared with his labours for the development of the agriculture, manufactures, commerce, and finance of his dominions. No sooner was the war at an end and the work of restoration set on foot than Frederick began to pour forth a flood of edicts for the regulation and advance of every department of national life, and to

THE NEW PALACE AT POTSDAM.

engage in incessant labours of inspection to see that they were carried out.

In promoting agriculture he was guided by principles with which we are already familiar. His prime rule was still to increase the number of tillers of the soil and to make them safe against starvation. He therefore continued to bring in colonists from far and near, to drain marshes, to reclaim wastes, and to build new habitations. It is computed that at the close of his reign one-fifth or one-sixth of his subjects were immigrants or the descendants of immigrants. Besides a knowledge of husbandry and handicraft which in many cases surpassed that of the Prussians, the aliens brought with them substantial additions to the material wealth of the land. The official inventory of their belongings, though incomplete, shows that 6392 horses, 7875 head of cattle, 20,548 sheep, 3227 pigs, and upwards of 2,000,000 thalers in money were thus added to the capital of the nation.

To provide for the accommodation of the recruits to his army of agriculture, the King applied every art of government to bring new land under cultivation and to increase the fertility of the old. The superior enlightenment of Prussia was attested by the curt refusal of Brunswick and Hanover to cooperate in works of drainage. No site for a farmstead was to be left vacant and in the forests—so ran the decree—"no place where a tree can stand, unplanted." The sterile nature of the soil challenged the unwearied industry of the King. Many centuries before blotting-paper came to be known,

Brandenburg was nicknamed "the sand-box of the Holy Roman Empire." Thousands of acres had to be set with bushes to prevent its surface from being blown over the neighbouring fields.

"I confess," wrote Frederick to Voltaire, "that with the exception of Libya few states can boast that they equal us in the matter of sand. Yet we are bringing 76,000 acres under cultivation this year as pasture. This pasture feeds 7,000 cows, whose dung will manure and improve the land, and the crops will be of more value."

The spectacle of the royal philosopher writing to Voltaire about manure and walking almost daily from Sans Souci to his turnip-field is a visible proof of Frederick's devotion to this branch of his steward-ship. He was wont to speak with authority as the leading agriculturist of the realm. Here, as else-where, his breadth of view often enabled him to discern the best product or practice in other lands, and his command of resources to transport it to his own. Having once attained his object by teaching his subjects to produce an article at home, he imper-atively forbade them to import it from abroad. The full reward of his policy would be reaped when Prussia began to supply it to other countries in exchange for gold and silver.

A single instance of the minuteness and imperious-ness with which the King applied this policy to agri-culture may be cited from Professor Koser's history of the reign. The Berlin egg-market was still de-pendent on foreign supply. In 1780 a royal hen-census showed that there were 324,175 hens in the

Electoral Mark and that 36,300 more were required to meet the demand for eggs. "What will it matter," asked the King, " if every peasant keep ten or twelve more hens? Their food does not cost much ; they can pick up most of it in the straw and dung of the farmyard." Prohibition of the import of foreign eggs followed. This caused the market price to rise and the ministers expressed the fear that the supply would not be sufficient. The King rejoined :

"It is all the fault of the farmers and peasants for not setting about it. I have laboured forty years to introduce things of this kind. If the ministers want to eat eggs, let them take more trouble with the Chambers to carry it through. The prohibition of foreign eggs remains as before."

Only a six months' interval was allowed later to give the new establishments time to develop.

All through his reign Frederick set his face firmly against any attempt to bridge over the gulf which, divided the country from the town. The tobacco and sugar with which the peasant solaced himself, the clothes he wore, the plough and hoe which served him to till the fields were all made more costly in order that the towns might thrive. The vast majority of handicrafts might be practised only within their walls. On the other hand, the King's ordinances against artisans who meddled with farming were so severe that they could not be strictly carried out. He also tried many measures with a view to conferring upon the peasant a secure position on the soil. He was successful in preventing the nobles from buying up

the holdings of the class below them. He established some three hundred new villages by breaking
up outlying farms. But in other directions even
his autocratic power failed to overcome the passive
resistance of the rural population.

In theory, Frederick was a champion of human
freedom. He condemned slavery in strong terms
and viewed askance the legal position of the Prussian countryfolk whom their lords regarded as so
many head of labour. But he dared not shake the
pillars of his army and of his treasury by giving the
peasant leave to quit the soil. He desired to retain
serfdom, but only in its mildest form. He set his
heart on making every serf a hereditary tenant at a
money rent. This was, however, repugnant both to
the nobles, who feared that they would not be able to
secure labourers for hire, and to the peasants, who
feared that they would in future be obliged to bear
the loss when their cattle died and to pay their arrears
of taxation themselves. The proposed reform, as
well as an attempt to assign limits to the labour that
the lords might lawfully exact, had therefore to be
given up.

A change of still more unquestionable benefit, of
which England had enjoyed the fruits for fully two
centuries, likewise proved impracticable in Prussia,
even on the domains of the Crown. Each holder,
whether noble or peasant, had a number of scattered
strips of land in huge fields which were unenclosed
and were ploughed and sown in common by the
labour of the whole village. The abuses of such a
system were manifold. It stereotyped the succes-

sion of crops, checked individual enterprise, prevented the high cultivation which depended on the aid of walls or hedges, and exposed the strips of the industrious to the spreading tares of his slothful neighbour. Frederick, once more guided by his loftier outlook on affairs, ordered commissioners to remedy this unprofitable system by a rearrangement of all the holdings. Peasants, bailiffs, ministers, all protested in vain, but Frederick in his turn commanded in vain. All that he could accomplish in his lifetime was the severance of noble from peasant land. He was compelled to content himself with abolishing practical slavery as distinguished from serfdom, with codifying the services due from the peasants, and with other minor reforms.

Whatever may have been its effect in the long run, however, there can be little doubt that it was Frederick's deeds rather than his laws which conferred the greatest immediate benefit upon Prussian agriculture. His subjects were assured, as were those of no other great monarch in Europe, that there would be a market for their produce in years of plenty, relief of their necessities in years of dearth, and succour from the State where fire or flood or pest would otherwise have ruined them. This sense of security against starvation, though now so common that it is difficult to appreciate it, was then so rare that thousands of freemen left their native lands for the despotism and sterile soil of Prussia.

In the sphere of industry Frederick was less hampered than in that of agriculture by the inertia of his people. He found Prussia making few commodities save the simplest and exporting only three,—wool, linen, and wood. Before he died his minister, Hertzberg, could boast that every conceivable manufacture found a home in his dominions.

The record of the steps by which the transformation was effected is simply a further series of illustrations of the autocracy and diligence of the King. He strove with might and main to reanimate and develop the old industries and to establish new ones. This involved incessant contrivance and inspection on his part, the free use of subsidies by the State, and the constant imposition of vexatious restrictions upon every form of trade.

One of the most conspicuous examples of Frederick's methods is the development of the porcelain industry of Berlin. During the Prussian occupation of Saxony the secret of the far-famed Dresden ware was extorted from the employees of Augustus. The King spared no effort to make the most of his prize. He bought up the manufactory at Berlin, forbade all purchase of rival goods from abroad, installed porcelain at his own table in place of the gold and silver associated with royal state, used porcelain snuffboxes, and bestowed samples of the finest products when convention prescribed a regal gift. To promote the welfare of Prussia, Jews who wished to marry were compelled to purchase a service of porcelain and to dispose of it abroad.

With the same unflinching resolution the King pursued his design of making Berlin a great industrial centre, of establishing manufactures in all his towns, and of forcing Prussia to provide for all her own

needs and for many of the needs of foreign lands.
Every industry, silk and satin, cloth and linen, ship-
building and mining, alike received the royal stimulus
and was compelled to submit to the royal interference. Frederick's success varied, for in some cases
it was more apparent than in others that precepts,
prohibitions, and subsidies could not make good
deficiencies of climate, skill, and enterprise. While
the production of porcelain was firmly established,
that of tobacco by no means fulfilled the expectations of the King. He commissioned a Prussian
chemist to find out a sauce which would make the
home-grown leaf at least comparable with the Virginian. The experiment, which occupied more than
two and a half years, was furthered by all the resources of Government. No less than 1180 samples
were tested. The report of the General Tobacco
Administration, however, stated that only 34 of
these were in any way better for the treatment, and
that these 34, "notwithstanding they made a brave
show to outward seeming," were too unsavoury even
to be mixed with the products of Virginia.

Twice a year the King with the aid of his ministers was wont to take stock of his kingdom, and to
measure the progress of all his schemes. In the interval he travelled through his provinces and issued
instructions for the amendment of all that he found
amiss. "Schweidnitz and Neisse are still very short
of tiled roofs, N. B., someone will have to look to
it" is one of fourteen points that he noted down in
the course of a visit to Silesia. No detail was too
trifling for his attention. At the time when a paper

manufactory was determined on, doubt was expressed whether sufficient raw material in the shape of fine rags would be forthcoming.

"The ill custom prevails among us," rejoined the King, "that both in town and country the servant-girls make the best rags into tinder to light the fire. We must try to break people of it, and therefore the rag-collectors must be provided with touch-wood, which is just as good as tinder for lighting a fire, to give to the girls in exchange for rags."

A king who took upon his own shoulders so vast a share as did Frederick in regulating the agriculture and industry of his subjects could not avoid concerning himself also with their foreign trade. The general principles of commercial policy which he followed were simple. He was determined to see that Prussian subjects sold as much as possible to foreigners and bought as little as possible from them in return. The latter part of his task could be, and was, accomplished by prohibiting the importation of certain commodities, such as salt, porcelain, and steel, and by appointing a host of customs-officers to make the prohibition effective. But to sell to foreigners goods which were produced in Prussia chiefly because the King willed that his subjects should forego the convenience of buying them from foreigners was a feat which taxed Frederick's statecraft to the utmost.

In general it may be said that Prussian commerce did not thrive. Thanks to the strenuous efforts of King and ministers, who imported foreign artisans, endowed them with implements and homes, compelled natives to learn crafts, bought sheep in Spain, forbade the export of raw material or the import of finished goods, forced the monasteries to support unprofitable industries, vetoed profitable industries that threatened in any way to prejudice their favourites, in short, exhausted the arts of government to foster production,—thanks to all this the Silesian export of cloth and linen rose to between five and six million thalers a year.

This result was not achieved by domestic interference only. The King did not shrink from tariff wars with Austria and Saxony, nor from much toil to procure commercial treaties. It often appeared, however, that there were spheres in which statecraft, even when practised by a Frederick, could accomplish little.

"When at that time a new republic arose across the ocean," writes Professor Koser, "King Frederick made haste to enter into commercial relations with it, in order to exchange cloth, woollen stuffs, and linen, iron goods and porcelain, for rice, indigo, and Virginian tobacco. The 'most favoured nation' treaty of 10 September, 1785, between Prussia and the United States of America fulfilled, it is true, few of the expectations which both parties formed of it, for the English, who from a seafaring and capitalist point of view were more competent, long continued to be the commercial intermediaries between those renegade colonies and the Old World."

In the course of his efforts the King endeavoured at different times to supplant Hamburg, to ruin Danzig, and to make Silesia an impenetrable barrier between Polish wool-growers and their customers in Saxony. It was a peculiar feature of Prussia that her straggling frontiers were crossed by many roads and rivers which connected foreign states. The Hohenzollern laboured to turn this fact to account and to favour Prussian merchants by hampering foreigners with enormous tolls. The result was that commerce was compelled to avoid the borders of his dominions.

Frederick was indefatigable in inciting his subjects to take up new enterprises as well as in striving to procure for them advantages abroad. As a rule, however, the commercial companies which he formed either decayed or relapsed into the position of State undertakings. It may be surmised that what might have been possible to the Frederick and the Prussia of 1740 had been rendered well-nigh impossible by the changes in both which a generation of militarism had produced. The system of despotic command and automatic obedience was fatal to the growth of a class of self-reliant merchants, and the King complained bitterly that neither individuals nor corporations would act with enlightened patriotism in developing the commerce of Prussia. Able advisers of the Crown, indeed, did something to atone for this lack of initiative. Thanks to the talent of Hagen, the Bank, which was established in 1765, survived its early perils and became serviceable to Prussian trade. The Marine Commercial Company also outlived many of Frederick's semi-official creations.

It is perhaps in the sphere of taxation that Frederick's unflinching autocracy is most remarkably displayed. He claimed not only to regulate the consumption of his people according to his own standard of propriety, but also to select agents to enforce his rules without the smallest consideration for their feelings. Frederick wished to make existence easier for the poor, especially for the soldier. He therefore abolished the tax on grain, but subjected meat, beer, and wine to progressive imposts. Every Prussian was forced to buy from the State a fixed quantity of inferior salt at a price equal to four times its cost of production. The King's delight in coffee did not make him blind to the fact that the State would gain more profit if his subjects were forced to abandon it in favour of Prussian beer. Accordingly in 1781 coffee became, like salt and tobacco, a monopoly of State and a tax of 250 per cent. upon its value was imposed. Frederick strove to refute the remonstrances of the Pomeranian gentry with the words: "His Majesty's high person was reared in youth on beer-soup, therefore the people in that part can equally well be reared on beer-soup; it is much more wholesome than coffee." The people, however, seem to have mitigated the inconvenience to which they were put by their King in part by brewing decoctions of herbs, but chiefly by smuggling. It has been estimated that no less than two-thirds of the coffee which they used was contraband. It boded ill for the State when to knock one of the King's spies on the head excited none of the odium of murder.

The measure which most of all estranged the hearts of the Prussians from their King dates, however, from the year 1766, when Frederick resolved to introduce the French system of farming out the indirect taxes, or Regie. Not the system alone, but also the chief agents who carried it into effect, were brought from France. The lessee-in-chief, de Launay, exercised great influence over the King, who accepted his opinion as to the possibilities of taxation in preference to that of his Prussian commissioners.

The people, as was natural, detested an innovation which both wounded their Teutonic sensibilities and raised the price of food. De Launay and his assistants were caricatured as marching behind beasts laden with rackets, foils, and fiddles, to avenge the shame of Rossbach on the inhabitants of Berlin. Patriots might well chafe at the thought that a new and foreign department was introduced into the General Directory itself, and that whereas a Prussian minister was paid only 4000 thalers a year, each of the four chief Frenchmen received 15,000. Less than ten per cent. of the 2000 tax-gatherers were foreigners, but the Germans were insulted at being deemed fit for the lower grades alone.

Their murmurs, however, were powerless to alter the purpose of the King. The innovation, indeed, was not recommended by conspicuous success. Though it simplified the fiscal administration, a large proportion of the returns was still swallowed up by expenses of collection. On a review of the twenty years, 1766–1786, the proceeds of the Regie seem to have been in no wise augmented by de Launay's hated invasion. Yet Frederick adhered to his plan, kept the taxes high, administered the funds of the

State in secret, and crowned all by bringing coffee under the control of the French. To his fiscal measures more than to all else was it due that the State which he had exalted drew a deep breath of relief when he died.

CHAPTER XI

FREDERICK AND EUROPE, 1763–1786

THE chief significance of the Peace of Hubertusburg for Prussia was not expressed in any of
its clauses. The signature of the treaty implied that Europe renounced the endeavour to deprive her of the rank among the Great Powers which
she had arrogated to herself in 1740. Their survival
of the great ordeal conferred a new consequence
upon Frederick and his State. "Frederick himself,"
Mr. James Sime happily says, "acquired both in
Germany and in Europe the indefinable influence
which springs from the recognition of great gifts
that have been proved by great deeds." The brief
sketch of his domestic labours that has been given in
Chapter X. suggests that he was not lacking in the
energy which was needed to maintain this influence
and to derive full profit from it. The history of his
dealings with foreign Powers during the latter half
of his reign is the story of how this was done.

From the moment at which he signed the treaty
down to the day of his death, Frederick felt that
Austria was still his enemy. Joseph II., the eldest
son of the Queen, who was unanimously elected

JOSEPH THE SECOND.

AFTER THE PAINTING BY LISTARD.

Emperor in 1765, had learned politics from the King of Prussia. He desired nothing so much as to restore the immemorial pre-eminence of his House by a sudden blow at its upstart rival. Frederick, who had spies everywhere, was soon acquainted with the ambitions of the restless youth. For the present he could place some reliance on the pacific influence of the Queen and more on the emptiness of the Austrian treasury, but he was none the less compelled to make it his foremost task to thwart successive Hapsburg schemes of aggrandisement.

His security was the greater, however, because the Peace of Paris of 1763 reconciled France and England as little as the Peace of Hubertusburg reconciled Austria and Prussia. Frederick, it is true, was still treated with coldness by the French, who clung to their alliance with the Queen, and he was resolved never again to trust an English ministry. With a rare access of spite, indeed, he condemned the charger which he had named after Lord Bute to be yoked with a mule and to perform humiliating duties in his sight. But though neither of the Great Powers of the West was his ally, their latent hostility was still too incurable to permit them to unite against him.

On the remaining Great Power, therefore, the well-being of Prussia depended. The Seven Years' War of the future, which Frederick was always labouring to avert by means of elaborate armaments, was improbable if Russia stood neutral and impossible if she became his ally. From 1763 onwards the Russian alliance was the prize for which he strove. He had to surmount the obstacle that as sovereign of Ost-Preussen he was the natural enemy of the Russian designs upon Poland. But Austria, on the other hand, besides being interested in Poland, was the natural enemy of the Russian designs upon the Turk. Frederick might reasonably hope that by humouring Russia to the extreme limit which the interests of his State permitted, he might establish a good understanding with her to the prejudice of the more formidable empire in the south.

Catherine, whose throne was far from secure, seemed at first resolved to shun a new connexion with the ally of her murdered husband. Early in October, 1763, however, her neighbour, Augustus, died, and the stress of the election to the throne of Poland compelled her to seek the aid of some foreign Power. France, Austria, and finally the Russian faction in Poland all disappointed her, and she feared a hostile combination between Prussia and the Turk. On April 11, 1764, therefore, Frederick's desire was gratified. He bound himself to aid Catherine in upholding the existing constitutional anarchy in Poland and in Sweden, and received in return the coveted Russian guarantee for Silesia. Then, by means of force and corruption, Stanislaus Poniatowski was installed as King of Poland (September 7, 1764). "God said, let it be light, and it was light," was Frederick's congratulation to Catherine. "You speak and the world is silent before you."

In accommodating himself without undue humility to the flighty humours of his imperious ally, and in appropriating for Prussia most of the benefits of the compact, Frederick showed that experience had taught him much. The state of Polish and Turkish affairs gave to the Eastern Question of that day two storm-centres which threatened wide and immediate disturbance. Frederick, who was deep in his labours of restoration and reform at home, desired above all to keep the peace. This imposed upon him tasks of the utmost delicacy. He had to prevent the formation of a Northern league which Russia desired, to cow Austria by means of the Russian alliance, to follow with the closest attention the turbulent course of politics in Poland, to keep Austria from acquiring influence there, to check the military ardour of the Turk, and to hinder a *rapprochement* between Austria and Russia. During more than four years (April, 1764–October, 1768), he was able to stave off war, and when at last France induced the Turks to attack Russia, he found himself liable only to pay an annual subsidy of less than half a million thalers. In 1769 the alliance was prolonged till 1780.

The war between Russia and the Turks seemed to Frederick a pitiable display of incompetence. "To form a correct idea of this war," he wrote, "you must figure a set of purblind people who, by constantly beating a set of altogether blind, end by gaining over them a complete mastery." But the triumph of Russia, however achieved, threatened to kindle the general conflagration which he dreaded. It was clear that if left to herself she would make conquests, and Austria was on the alert for compensation. The Hapsburg claims might possibly be satisfied at the expense of the Turk, but this resource was of no avail to furnish the compensation which Prussia herself would not forego. Frederick cast longing glances towards West - Preussen, but could not bring himself to believe that Russia would consent to an acquisition which would add immensely to the power of a rival state. He therefore feared that the knot would yield only to the sword.

At this crisis the King twice met Joseph II. face to face. At Neisse, in August, 1769, little save a personal introduction was effected. Frederick professed to be charmed with the beautiful soul and noble ambitions of the young Emperor, while Joseph reported to his mother that the King talked admirably, but betrayed the knave in every word he spoke. At the second meeting, which took place in Moravia in September, 1770, Frederick spared no effort to captivate Joseph and Kaunitz. He donned the Austrian uniform of white, though he smilingly confessed that his mania for snuff made him too dirty to wear it. He extolled the Imperial grenadiers as worthy to guard the person of the God of War. He made Laudon sit beside him, saying in graceful allusion to Hochkirch and Kunersdorf, that he would rather have General Laudon at his side than be obliged to face him. After sacrificing to the vanity of the Chancellor by listening for an hour to a monologue on political affairs, he won his heart by posing as a grateful convert to his views.

The result was that Frederick was able to offer Catherine the joint mediation of Austria and Prussia to end the war. The offer was not accepted, but it proved that the two foes were not irreconcilable.

WENZEL ANTON, PRINCE VON KAUNITZ.

AFTER THE PAINTING BY STEINER.

The mere hint that Austria might compete for the
Prussian alliance was enough to raise its value at St.
Petersburg. It became clear, too, that only the fear
of Prussia was preventing Austria from interfering
on behalf of the Turk. Urged on by his brother
Henry, who had just returned from the Russian
capital, Frederick determined early in 1771 to take
the risk of offending Russia and provoking Austria
to war, in order to net his profit from this advantageous situation ere it changed.

In the summer of 1770 Austria had drifted, half
involuntarily, into an occupation of Zips, a portion
of the territory of Poland which was almost surrounded by her own, and of some of the adjacent
districts. Frederick now seized upon this, though
the Queen was willing to draw back, as an excuse
for pressing upon Russia a plan which he had pro-
mulgated under an alias at an early stage in the war.
On February 1, 1769, he had suggested to his
ambassador at St. Petersburg

"that Russia should offer to the Court of Vienna
Lemberg and the surrounding country in return for
support against the Turks ; that she should give us
Polish Preussen with Ermland and the protectorate over
Danzig; and that she should herself incorporate a suitable part of Poland by way of indemnity for the expenses
of the war."

The plan of dismembering Poland because the
Turks were defeated was, as Frederick knew full
well, distasteful to both of the Powers whose com-
plicity he desired. Russia was strongly opposed to

any aggrandisement of Prussia to the eastward. Austria, besides being averse to the aggrandisement of her rival in any quarter, preferred any lands to the Polish and any method to that of naked force. Yet the King, while professing that he was an old man whose brain was worn out, secured the co-operation of Russia within a year (15th January, 1772), and of Austria less than eight months later.

The triumph of his diplomacy was enhanced by the fact that he would have been completely foiled if Austria had consented to join Russia in dismembering the Turk. As it was, he was permitted to enjoy the spectacle of the Queen struggling with her conscience and upbraiding herself, her Chancellor, and her son. She complained that they had aimed at two incompatible objects at once, " to act in the Prussian fashion and at the same time to preserve the semblance of honesty." The prospective additions to her domains were to her odious, since they were " bought at the price of honour, at the price of the glory of the monarchy, at the price of the good faith and religion, which are our peculiar possession." "She is always weeping, but always annexing," sneered the triumphant King.

On August 5, 1772, Austria signed the Treaty of Partition. By agreeing upon their demands the three Powers had accomplished the hardest part of their enterprise. The strength of Poland had been wasted by the anarchy which Russia and Prussia had studiously conserved. Since 1768, Romanists and Dissidents had been engaged in a bloody and desolating war in which Russia, the protector of the

Greek Church, played the decisive part. No party among the Poles still retained sufficient energy to oppose in arms the claims to Polish provinces which, in order to save appearances, were formulated by the Powers. Frederick even put forward a double title to Pomerellen, alleging that it had been wrongfully alienated by the Margrave of Brandenburg in 1311, and that if he as suzerain consented to overlook this irregularity, he would still be entitled to the province as heir, since 1637, to the elder branch of the House of Pomerania. He claimed Great Poland as heir of the Emperor Sigismund, who had pawned it to the Teutoniç Order, from which the Poles had wrested it by force. The remainder of his share was due to him as compensation for the loss of the revenues of these two provinces for so many centuries.

The Polish statesmen had no difficulty in refuting such nonsense as this. But King Stanislaus was convinced that true patriotism dictated obedience in order to save what remained. France and England were too intent on their own affairs to interfere by force. Hence a mixture of persuasion, bribery, and the presence of 30,000 soldiers was sufficient to procure the unanimous acquiescence of the Diet after six months' negotiation (September 30, 1773). The Austrian ambassador was astonished at the trifling sums for which the nobles sold their votes. His Saxon colleague lamented that they shamelessly laid upon the gaming-tables the foreign gold with which they had just been bribed.

Frederick's share of the spoil amounted to more

than sixteen thousand square miles, and in 1774 he
was able quietly to filch two hundred additional villages from Poland.   Long before the Diet consented
to the cession he had inaugurated Prussian rule.   In
June, 1772, he made a triumphal entry into his
new province.   He gave out to all and sundry that
no one could envy his good fortune, for as he came
he had seen nothing but sand, pines, heath, and
Jews.   "It is a very good and very profitable acquisition," he wrote to Prince Henry, "both for the
political situation of the State and for its finances."
Men said that without Danzig, which along with
Thorn remained Polish, West-Preussen was but a
trunk without a head, but the King was full of
schemes for partitioning the trade of Danzig among
his own ports.   Voltaire, finding him deaf to his
exhortations to free the Greeks, lamented that the
harbour of Danzig lay nearer his heart than the
Piræus.

Soon the poverty-stricken land echoed to the un-
tiring march of Hohenzollern progress.   The contempt which the King openly expressed for "this
perfectly imbecile set with names ending in ki"
was apparent in all his dealings with the privileged
classes.   His treatment of private estates as well as
of provinces seemed to warrant the Poles who added
the word *Rapuit* to the *Suum Cuique* which they saw
inscribed beneath the Prussian eagle.   The local officials were simply dismissed from office, and their
lands appropriated at the cost of a trifling compensation. Though Frederick bound himself to respect
the existing rights and property of the Roman

Catholics, the bishops and abbots likewise lost their
lands, but in their case an allowance amounting to
nearly half of their previous incomes was conceded.
Upon the nobles a tax of one-quarter of their net
revenues was imposed, but Protestants were entitled
to a discount of twenty per cent. In the hope of
cleansing West-Preussen of its Polish inhabitants,
the King went so far as to favour the purchase of
noble lands by German peasants. Strict watch was
kept on the frontier for Polish immigrants who might
try to enter the country.

The common people, however, could not but gain
from the introduction of that policy of developing
all the resources of the land which formed the Hohenzollern ideal of domestic government. Slavery
was abolished and serfdom regulated. New water-
ways were dug. Colonists were brought in by
thousands. Prussian soldiers scoured the country
in search of gipsies, tramps, and begging Jews.
Toleration, justice, and education were established
where all three had been far to seek. The peasants
and townsmen were subjected to the Prussian system
of taxation, which laid upon their shoulders a burden heavy indeed, but steady and not beyond their
strength. Soon the royal revenue from West-Preussen
amounted to more than two million thalers a year.

But for a timely revival of energy in her royal
House, it is not impossible that Sweden, like Poland,
would have been the poorer for the Russo-Prussian
alliance. In 1769 Catherine and Frederick had
pledged themselves to maintain anarchy in Stockholm as well as in Warsaw. Should the existing

constitution be modified, Russia would take up arms and Frederick's contribution to the war was to be the invasion of Swedish Pomerania. It is easy to imagine that with Russia and Prussia in cordial agreement and France and England embroiled or apathetic, a war with Sweden might have resulted in the annexation of Finland and the remainder of Pomerania by the allies. In 1772, however, young Gustavus III., the son of Frederick's sister Ulrica, delivered Sweden from the trammels of her constitution by an unlooked-for *coup d'état*. Russia, which was still hampered by the Turkish war, was unable to wage war against the revolution, and Frederick, who for once was taken by surprise, grudgingly accepted the apologies of his nephew.

The remainder of Frederick's life was dedicated to the defence of the position that he had already attained. He was determined to do nothing that could prejudice his cause in a future struggle with Austria. He therefore looked on while Russia and Austria despoiled the Turk in 1774, while England and her Colonies fell to blows in the next year, and while France joined in the fray in 1778. His private opinion, indeed, was that the country which could commit its destinies to a Bute could hardly fail to be in the wrong. He blamed the English both for political and military folly—for beginning a terrible civil war with no settled plans or adequate preparations, for underestimating the enemy's force, for dividing her own and for trampling upon the rights of neutrals. But he avoided with the most scrupulous care any action that could give offence to either combatant, and declared to his ministers that he intended to await the issue quietly and to throw in his lot with the side which fortune favoured.

In the very year in which France allied herself with the Colonies against England (1778) Frederick's long-expected struggle with Austria came to pass. Joseph II., whose restless desire to imitate the achievements of the King of Prussia was not satisfied by his gains from Poland and the Turk, thought that the moment had arrived for acquiring a portion of Bavaria, the great geographical obstacle to the consolidation of the Hapsburg lands. At the close of the year 1777 the Elector of Bavaria died, and his lands passed by right to the aged and childless Elector Palatine. Austria, however, furbished up a claim to a considerable portion of eastern Bavaria, and on January 14, 1778, the Elector was half bribed, half frightened into acquiescence. Two days later 10,000 Austrian troops occupied the ceded districts. Joseph's triumph seemed to be assured.

Frederick, however, had still to be reckoned with. Though his health was indifferent and his desire was all for peace, he took up the challenge without an hour's delay. Determined, as he said, "once for all to humble Austrian ambition," he assumed his ancient pose as champion of the German princes against an Emperor who was trampling upon their constitutional rights. "I know very well," he owned to Prince Henry, "that it is only our own interest which makes it our duty to act at this moment, but we must be very careful not to say so." Few volunteers, however, declared themselves on his side.

The Elector's cousin and heir, Duke Charles of Zweibrücken, became a pawn in Frederick's hands, and the Elector of Saxony, who had claims on the estate of the dead prince, promised 21,000 men. But his only other ally was Bavarian public opinion, which was shocked at the idea of partition. The Bavarians, according to the current jest, left off their pious invocation of " Jesu, Mary, Joseph," and cried to " Jesu, Mary, Frederick " to deliver them.

The Austrian statesmen were willing enough to negotiate, but they clung to the gains which they had made. Their preparations for war were not complete, but they did not believe that Prussia meant to fight. Both sides, indeed, hoped more from negotiation than from battle. It became evident, too, that Frederick was no longer the general whose delight was in swift and resolute movements. Not till April 6, 1778, did he march from Berlin, and then he drew rein in southern Silesia, and spent three months more in fruitless haggling. At last, on July 3rd, he made a declaration of war, and two days later completed his march across the mountains into Bohemia. Even then the Queen brought herself to beg for peace, so that, although hostilities continued, August was half gone before the diplomatists finally dispersed.

The War of the Bavarian Succession formally began, however, when Frederick set out for Bohemia, on July 3, 1778. He was attacking with two armies, each about 80,000 strong. Earlier in the year he had hoped that the main Austrian force would assemble in Moravia. In that case his plan was to lead his own army from Silesia against it, to win a great victory, and thus to compel the enemy to call back their troops from Bohemia. This would make it easy for Prince Henry with a combined host of Prussians and Saxons to advance on Prague while the King made progress in Moravia. The two armies, if all continued to go well, would then press forward towards the Danube.

The plan was spoiled, however, because the Austrians were bold enough to choose north-eastern Bohemia for their place of concentration. There they were indeed further from Vienna, but they secured greater possibilities of offensive action. If Frederick invaded Moravia they could overrun Silesia behind his back or fall upon Prince Henry and Saxony in overwhelming force. The King, therefore, reluctantly turned aside into Bohemia by way of Nachod in order to engage the enemy's attention until his brother, marching from Dresden, should have established himself firmly in the north.

On his arrival in Bohemia, Frederick found the Austrians some 250,000 strong. Joseph and Lacy with the bulk of the troops confronted him in a position on the Elbe nearly fifty miles in length and as strong as water, earthworks, and cannon could make it. Judging it impregnable, Frederick waited impatiently for his brother to get the better of Laudon, who was guarding the northern gate into Bohemia. The army chafed at the enforced inaction, but the King still hoped by sending repeated detachments to Moravia to compel the enemy to meet him there in the field.

Prince Henry, after hesitating for some time between different routes, performed his task to perfection. Early in August he led his army over the
mountains to the east of the Elbe by ways hitherto
reputed impassable. Laudon was at his wits' end.
He fell back upon the line of the Iser, but on August
14th, Joseph himself admitted that he was too weak
to hold it. If Laudon were driven off, the great
position on the Elbe would be untenable, but Prince
Henry lacked the hardihood to venture the decisive
move. Dissensions between the royal brothers and
the failure of their efforts to effect a junction justified the policy of their opponents, who, Frederick
sneered, seemed to be turned into stone. Soon the
movements of the Prussians were dictated largely
by hunger and the conflict earned its nickname of
the Potato War. Heavy rains completed their dis-
comfiture. By the middle of October the exultant
Austrians had seen the last of the invaders.

The campaign of 1778 cost the combatants some
20,000 men and 29,000,000 thalers in money. Frederick had shown himself captious and irresolute.
His brother declared that he was more on his guard
against the treachery of the King than against the
enterprises of the enemy. The army had become
dejected, ill-disciplined, and disaffected. Frederick,
though he prepared to invade Moravia in the spring,
spent the winter in working his hardest for peace.
France and Russia lent their aid. In March, 1779,
a congress of the four Powers met at Teschen, and
on May 13th peace was signed.

The Peace of Teschen was in some degree a

triumph for Frederick. The chief points for which
he had taken up arms were secured at no great cost.
The Austrian acquisitions were limited to the Quarter of the Inn, a strip of territory bounded on the
west by that river, while Bavaria was obliged to pay
4,000,000 thalers in settlement of the Saxon claims.
Prussia seemed thus to have maintained the rights
of two great German princes from motives of pure
patriotism. Her military prestige, on the other
hand, had suffered. She had not derived prompt
support from her intimacy with Russia and she had
failed to disturb the connexion between Austria
and France. No less than four royal marriages
now linked the Bourbons to their secular foes the
Hapsburgs. By accepting the guarantee of France
and Russia to a treaty in which the Peace of
Westphalia was once more confirmed, Prussia had
moreover paved the way for unwelcome foreign
intrusions into German affairs.

Frederick saw good reason to fear that the danger
from Austria would be renewed so soon as Joseph
should be emancipated from the restraining influence of the aged Queen. For the time being, however, he was free to resume his round of toil, to
mourn the loss of Voltaire, to correspond with the
philosopher d'Alembert, and to pursue reforms in
law and education. The Prussian judges were now
empowered to interrogate the parties to suits and
compelled to hear what they had to say. A codification of the law and a Book of Rights which
should stereotype the existing feudal system of
society in Prussia were set on foot. And at the

moment when Romanist sovereigns drove out the Jesuits, Frederick welcomed the fugitives as harmless individuals, who could help to supply one of the most pressing needs of the State by instructing the common people.

The lack of qualified elementary teachers in Frederick's dominions was attested by the fact that in 1763 an edict of educational reform in Silesia permitted them to continue such employments as tailoring, but forbade them to eke out their incomes by peddling, by selling beer or brandy, or by fiddling in public-houses. A counsel of despair had been to set the worn-out sergeants to keep school. Out of 3443 of them, however, only 79 were reported by the military officials as possibly fit to serve, and investigation by the civil authorities still further reduced the number. Under such conditions as these the influx of members of an order which had long been famous for its schools was regarded by the King as a boon to Prussia. To grant them an asylum gratified his real love of toleration, without in his opinion involving the smallest peril to the allegiance of his subjects.

From time to time, however, Frederick was unpleasantly reminded of his insecurity. In the summer of 1780, Austria secured a portion of the Bavarian inheritance which it was beyond his power to take away. In spite of all his diplomacy, the mighty sees of Cologne and Münster fell into Hapsburg hands. At this moment of triumph, Maria Theresa died (November 29, 1780). "She has done honour to her throne and to her sex," wrote the King to d'Alembert. " I have made war against her, but I have never been her enemy."

Though Frederick regarded his great antagonist as bigoted and hypocritical, he mourned her sincerely, for her death removed the most potent check upon her son. Joseph seemed to have inherited his mother's energy, without her reverence for existing institutions. He now plunged into a medley of hasty and sweeping reforms, treating the inhabitants of his miscellaneous provinces as cavalierly as though he were a Frederick and they submissive Prussians. The King could afford to look on while Joseph and Kaunitz embroiled themselves with the landowners, the Hungarians, and the Church. It was not long, however, before their foreign policy compelled him to active interference.

Since 1780 the Russian alliance had failed him. He valued it as a means of preserving peace, but the policy which now prevailed at St. Petersburg looked towards war. Frederick, who was strangely blind to this, declared in response to the blandishments of the Czarina that the time was not ripe to seize more of Poland (1779). He proposed the admission of the Turk into the league at the moment when Catherine was dreaming of a new crusade. In Joseph, on the other hand, the Czarina found a willing partner in a policy of adventure. From the time when he visited her in the summer of 1780, the alliance between Russia and Prussia was practically dead. Frederick sacrificed to it in May, 1781, by joining the Armed Neutrality which

Russia had organised in order to check the high-handed treatment of neutral vessels by Great Britain. But in the same month Catherine and Joseph made a defensive alliance for eight years. Frederick rightly divined that the ambitious Czarina had won the Emperor's countenance to the scheme of a revival by Russia of the old Eastern Empire. Her eldest grandson was destined to be Czar of all the Russias. Her second was named after the founder of Constantinople and suckled by six Greek nurses. The third, sneered the King, when another was expected, would presumably become Great Mogul.

But though Frederick regarded Catherine as pretentious, saying that if she were corresponding with God the Father she would claim at least equal rank, none knew better than he the value of her alliance. In 1762 Russia had turned the scale, and had she been favourable to the plan, Joseph's bold throw for Bavaria might have been successful. It was no light matter for Frederick that in his old age his State was threatened by an Emperor whose thoughts were still running on Silesia and who had succeeded in seducing his sole ally. France and England were beyond the range of his overtures, and when the Russian armies moved in 1783 Europe believed that the Turk was about to be finally expelled. Frederick, it seemed, was doomed to perilous isolation.

One force indeed remained—a force difficult to marshal, but as Charles V. had found, formidable when marshalled — which Frederick might hope to rally to his side. The tilted balance of Europe

UNTER DEN LINDEN IN 1780.

FROM AN ETCHING BY ROSENTAG.

might still be redressed in Germany. By his conduct in the affair of the Bavarian Succession Frederick had proved that it was not impossible for
Germans to trust him, and since that time Austria
by fresh aggressions had alienated from herself the
general body of Romanist opinion among them. It
appeared that the Empire which was a corporation
for the preservation of rights had acquired in Joseph
a head who set at naught all rights save those of
Austria. The inevitable result was that the princes
began to think of uniting in self-defence.

From the beginning of the year 1784, Frederick
devoted himself to the task of organising a con-
federacy of German States to defend the existing
constitution. This was a far more arduous undertaking than any negotiation with a single Great
Power. It was always difficult to induce a number
of naturally jealous neighbours to combine. In 1784
the difficulty was increased threefold. The danger
from Austria was general and prospective, rather
than specific and imminent. It might be averted,
indeed, by maintaining an equality of strength between Prussia and Austria, but the princes would
beware of embarking upon a course which might
make Prussia the stronger of the two. Frederick,
moreover, was compelled to entrust a great share in
the negotiations to his ministers. His chief agent,
Hertzberg, had dared to form political ideas of his
own. In the hope that a *rapprochement* with Austria would lead to further gains in Poland, he quietly
obstructed the measures of the aged King.

The inactivity of the Prussian ministers might

have delayed the confederation indefinitely had not all Germany been shocked by the sudden revival of the Emperor's designs upon Bavaria. Again, just as seven years earlier, Austria corrupted the Elector Palatine without the privity of his heir and again her acquisition of the Electorate was paraded before the world as an accomplished fact. In the first days of January, 1785, Rumianzow, the Russian agent at the German Diet, suddenly presented to the Duke of Zweibrücken a joint demand of Austria and Russia for his acceptance of a bargain to which the Elector Palatine had already consented. The substance of this was that Bavaria was assigned to the Emperor in return for the Austrian Netherlands, the title of King, and handsome rewards in money.

"I, who am already more than half beyond this world," complained Frederick to his brother, "am forced to double my wisdom and activity, and continually keep in my head the detestable plans that this curséd Joseph begets afresh with every fresh day. I am condemned to enjoy no rest before my bones are covered with a little earth." His energy, none the less, was as great as the crisis demanded. Austria was always hampered in time of war because the distant Netherlands were hers as much as because the adjacent Bavaria was not. The exchange was therefore most alluring, but the opposition of Prussia to the scheme was so stout as to evoke disclaimers from all the parties to it. Catherine protested that she would countenance no violation of the Peace of Teschen. Louis XVI., whom Frederick believed to have been bribed by the offer of

Luxemburg, stated in answer to his protests that the Emperor renounced the scheme. Before the end of February, 1785, the danger was past.

To guard against its recurrence Frederick none the less completed the *Fürstenbund* or League of Princes. On July 23, 1785, Prussia, Saxony, and Hanover entered into an alliance, with the object of safeguarding the lands and rights of every member of the Empire. By separate articles the three Electors bound themselves to act together in Imperial business. The accession of the Archbishop of Mainz, who as president of the Electoral College had a casting vote, both gave the League a majority at the election of the Emperor, and prevented it from being regarded as a mere clique of Protestants. Frederick's triumph was complete when, in spite of the diplomatic opposition of the Emperor, a host of German princes accepted the result of his work. The rulers of Zweibrücken, Hesse-Cassel, Gotha, Weimar, Brunswick, Ansbach, Baden, Anhalt, Mecklenburg, and Osnabrück formed with the four protagonists a great body of organised German conservatism led by the King of Prussia. Frederick in his old age had improvised with marvellous success a temporary insurance against the greatest danger that visibly threatened his State.

CHAPTER XII

FREDERICK'S DEATH AND GREATNESS

THE League of 1785 was Frederick's last contribution to the politics of Europe. He felt that his days were numbered, but answered the summons of Death only by quickening the step with which he had long traversed the routine of daily duty. In his last months he remained true to his long-cherished ideal of life and still proved himself diligent, imperious, stoical, and even gay.

The fatal shock to his health, which was already shaken by gout and dyspepsia, seems to have been given at a review in Silesia on August 24, 1785. After the manœuvres of the previous year he had written to the Infantry Inspector-General of the province that he was more dissatisfied with his troops than ever before. "Were I to make shoemakers or tailors into generals, the regiments could not be worse," declared the King by way of prelude to more particular strictures. He threatened court-martial in the following year to whomsoever should not then fulfil his duty.

When the time arrived for the visit of 1785 to Silesia, no symptoms of disorder could keep the

DEATH-MASK OF FREDERICK THE GREAT.
FROM THE ORIGINAL IN THE HOHENZOLLERN MUSEUM, BERLIN.

King from his post. As he made his usual tour
of inspection, thousands of the country-folk flocked
in to see him pass and to utter their gratitude for
his subsidies. So he arrived at the review of August
22nd–25th, which was held in the plain that lies
south of Breslau, and which military Europe regarded
as one of the greatest tactical displays of the year.

On the third morning of the four, Frederick insisted on teaching his men their duty by sitting his
horse for six hours in a deluge of rain without the
shelter of a cloak. In spite of the inevitable chill,
he then presided at dinner, at which the Duke of
York, Lafayette, and Cornwallis were among the
guests. Fever and ague followed, but he shook
them off in a night and completed the review, the
progress through Silesia, the journey to Potsdam,
and the inspection of artillery at Berlin. On September 10th, he left his capital for the last time.

At Potsdam, on the eve of the Grand Review,
the blow fell. Within a month of his indiscretion
in Silesia he was seized in the night with a fit of
apoplexy (September 18–19, 1785). Gout, asthma,
dropsy, and erysipelas set in, and after days of torment he was compelled to spend his nights in fighting for breath in an armchair. Yet no disease could
break his spirit. " There is traceable," says Carlyle
with fine insight, " only a complete superiority to
Fear and Hope."

Partly, perhaps, because Austrian troops might
menace the frontiers if his weakness were known,
but doubtless in part out of fortitude and pride,
he concealed his illness so far as possible from his

subjects and from his friends. He performed the
labours of the Cabinet with unclouded brain and
with a growing fever of energy. His mind was
full of plans for establishing new villages upon
the districts reclaimed from the sand, for providing
technical instruction in agriculture, and for arranging
the coming manœuvres in Silesia. He continued
to read history day by day, and to converse cheerfully with his friends. Once he enquired of the
Duke of Courland whether he needed a good watch-
man, maintaining that his sleeplessness at nights
qualified him to fill the post. After seven months of
suffering he entertained Mirabeau with lively conversation, though his state was so pitiable as to
render the interview painful to his favoured guest.

Very early on the morning of April 17, 1786, he
left the palace in Potsdam town, where he had passed
the winter, and made a long, circuitous journey to
his favourite abode, Sans Souci. But the change
was powerless to bring relief. Some days he was
too weak to converse as usual with his guests.
On June 30th, however, he shocked his doctor by
taking a copious dinner of strong soup full of spices,
beef steeped in brandy, maize and cheese flavoured
with garlic, and a whole plateful of pungent eel-pie.
Four days later he actually quitted his chair for a
short gallop on horseback, but the exertion left him
prostrate.

Again he rallied, and until the middle of August
disease and his inflexible determination to accomplish the daily routine struggled for the mastery.
On August 10th, he sent a tender little note to his

widowed sister Charlotte of Brunswick. " The old," wrote the dying King, " must give place to the young, that each generation may find room clear for it : and life, if we examine strictly what its course is, consists in seeing one's fellow-creatures die and be born." By an almost pathetic chance his last letter, written on August 14th, was to de Launay, demanding more minute accounts of the hated excise.

Frederick, like his ancestors, died at his post. The Great Elector, whose only fear was that dropsy might unfit him to govern, held a Privy Council within two days of the end. Frederick William amid all his torments spent his last days in private conference with his heir. Frederick, an older man than either, began work at five o'clock on the morning of Tuesday, August 15th. He made the arrangements for a review at Potsdam and dictated despatches of weight with all his wonted clearness. On Wednesday he failed, struggling in vain to give his weeping general the parole. All that day he lay in his chair dying, attended by valets, ministers, and physicians. In the evening he slept, and when eleven o'clock struck he enquired the time and declared that he would rise at four. Towards midnight he asked for his favourite dog and bade them cover it with a quilt. Then for more than two hours his faithful valet Strützky knelt by his chair to keep him upright, passing both his arms around the half-unconscious King. At twenty minutes past two in the morning of August 17th, Frederick passed quietly away.

Hertzberg closed his eyes and led his nephew and

successor, Frederick William, to the corpse. The King had willed to be buried on the terrace of Sans Souci, but he could now command no longer. Throughout one day, August 18th, he lay in state at Potsdam. In the evening his coffin was borne to a vault in the garish church of the Potsdam garrison, where it rests by the side of his father's.

Frederick's fame, as was inevitable in the case of one who died on the eve of the French Revolution, has fluctuated with the current of subsequent events. The world that he quitted paid to his memory the homage due to one who had been for a generation the foremost among its princes. Among his poorer subjects traces of a warmer feeling may be discerned. The legend of the Prussian soldier who boasted all his life that Frederick had answered his challenge with the words, " Dog, hold thy peace," is doubtless symbolic of the attitude of many of the rank and file. It would be idle to imagine that multitudes of humble serfs did not bewail the loss of the Father whose charity succoured them in time of need and whose equity they could always invoke against oppression. It would be no less idle to imagine that among his veteran servants no hearts beat in unison with the heart of General Lentulus, who craved the honour of following his great chief as rear-guard, since Zieten, who died earlier in the year, had secured the place of pride in the van.

Berlin, however, rejoiced that Frederick was no more. The cry of the hour was, Back to Frederick William I! Led by a silly King (1786–1797) Prussia plunged into a Teutonic reaction. Good-humour,

COFFINS OF FREDERICK THE GREAT (RIGHT) AND FREDERICK WILLIAM I. (LEFT) IN THE GARRISON CHURCH AT POTSDAM.

pomp, aggressive orthodoxy, the use of the German speech, and a grandiose foreign policy marked the royal condemnation of Frederick's practices. Prussia was tempted by profits in Poland and in Germany to regard the convulsions of France with narrow selfishness. On the field of Jena, twenty years after Frederick's death, she paid the price of all her errors (1806). Next year her Russian ally agreed with Napoleon that she should lose half her land, forego the right to arm, and submit for the future to be hemmed in by four hostile States.

Prussia was rescued from this plight by forces which found no place in Frederick's system. Great ministers now gained ascendancy over the King. The nation flung off the fetters of feudalism, all classes joined in the War of Liberation, and the final triumph in 1813–1815 was inspired by the spirit not of autocracy but of German nationality. The memory of Frederick faded into that of a ruler of that old despotic type which the sovereigns, in defiance of the claims of their people, were striving to restore.

It was the spirit of nationality, however, that in the long run revived Frederick's renown. The German people cried out for an organisation that should be closer and more virile than the federation into which they had been formed after the overthrow of Napoleon. In 1848–49, while Austria was paralysed by revolt, they turned hopefully to Prussia for leadership, but the reigning King refused to accept an Imperial crown at the hands of the mob. From that time onwards, however, the theory gained wide credence that it was the destiny of Prussia to unite and to regenerate Germany.

When in 1866 she worked her will with Austria, and when in 1871 the Imperial crown was handed to her over the body of prostrate France, the Hohenzollern legend grew. Results so glorious, men thought, could have been achieved only because a long series of national heroes had worked towards a common goal. The Hohenzollerns, and Frederick chief among them, were extolled by a thousand pens as the pioneers of a solid and triumphant Germany. A generation which salutes by the title of "Great" the Emperor whom Bismarck was wont to hoodwink and cajole is logically compelled to regard Frederick as superhuman.

The student who reviews the life-work of Frederick without either the sympathy or the bias of German patriotism may return a calmer answer to the question,—Is Frederick rightly termed "The Great"? Having followed the main steps in his long career, we may at its close sift out and set down those qualities and achievements, if such exist, which entitle him not merely to a place among the great, but to a place in that small circle of the world's heroes whose memory is so illustrious that greatness is always coupled with their names.

As a thinker, Frederick falls very far short of greatness. Though he struggled all his life with the problem of the World and its Maker, he convinced himself only that nature furnished irresistible proof of an intelligent Creator, but that the idea of an act of creation was absurd. In no department of thought was his range of vision long, but he saw with wonderful clearness so far as his sight could penetrate. The very fact that all objects within his ken seemed so distinct prevented him from realising that great forces might lie beyond. Thus the method of progress which he followed was that of devising ingenious improvements in a world that was settled and known. Though he witnessed the American Revolution and died within three years of the great explosion in France, he seems to have had no suspicion that the framework of the world might change.

This lack of sympathy with the deeper currents of human progress reveals itself by many signs in almost all the phases of Frederick's activity. In the art of war, indeed, he had witnessed too great an advance during his own career not to suppose that further advance was possible. He had himself given the infantry a mobility then unrivalled. He had introduced horse-artillery, and created the finest cavalry in the world. In his old age he turned to account the lessons of wars in both hemispheres, by raising his artillery to the importance of a separate arm and experimenting with the straggling tactics of the Americans.

Literature and learning, however, he regarded with a less open mind. While Voltaire lived, he viewed him as the sole surviving man of letters. He treated the work of young Goethe, his own fervent admirer, with contempt and showed himself no less blind to the latent possibilities of natural science and mathematics. What he saw clearly was that these studies claimed much devotion, but sometimes failed to

produce practical results. " Is it not true," he demanded of d'Alembert, " that electricity and all the
miracles that it reveals have only served to excite
our curiosity? Is it not true that the forces of at-
traction and gravitation have only astonished our
imagination? Is it not true that all the operations
of chemistry are in the same câse? " Euler himself
had failed to make the fountains at Sans Souci play
successfully, and the King jeered at geometricians
as the very type of the pig-headed. In the campaign of 1778 an officer who trusted his theodolite
in preference to his eye was bidden to go to the
devil with his trigonometry.

None of Frederick's opinions or whims can be
termed unimportant, for his power was so unfettered
that he could embody any of them in acts of State.
The building of the New Palace furnishes a hint of
how great might have been the consequences had he
given rein to a single enthusiasm in the sphere of
art. But with this reservation it is in the domain of
statecraft, especially in his system of foreign policy,
his economic doctrine, and his theory of the organisation of the State, that we must seek the true measure of his mind.

In his conception of the political world and of
Prussia's place in it, acuteness and lack of profundity
are again apparent. The acuteness is indeed im-
paired because of the existence of two political
factors, honesty and women, that Frederick never
understood. The former, it is true, was so rare that
his ignorance of its nature hampered him but little,
save when Augustus frustrated all his plans in 1756,

and when in the later stages of the Seven Years' War Louis XV. fulfilled his unprofitable engagements with the Queen. But during Frederick's lifetime women played an unusually prominent part in Europe, and his misjudgment of them was a serious political defect. Prussia suffered severely for his belief that Maria Theresa was pliable, Elizabeth of Russia incapable, the Pompadour insignificant, and Catherine II. shallow.

In general, however, Frederick was as gifted a tactician in politics as in war, and in both he knew how to profit by experience. Compared with his handling of France in his early years, his handling of Russia from 1762 to 1779 shows an advance as marked as that of his guardianship between Mollwitz and Leuthen. The circumstances of the age favoured a policy of opportunism for Prussia. Dexterity, not depth, was profitable, and Frederick therefore earned handsome rewards—Silesia, East Frisia, and West-Preussen.

The pillars of his system, none the less, were built of crumbling stone. The triumphs of his successors have to this day shored up some among them — that profit ranks before promises in affairs of State, that morals are to be reserved for manifestoes, and that the rectitude of an act is determined by its success. Some, on the other hand, were swiftly demolished by the course of subsequent events. That Austria was Prussia's most dangerous foe, that the German princes were her least desirable allies, and that lasting concord with Russia was expedient, may be regarded as mistakes, natural enough but damaging to Frederick's reputation for profound statesmanship.

His economic errors have been discussed in earlier chapters of this book. Where an original thinker would have reflected and enquired, Frederick plunged into ill-judged action. While he claimed for Prussia a place among the Great Powers, he was bent on administering her resources as despotically as though she were a farm and he the steward. His thrift and industry palliated but could not cure the evils which flowed from this confusion. The birth of individual enterprise was retarded, while by the concentration of its attention upon petty cash the hereditary tendency of the Prussian Government to be sordid was intensified. The King, though admirably acquainted with the details of the production of material wealth, was insensible to the vastly greater value of goods which cannot be seen or handled. How, it may be wondered, could his Government foster honour, initiative, or independence — qualities which in the long run are the fundamentals even of material success?

In foreign policy Frederick was successful, and in economic practice his failure was qualified. But his lack of true insight into the functions of government was fraught with terrible consequences for Prussia. Judged by the standard of the age, it is true, Frederick's administration was a pattern to the world. The State, as the fashion then was, interfered everywhere and with irresistible strength. Its machinery, though cumbrous, ran smooth and true, and the actual expense was small. "If Prussia perishes," wrote Mirabeau, "the art of government will return to its infancy."

From the same pen, however, came a verdict, damning, indeed, yet unshaken by appeal to reason or to the event. " If ever a foolish prince ascends this throne we shall see the formidable giant suddenly collapse, and Prussia will fall like Sweden." Frederick secured his own triumph by making it impossible to succeed him.

Against this department of his statecraft a double indictment must be brought. He was not profound enough to see that the machine which he laboured to render indissoluble was such that only an unbroken series of monarchs as gifted as he could guide it. Nor was he wise enough, though he knew that the next steersman of the State would be a fool, to alter the machine so as to give it some power of self-direction.

The folly of tacitly assuming that successors like himself would be forthcoming was shared by Frederick with many of the great autocrats of history. Men abhor the thought of a vacuum created by their own disappearance. The self-abnegation of a Washington is as much rarer as it is wiser than the augmented industry of an aged Louis XIV. Yet the sketch that has been given in this book of the all-embracing activity of the King, who nominated even the sergeants and corporals in an army of 200,000 men, and allowed no branch of his civil hierarchy the least real independence, suffices to show how improbable it was that an ordinary prince could put himself in Frederick's place, and how fatal it would be to the Government if he did not.

Frederick himself stated clearly the ruin that would ensue if a King of Prussia relaxed his grip on the finances, embarked upon schemes of premature aggression, or paused to enjoy his kingship. His nephew and heir, to look no further into the future, was a man whom he knew to be likely to commit all these faults. The remedy was to call into existence a body outside the throne and to entrust to its keeping some share in the power which had grown too great for the monarchy to wield. In the bureaucracy Frederick possessed a body of loyal and upright men who were not connected with any dangerous caste. Yet so far from training them for partial independence, he continued to treat them, from the General Directory downwards, like schoolboys who deserved to be flogged. His standing recipe was to keep them between fear and hope. In 1780, to cite only one instance from many, he wrote to the Chamber for West-Preussen: "Ye are arch-rogues not worth the bread that is given you, and all deserve to be turned out. Just wait till I come to Preussen!" It is not surprising that men of birth and capacity hesitated to serve in the administration during Frederick's lifetime and that narrow-minded pedantry soon became its distinguishing feature after he died. The King bequeathed an impossible task to posterity and the catastrophe of the Prussian State at Jena was the result.

As a thinker, then, even in politics and administration, Frederick falls very far short of greatness. His powers were, in reality, those of a man of action. The versatility with which he entered into every

FREDERICK THE SECOND, KING OF PRUSSIA.
AFTER THE PAINTING BY CHODOWIECKI.

department of government in turn is no more astounding than the clearness with which he perceived the immediate obstacles to be overcome in each, the courage with which he faced them, and the force, swift, steady, and irresistible, by which he triumphed. The wonderful energy which prompted him to bear on his own shoulders all the burden of the State in war and peace, and to put forth all his strength at every blow, was yet more marvellous because it was susceptible of control. Frederick, as we have seen, ceased from the labours of the Seven Years' War, only to undertake the reconstruction of the economic life of a great kingdom. By mere overflow of force he finished his *History of the War* early in the year after that in which peace was made. Yet, with all his energy, he was able to realise that not seldom force needs the help of time. He was gratified when some of his enterprises began to repay him after twenty years, and he declined to aggrandise Prussia beyond the limit which his statesmanlike instinct taught him that her strength would warrant.

Among Frederick's powers, then, energy alone is truly great, but his energy was such that to him few achievements were impossible. If we turn from his powers to his performance, we find his name associated with three great phenomena of history. Under his guidance Prussia rose at one step from the third to the highest grade among the Powers. He was, moreover, the pattern of the monarchs of his time, the type of the benevolent despots of the later eighteenth century. Finally, in the great series of events by which Germany has become a united military Empire his life-work fills a conspicuous place. How far, we may enquire, should his work in any of these three fields compel the admiration of succeeding ages?

That part of the Hohenzollern legend which portrays Frederick as the conscious or semi-conscious architect of the modern German Empire finds little support in the record of his life. Sometimes, it is true, he used the language of Teutonic patriotism and posed as the indignant defender of German liberties against the Hapsburg. But he posed with equal indignation as the protector of Polish or Swedish "liberties" against a reforming king or as the champion of Protestantism against Powers who might be represented as its foes. The whole course of his life witnessed to his preference for French civilisation over German, and to his indifference as to the race of his subjects and assistants, if only they were serviceable to the State. His point of view was invariably and exclusively Prussian. It would never have occurred to him to refuse to barter his Rhenish provinces for parts of Bohemia or Poland because the former were inhabited by Germans and the latter by Slavs. He was far from being shocked at the suggestion that he might one day partition the Empire with the Hapsburgs. He struggled for equality with Austria, never dreaming of the time when his descendants should expel her from Germany and assume the Imperial crown. Thus, though his work was a step towards their triumph, it was unconscious. He must be judged by viewing his achievements in relation to his own designs.

Frederick's influence upon his contemporaries was enormous, and in many respects it cannot be over-praised. He found what has been styled "Sultan and harem economy" prevalent among his peers, together with a tendency to regard the income of the State as the pocket-money of the ruler. For this he substituted in Europe a great measure of his own ideal of royal duty. Fearing nothing and hoping little from any future state, he was yet too proud to flinch from an atom of the lifelong penance that he believed was prescribed for kings by some law of nature. Duty to his House and duty to his State were to him the same, and they dictated a life of incessant labour for his subjects' good, and forbade the appropriation of more than a living wage. Other sovereigns followed the Prussian mode, and "benevolent despotism" came to be regarded as the panacea for the ills of Europe. Though it hardly survived the storm of the Revolution, it was instrumental in removing many abuses and in promoting during several decades the comfort of the common people. Thanks in great part to Frederick, irresponsible monarchy became impossible for ever.

Frederick's fame, none the less, finds its most solid basis in the achievement to which all else in his life was subordinate,— the successful aggrandisement of Prussia. Though it may be true that another and a better way lay open to him, that the path which he marked out led straight to Jena, that he owed much of his success to fortune, and that his work was rescued by forces which he had not prized, in spite of all it is to him that Prussia owes her place

among the nations.   By his single will he shaped
the course of history.   His rule completed the fusion
of provinces into a State, his victories gave it prestige, and the success of his work of aggrandisement
was great enough to consecrate the very arts by
which it was accomplished.   Two decades after his
death a king of Prussia entered his tomb by night,
seeking inspiration to confront Napoleon.   The archi-
tects of modern Germany declare that all that they
have built rests upon the foundations that he laid.
As long as the German Empire flourishes and the
world is swayed by the principles of its founders, so
long will the fame of Frederick the Great remain
secure.

INDEX

A

Agriculture, Prussian, 309 *ff.*
Aix - la - Chapelle (Aachen), 129; Peace of (1748), 156, 157, 194
Alembert, d', 160, 337, 339, 352
Algarotti, 82, 160
Amelia, Princess, 31
Anhalt-Dessau, Leopold, Prince of ("the Old Dessauer"), 78, 82, 109, 116, 126, 140, 143, 150 *ff.*
Anhalt-Dessau, Leopold, Prince of ("the Young Dessauer"), 104, 105, 109, 115, 262
Anne of Russia, 44, 91
Ansbach, Margravine of, 81
Anti-Machiavel, 53
Archenholtz, cited, 289
Armed Neutrality of 1780, 339
Army, Prussian, 15, 19, 22, 66, 78, 81, 104, 109, 114, 117, 126, 147, 150, 165 *ff.*, 188, 203, 221, 243, 247, 267, 271, 289, 293, 302 *ff.*, 336, 344, 351
Augustus III., Elector of Saxony and King of Poland, 66, 67, 130, 138, 148, 151, 153, 204, 206 *ff.*, 324, 352

Augustus William, Prince, 112, 203, 228, 230 *ff.*, 251, 264

B

Baireuth, 81, 82, 135
Baireuth, Margrave of, 41, 43, 82
Bank, Prussian, 318
Barberina, 131, 132
Baumgarten, 109
Bautzen, 230, 232
Bavaria, in 1778, 333, 334; in 1785, 342, 343
Bavarian Succession, war of the, 334 *ff.*
Belleisle, Marshal, 118, 121, 139
Berg, 61 *ff.*, 76, 85, 98
Berlin, 28, 35, 80, 98, 129, 150, 171, 173, 233, 290, 307, 314, 345, 348; treaty of (1728), 62; treaty of (1742), 127, 136, 149, 153
Bevern, Duke of, 212, 219, 220, 224, 232, 238
Bismarck, 3, 94, 350
Black Eagle, Order of the, 20
Bohemia, campaign in (1778), 334 *ff.*
Book of Rights, Prussian, 337
Borcke, 100, 102, 205
Botta, Marquis di, 98–100